Pre-publication REVIEWS, COMMENTARIES, EVALUATIONS . . .

"Hertlein and Viers have put together an excellent workbook for therapists. Each chapter, written by seasoned therapists, includes a section on the objective of the activity, its theoretical foundation, how to do the technique, an exemplar, contraindications, and references. Many models of family therapy are included in this book. The activities can be used in-session and for tasks between sessions. This book is an outstanding resource for therapists seeking to expand their repertoire of skills and when encountering new clinical populations."

Jerry Gale, PhD
Director, Marriage and Family Therapy Doctoral Program,
Department of Child and Family Development,
The University of Georgia

"This book provides a plethora of ideas for therapists and clients in concrete, accessible form with rationale, instructions, and further information for each intervention. The readings and resources for clients as well as therapists are especially helpful. This book is useful for therapists of all experience levels who are interested in new ideas. I particularly like the consistency of the format for the chapters and the concrete nature of the interventions. I have already used some of the ideas in my own practice and teaching."

Thorana S. Nelson, PhD
Director, Marriage and Family Therapy Program,
Department of Family, Consumer, and Human Development,
Utah State University

"In *The Couple and Family Therapist's Notebook,* Drs. Hertlein and Viers, along with their associates, invite therapists of all levels of experience to explore a clinical world in which healing practices help clients to create therapeutic connections. The contributors present their real-world tested techniques, exercises, and metaphors through the effective use of practice-based evidence, including colorful case examples and therapists' insightful commentaries. In doing so, they take their readers into therapy rooms across the country to experience firsthand how resourceful therapists, couples, and families work together to produce significant therapeutic outcomes."

Ronald J. Chenail, PhD
Editor, *Journal of Marital and Family Therapy;*
Vice President for Research, Planning,
and Governmental Affairs and Professor of Family Therapy,
Nova Southeastern University

"Once again, the *Therapist's Notebook Series* has put forth another creative compilation of field-tested interventions to help therapists enhance their clinical effectiveness. This is a great resource for couple and family therapists, regardless of experience, theoretical orientations, or educational backgrounds.

As an educator, clinical supervisor, and therapist in private practice, I have often needed a book like this to help me get through a clinical impasse, jumpstart my creativity in therapy, or offer innovative and theoretically informed ideas to students. Each chapter is well written, scholastically sound, grounded in a specific theoretical approach, and includes a clinical vignette with a rich description of a clinical intervention. This book is a must for any therapist wanting practical and creative ideas to apply in therapy with couples and families."

J. Maria Bermúdez, PhD
Assistant Professor of Marriage and Family Therapy,
Texas Tech University

The Couple and Family Therapist's Notebook

Homework, Handouts, and Activities for Use in Marital and Family Therapy

HAWORTH Practical Practice in Mental Health
Lorna L. Hecker, PhD
Senior Editor

101 Interventions in Family Therapy edited by Thorana S. Nelson and Terry S. Trepper

101 More Interventions in Family Therapy edited by Thorana S. Nelson and Terry S. Trepper

The Practical Practice of Marriage and Family Therapy: Things My Training Supervisor Never Told Me by Mark Odell and Charles E. Campbell

The Therapist's Notebook for Families: Solution-Oriented Exercises for Working with Parents, Children, and Adolescents by Bob Bertolino and Gary Schultheis

Collaborative Practice in Psychology and Therapy edited by David A. Paré and Glenn Larner

The Therapist's Notebook for Children and Adolescents: Homework, Handouts, and Activities for Use in Psychotherapy edited by Catherine Ford Sori and Lorna L. Hecker

The Therapist's Notebook for Lesbian, Gay, and Bisexual Clients: Homework, Handouts, and Activities for Use in Psychotherapy by Joy S. Whitman and Cynthia J. Boyd

A Guide to Self-Help Workbooks for Mental Health Clinicians and Researchers by Luciano L'Abate

Workbooks in Prevention, Psychotherapy, and Rehabilitation: A Resource for Clinicians and Researchers edited by Luciano L'Abate

The Psychotherapist as Parent Coordinator in High-Conflict Divorce: Strategies and Techniques by Susan M. Boyan and Ann Marie Termini

The Couple and Family Therapist's Notebook: Homework, Handouts, and Activities for Use in Marital and Family Therapy by Katherine A. Milewski Hertlein, Dawn Viers, and Associates

Therapy's Best: Practical Advice and Gems of Wisdom from Twenty Accomplished Counselors and Therapists by Howard Rosenthal

Interactive Art Therapy: "No Talent Required" Projects by Linda L. Simmons

The Therapist's Notebook for Integrating Spirituality in Counseling: Homework, Handouts, and Activities for Use in Psychotherapy edited by Karen B. Helmeke and Catherine Ford Sori

The Therapist's Notebook for Integrating Spirituality in Counseling II: More Homework, Handouts, and Activities for Use in Psychotherapy edited by Karen B. Helmeke and Catherine Ford Sori

The Couple and Family Therapist's Notebook

Homework, Handouts, and Activities for Use in Marital and Family Therapy

Katherine M. Hertlein, PhD
Dawn Viers, PhD
and Associates

Routledge
Taylor & Francis Group
NEW YORK AND LONDON

First published 2005 by The Haworth Press, Inc.

This edition published 2012 by Routledge
605 Third Avenue, New York, NY 10017
2 Park Square, Milton Park, Abingdon, Oxon OX14 4RN

Routledge is an imprint of the Taylor & Francis Group, an informa business

First issued in hardback 2015

Cover design by Kerry E. Mack.

Library of Congress Cataloging-in-Publication Data

The couple and family therapist's notebook : homework, handouts, and activities for use in marital and family therapy / [edited by] Katherine A. Milewski Hertlein, Dawn Viers, and associates.
p. cm.
Includes bibliographical references and index.
ISBN 978-0-7890-2236-3 (pbk)
ISBN 978-1-138-12956-6 (hbk)
1. Marital psychotherapy—Problems, exercises, etc. 2. Family psychotherapy—Problems, exercises, etc. I. Hertlein, Katherine A. Milewski. II. Viers, Dawn. III. Series.
[DNLM: 1. Family Therapy—methods. 2. Couples Therapy—methods. 3. Marital Therapy—methods. WM 430.5.F2 C857 2005]

RC488.5.C638 2005
616.89'1562—dc22

2005000064

ISBN 13: 978-1-138-12956-6 (hbk)

To my parents, Robert and Nancy Milewski,
who, through their support, love, and example,
gave me my love for families (KH)

To Brynn and Mia (DV)

CONTENTS

SECTION II: INTERVENTIONS FOR FAMILIES

ABOUT THE EDITORS

Katherine M. Hertlein, PhD, is Assistant Professor in the Department of Counseling at the University of Nevada, Las Vegas. She formerly served as a family therapist at Family Service of Roanoke Valley and a day treatment manager for a children's after-school treatment program in Roanoke, Virginia. She has been published in several journals, including *Journal of Couple & Relationship Therapy, Journal of Feminist Family Therapy, American Journal of Family Therapy, Contemporary Family Therapy,* and *Journal of Clinical Activities, Assignments & Handouts in Psychotherapy Practice,* and has contributed chapters to *The Therapist's Notebook for Children and Adolescents.* She is currently co-editing a book on infidelity treatment. She is a member of the American Association for Marriage and Family Therapy and has presented at local and national conferences in the areas of MFT training, infidelity, cognitive, and social psychology. She has won three awards for her research in infidelity, including the American Association for Marriage and Family Therapy Graduate Student Research Award. Dr. Hertlein's areas of interest include research methodology and measurement, training in Marriage and Family Therapy, infidelity treatment, child-centered play therapy, and Bowen family systems theory.

Dawn Viers, PhD, is Prevention Specialist with New River Valley Community Services, where she facilitates parent education groups. She has been published in *Journal of Feminist Family Therapy, Journal of Clinical Activities, Assignments & Handouts in Psychotherapy Practice, American Journal of Family Therapy,* and *The Therapist's Notebook: Homework, Handouts, and Activities for Use in Psychotherapy.* Her research interests include the career satisfaction of female MFT faculty, divorce education, and grandparents as caregivers.

CONTRIBUTORS

Pam Black, MSW, is an assistant professor at Eastern Kentucky University, Department of Anthropology, Sociology, and Social Work in Richmond, Kentucky. She holds a master's degree in social work and has vast experience as a trainer and facilitator. Her practice experience is in family and children services.

Andrew S. Brimhall, MS, is a second-year doctoral student in the Marriage and Family Therapy Program at Texas Tech University. His clinical experiences include positions at Catholic Family Services (Lubbock, Texas), Aspen Achievement Academy (Loa, Utah), and the Turning Point (Orem, Utah). He has worked extensively with couples, families, and at-risk adolescents. Previous works include exploring the role of enactments in therapy and the effect of spirituality on the marital relationship. He is currently developing a Q-sort methodology for ethnically diverse therapy as well as documenting the historical perspective of neutrality in marriage and family therapy. Andrew, his wife, Heather, and their beautiful daughter, Katie, reside in Lubbock, Texas.

Rudy Buckman, EdD, is a therapist at a nonprofit community agency (Salesmanship Club Youth and Family Centers, Inc.) in Dallas, Texas. He has presented numerous workshops on narrative therapy at the state and national levels, and has published several journal articles and a book chapter on narrative therapies.

Wan-Juo Cheng, MS, is a PhD student in the Marriage and Family Therapy Program of the Department of Human Development and Family Studies at Iowa State University, where she enjoys the cultural shocks of living in a small midwestern town. Her professional interests include theories of social construction and constructivism, and the practice of narrative and collaborative language systems therapy.

Abigail Tolhurst Christiansen, BS, is a graduate student in marriage and family therapy at Purdue University in West Lafayette, Indiana. She is a student member of the American Association for Marriage and Family Therapy, the American Psychological Association, and the National Council on Family Relations. She has also presented at the Business and Professional Women's conference. Current research interests focus on the intersection between marriage and work. She has co-led a community women's support group for childhood incest survivors.

Patricia A. Craven, MA, is a PhD student at Florida State University pursuing a degree in marriage and family therapy. Patricia is a pediatric nurse. She received her BA at University of Central Florida in psychology. She received her MA at Appalachian State University in marriage and family therapy. She is involved in research developing a group intervention for foster children. Patricia was previously a foster parent for chronically ill children in Florida. She is also conducting research investigating the mother's role in major clinical journals. She currently works at Intensive Crisis Counseling Service where she does home-based therapy with families at risk. Her work with healing rituals with couples has developed out of a collaborative effort with her major professor while attending Appalachian State University. This work has expanded into a publication in *Contemporary Family Therapy* and continues to be a useful intervention with couples who have experienced infidelity and want to work on their relationship.

Erin Cushing, BA, is currently completing her master of arts in marital family therapy at the University of San Diego. She is working on her traineeship at Children's Hospital Outpatient

Psychiatry in Oceanside, California. Her professional interests include the treatment and diagnosis of attachment disorders, trauma and child abuse treatment, and conducting specialized groups for children with Asperger's disorder.

Christina Dust, BA, is a master's candidate in the Marriage and Family Therapy Program at Purdue University–Calumet. She is finishing her master's thesis and is interested in narrative therapy and the influences of relationship priorities.

Cezanne Elias, BS, is a master's student and therapist intern in marriage and family therapy at Purdue University–Calumet. She received her BS in human development from The University of California at Davis and was a child development intern and teacher's assistant at the University of California at Davis Center for Child and Family Studies. She has also interned in Child Life at Shriner's Children's Hospital in Sacramento, California, and the University of New Mexico Children's Hospital.

Wendy Danto Ellis, MC, CPC, is a certified professional counselor in Arizona. She received her master of counseling degree from Arizona State University. For more than twenty years, she has divided her professional activities between graduate and postgraduate education and training, as well as clinical private practice. Her clinical areas of interest include individual and family therapy, women's issues, change management, and the enhancement of coping and adjustment to chronic and critical illness. Wendy is the Behavioral Science Director for the Scottsdale Healthcare Family Practice Residency Program, in Scottsdale, Arizona. Her academic interests include collaborative and relationship-centered care, the process of change, and the social construction of illness. In all aspects of her teaching, Wendy utilizes a collaborative approach and enjoys learning with her students. In her free time she enjoys movies, reading, writing (she authored an organizer book for people with cancer), and traveling, as well as spending time with family and friends. Wendy and Muriel S. McClellan, PhD, are the cofounders of the consulting group The Changetalk Way, which provides energizing consultations to organizations. Through their collaborative work, they are committed to encouraging cutting-edge approaches that deal effectively with life events in positive and affirming ways. They appeared in the April 2002 issue of HEMALOG in an interview about change, "Getting Unstuck—For Good."

Bill Forisha, PhD, is a licensed marriage and family therapist (Washington), a licensed psychologist (Minnesota), and an AAMFT-approved supervisor. He serves on the core faculty of the Psychology Program, Antioch University, Seattle, Washington.

Brandt C. Gardner, PhD, is an assistant professor at Oklahoma State University. His previous works include empirical and conceptual articles exploring the influence of spiritual practices on conflict resolution in religious couples, the clinical process of enactments, and family-of-origin influences on premarital relationships. Brandt, his wife, Mary, and their four children reside in Lubbock, Texas.

Kevin A. Harris, MS, NCC, is a doctoral student in the Counseling Psychology PhD Program at Ball State University in Muncie, Indiana. He received his MS in counseling from Indiana University–Bloomington in 2002 and is a National Certified Counselor. His counseling experience includes working with adults with autism, adolescent male sex offenders, and adult individuals and families from the Delaware and Monroe County areas. He has also counseled groups of middle-school boys and has worked with adult males in a residential drug and alcohol treatment center. His research interests include spirituality and religiosity, human sexuality, and multiculturalism. He is a cofounder of Project Rainbow, an interdisciplinary collaboration between theater, therapy, and theology stressing dialogue and social responsibility between the three fields.

Darryl R. Haslam, MSW, is a doctoral student in the Marriage and Family Therapy Program at Texas Tech University in Lubbock, Texas. He received his master of social work degree from Brigham Young University in Utah with an emphasis in clinical social work. He has had more than ten years of clinical experience working with children, couples, and families in a wide range of settings and has extensively studied play therapy approaches. He has trained numerous professionals about play therapy concepts and methods and holds the certification of Registered Play Therapist from the Association for Play Therapy.

Liddy B. Hope, MS, is a doctoral candidate in the Family Social Sciences Department at the University of Minnesota. She received her master's in marriage and family therapy from Purdue University–Calumet. Her main area of research interest is familial body image, focusing on the transmission, maintenance, and formation of body image within families. She teaches at several universities and colleges within the Twin Cities area and is also the research analyst for a national adolescent sex offender treatment program.

Z. Vance Jackson, MA, is a second-year doctoral student in the Counseling Psychology PhD Program at Ball State University in Muncie, Indiana. He received his MA in counseling from Ball State in 2002 and has been counseling since 2000. He has counseled college students from Ball State and individuals and families from the Delaware County area. He has also worked on speech development programs for children with autism and served as a counselor for a substance abuse rehabilitation program for college students in the Muncie area. His research interests include looking at stereotypes, prejudice, discrimination reduction, how multicultural programs can be taught more effectively, and applying psychological principles and theories to counseling techniques. He is a member of Project Rainbow.

Lisa Jameyfield, BS, is a master's student in marriage and family therapy and a therapist intern at Purdue University–Calumet. She received a BS in special education with licenses in the areas of mild/moderate/severe profound, multiply handicapped/physically handicapped. She is also a developmental specialist in the early intervention program for the state of Indiana. She has fifteen years of experience working with special needs children and their families. She has served in many community-based capacities, such as board president for Lake County First Steps for seven years, member at large for Lake County Step Ahead, member of the local chapter of National Association for the Education of Young Children (NAEYC), and an officer on the mayor of Hammond's Commission on Disabilities for three years. She also served as a classroom teacher in public schools for two years and was director/developmental therapist for a private, nonprofit early intervention agency.

Glenn W. Lambie, PhD, LPC, NCC, NCSC, CCMHC, is an assistant professor in the Counseling and School Psychology Program, School of Education, at Chapman University in Orange, California. His areas of specialty and interest include professional school counseling; individual, group, and family therapy with children and adolescents; and counselor development.

Nicole Lynn Lee, PhD, is an adjunct faculty member at Virginia Commonwealth University. Her areas of research include intersectionality and its relevance to oppressed populations, mental health interventions for African Americans, and art and movement therapies. Her current work is at a day treatment program for children with severe emotional disturbances (SED).

Muriel S. McClellan, PhD, is a licensed psychologist who practices in Phoenix, Arizona. Her clients come with a variety of dilemmas including relationship issues, marriage concerns, recovery from affairs, reducing conflict with divorce, creating successful stepfamilies, parenting issues, and work-related challenges. Dr. McClellan received her PhD from Arizona State University in counseling psychology and her master's degree from UCLA. She has completed postdoctoral training at the Phoenix Gestalt Institute, the Post Graduate Institute for Family

Therapy in Phoenix, and the Family Therapy Program, Medical School, University of Calgary, Canada, with Dr. Karl Tomm. Dr. McClellan and Wendy Danto Ellis, MC, CPC, are the co-founders of the consulting group The Changetalk Way, which provides energizing consultations to organizations. Through their collaborative work, they are committed to encouraging cutting-edge approaches that deal effectively with life events in positive and affirming ways. They appeared in the April 2002 issue of HEMALOG in an interview about change, "Getting Unstuck—For Good."

Lenore M. McWey, PhD, is an assistant professor in the Marriage and Family Therapy Doctoral Program at Florida State University. She received her doctoral degree in marriage and family therapy from Florida State University. Her areas of clinical and research interests include working with families involved in the foster care system and in-home family therapy with families in crisis.

Judy Meade had a private practice in northern Virginia for fifteen years counseling individuals and couples. After losing a client to suicide, she became involved with the American Association of Suicidology. She is the task force chair for a Support System for Clinician Survivors of the American Association of Suicidology. She has presented locally and nationally at conferences on the dynamics of loss, grief, and healing for clinicians in the loss of a client to suicide. In addition, Ms. Meade has developed a day workshop for clinicians who have lost or who will lose a client to suicide. She has served as a consultant for the Organization of Attempters and Suicide in Interfaith Services (OASSIS). She has also spoken with local churches and service clubs regarding suicide awareness and prevention.

Marta M. Miranda, LCSW, is a licensed clinical social worker with twenty-seven years of clinical and organizational experience in mental health and substance abuse practice. She is a tenured professor in the department of Anthropology/Sociology and Social Work at Eastern Kentucky University. Ms. Miranda has been in private practice for the past eighteen years providing individual, family, and group mental health services. She has facilitated trainings, workshops, and organizational development seminars to both private and nonprofit organizations in Florida and Kentucky. She is currently on sabbatical completing her doctoral dissertation for her PhD in social work.

Megan J. Murphy, PhD, is an assistant professor in the Marriage and Family Therapy Program at Iowa State University. Her current work focuses on power in couples' relationships.

Devon J. Palmanteer, BA, is a master's candidate in marriage and family therapy at Iowa State University. She is currently working on her master's thesis on the perceived preparedness of MFT students to work with clients from other cultures. Her other clinical interests include aging, intergenerational caregiving, gender roles, and parenting.

Margaret Shapiro, LCSW, is a licensed clinical social worker in Massachusetts and Pennsylvania and has been a practicing psychotherapist for twenty-five years. For the past ten years, she has been assistant director at the Council for Relationships in Philadelphia. She was formerly director of the Couples Communication Course, and is presently director of the Council for Dialogue at the Council for Relationships. Prior to moving to Philadelphia, Ms. Shapiro was the director of social work at Pembroke Hospital in Massachusetts and director of residential services at Mass Mental Health Center. She received her MSW degree from the University of Chicago School of Social Service Administration, and her BA from Smith College. Her current interests include working with couples of different ethnic backgrounds and exploring the impact of money on couples' relationships. She frequently presents on this latter subject at conferences.

Shari Sias, PhD, LPC, is an assistant professor in the Department of Rehabilitation Studies at East Carolina University in Greenville, North Carolina. Dr. Sais's areas of specialty and interest include substance abuse counseling, individual and family counseling, and counselor development.

R. Valorie Thomas, PhD, LMFT, LMHC, is a clinician and counselor educator. She is a faculty member in the Counselor Education Department at Rollins College in Winter Park, Florida, and has thirteen years of clinical experience working with individuals, couples, and families. She has been consulting with women experiencing fertility problems.

Margaret Tucker, BA, is a recent graduate of the Couple and Family Therapy Program in the Center for Psychological Studies, Antioch University, Seattle, Washington.

Charles F. Vorkoper, LCSW, LPC, LMFT, is a counselor in private practice in Dallas, Texas. He is a certified gambling counselor and a supervisor for the National Council on Problem Gambling and has trained mental health professionals for certification in several states. He served as chair of the Public Information Committee of the American Association of Suicidology (AAS) and is an active member of that organization. He has made frequent presentations at the national meetings of the AAS, has conducted workshops on the subject of suicide across the country, and has published chapters in two books on this subject. He is a member of the Task Force for Clinician Survivors of Suicide, developing strategies to serve helping professionals who are impacted by suicide. Currently, he is on the steering committee to create a suicide prevention plan for the state of Texas and is cochair of the committee to involve stakeholders and the public in the development of a Texas Network of Suicide Prevention Networks. In addition, he serves as a mental health volunteer for the Red Cross Disaster Services in Dallas. He helped develop their crisis mental health response approach to major disaster after a Delta airplane crashed in Dallas. He has been active as and is certified as a group psychotherapist. He has served as president of the Dallas Group Psychotherapy Society and has presented at the American Group Psychotherapy Association. He has trained professionals as group psychotherapists.

Lee Williams, PhD, is an associate professor in marital and family therapy at the University of San Diego. He is a co-author of *Essential Skills in Family Therapy,* a popular text for beginning family therapists. He has also published several journal articles and book chapters, primarily in the areas of premarital counseling, interchurch couples, and family therapy training/supervision. Dr. Williams also volunteers as a therapist for the Department of Veterans Affairs.

Laurie L. Williamson, EdD, is an associate professor in the Department of Human Development and Psychological Counseling at Appalachian State University. She is the coordinator of the School Counseling Program and has experience in both school and mental health settings. Previous works have been published in *Professional School Counseling* and *The Journal of Multicultural Counseling and Development.*

Paul W. Wilson II, BA, is a professional director, acting teacher, and theater scholar and is currently pursuing his doctoral degree at the University of Pittsburgh. He is the former production chair of Curtain Call Children's Theatre in Indiana and is the founder of the Abraxas Project for Theatre Outreach. He received his BA in theater and classics from Butler University in 2000 and his master's degree from Miami University in Oxford, Ohio. He has worked for nearly fifteen years with children's theater initiatives, using his training to merge the dramatic arts with projects for literacy, youth empowerment, and occupational therapy. He also has several years of training and experience with Theatre of the Oppressed and special education efforts. His academic specialization involves the dramatic portrayal of intercultural spiritual crises. He is the cofounder of Project Rainbow.

Jon L. Winek, PhD, received his doctorate in sociology from the University of Southern California. He lives in North Carolina with his wife, three sons, and golden retriever. He is the director of the Marriage and Family Therapy Program at Appalachian State University. His research interests include therapeutic process and supervision.

Carol Wright, MA, is a licensed marriage and family therapist (Hawaii) and serves as the Director of Family Services and School-Based Programs, Maui Youth and Family Services.

Chunhong Zhang, MA, is a doctoral student in marriage and family therapy at Purdue University, West Lafayette, Indiana. She is a student member of the American Association for Marriage and Family Therapy and the National Council of Family Relations. Her previous work includes research and clinical work in the following areas: family therapy with Alzheimer's disease, family therapy with sexual minority youth, family group therapy with incarcerated adolescents, and cross-cultural application of emotionally focused couple therapy. She also conducted several presentations at local and national conferences. Her current research interests focus on work and family interface, family resiliency, and marriage and family therapy training and supervision. She co-led a community women's support group for childhood incest survivors during the past year.

Foreword

When I was a university marriage and family therapy (MFT) faculty member, I was cognizant of the need for evidence-based therapy in our field. I have to admit, however, that as a clinician, I found the clinical stories of marriage and family therapists to be the most helpful in my practice. Beginning with the case reports of Milton Erickson found in *Uncommon Therapy,* the teaching tales of the many creative therapists in the MFT field have sparked my own clinical thinking. I have cherished those earlier editions of *Journal of Marital and Family Therapy,* along with current clinical journals, such as the *Journal of Family Psychotherapy,* that provide unique and imaginative ways of conceptualizing clinical cases. Thus, I read with excitement the latest version in The Therapist's Notebook series in which the editors, Kat Hertlein and Dawn Viers, provide a collection of field-tested MFT interventions that will assist therapists at all levels of experience in their quest to enhance clinical effectiveness.

The creation of effective MFT approaches often begins with the first step in task analysis—the implementation by a clinician of an important intervention that is based on the clinician's experience, theory, or model of therapy, but not yet empirically tested. This criterion is fulfilled as, collectively, the authors of *The Couple and Family Therapist's Notebook* provide a variety of therapeutic strategies and techniques for use in the change process. Along with detailed descriptions of the clinical interventions, the reader will find clear and meaningful discussions of the objectives, rationales, implementation details, case examples, suggestions for follow-up, and contraindications.

I have known Kat Hertlein and Dawn Viers long enough to be impressed by their abilities as creative and effective therapists, writers, and educators. These attributes are evident in their selection of the chapter authors and in their organization of this book. They provide contributors who are diverse in clinical training, experience, work environments, and clinical and research interests. The chapters are organized around effective interventions that can be applied with couples, families, or larger systems. The techniques and strategies are many, including changing communication patterns, externalizing interactional cycles, developing and implementing rituals, as well as using family drawings and acting techniques. Theoretical variety encompasses the Bowen theory, social constructionism, structural and strategic theories, and cybernetics, among others, while interventions emerge from such models as narrative, emotionally focused therapy, Satir, and experiential.

One of the consistent joys I experienced as an MFT professor was the continual contributions of my students to my learning. Often, in a clinical seminar, I would present one of my more difficult cases for the class to consider and I learned very quickly not to be surprised by the fresh and helpful viewpoints presented by class members, regardless of years of clinical experience. For this reason, I am especially pleased that the editors have chosen to include therapists who have a range of years of experience and who practice in a variety of clinical settings. Such inclusion is an important strength of this book.

Creative thinking has been one of the hallmarks of the field of marriage and family therapy since its inception. The clinical stories told in *The Couple and Family Therapist's Notebook* provide a sound base for the emergence of clinical creativity in the reader. While it is important to have research validation for our approaches, it is equally important that our clinical narratives continue to have a voice. Books like this allow such stories to be heard and the clinician to be enriched.

Howard Protinsky, PhD
Hardy, Virginia

Preface

Couples and families present unique challenges for counselors, social workers, and psychotherapists. With numerous clients and the interface of individual and family issues, therapists must be cognizant of how events, individual personalities, and social dynamics influence their case conceptualization and treatment. Working with couples and families, however, may provide the therapist with better treatment outcomes. Treatment that includes multiple systems allows the practitioner a fuller opportunity for assessment, a diffusion of the blame from one person, a chance to work on interactive components in treatment such as communication, and the opportunity to have more people supporting changes.

There are a multitude of theoretical paradigms, models, and ideas to work with couples and families, including general systems theory, cybernetics, developmental theory, object relations, postmodernism, and feminist theory, to name a few. Each of these theories gives practicing clinicians a lens through which to organize their treatment. Even with an understanding of theory, it is still helpful to have a toolbox from which to pull ideas and interventions. This book will help clinicians who work with couples and families to come up with creative activities, suggestions, and assignments. It is our hope that this book will help therapists supplement the theories they use to generate creative alternatives and innovative solutions to complex clinical problems.

The purpose of this book is to provide couple and family therapists with a repertoire of field-tested interventions based on theoretical underpinnings. Rather than providing a series of disjointed steps in an intervention, each activity, assignment, or handout is grounded in one or more specific theoretical approaches. These approaches include emotionally focused therapy, symbolic-experiential therapy, transgenerational theory, solution-focused therapy, narrative therapy, and many others. We believe that by incorporating this component, practitioners have a starting point to get their creative juices flowing and the opportunity to tailor the interventions to their clients.

Although several books on the market compile interventions for couple and family therapists, this book is a departure from those in that every chapter provides a clinical vignette describing the use of the intervention. These vignettes demonstrate the power of the intervention and offer readers a "sneak peek" of how this intervention is used in therapy, under what circumstances it is effective, and a better understanding of how the intervention benefits the couples and families for whom it is used. Clinicians whose clients differ from the couples and families in the vignettes can adjust the interventions to better suit their needs.

Organization

This book is organized into three major sections. The first section describes interventions that were generated for use with couples in therapy. The first three chapters in this section provide interventions for working with communication and interaction cycles. The fourth chapter deals with finances, often a difficult issue for couples to discuss. The next two chapters provide clinicians with ways to use metaphors, and the remaining two chapters explore using rituals, specifically targeted at infidelity and early pregnancy loss.

The second section details a wide variety of interventions for use with families. The first chapter describes an intervention for parenting and is followed by an intervention identifying the family rules. These are succeeded by two interventions based on the techniques of sculpting and three chapters describing creative games as interventions. The next four chapters utilize family creativity by engaging in art activities. The following five interventions encompass books, drawing, and writing activities. Working with adolescents in therapy is the next topic and the section concludes with interventions that challenge clinicians with new viewpoints, such as reflecting teams or work with other cultures.

The last section includes chapters that incorporate larger systems in couple and family therapy. These chapters explore working in the group therapy context, the school systems, and the role of the therapist after the loss of a client to suicide.

Chapters are divided into distinct sections. Each chapter begins with an objective orienting the reader to the homework, handout, or activity, followed by a brief rationale. Instructions, a clinical vignette, a section highlighting contraindications, and a list of resources for both the practitioner and the client conclude each chapter.

Audience

This book is intended for any clinician who works with couples and families. This can include practitioners in private practice, those who work within the school system, hospital or government settings, homeless shelters, or in not-for-profit agencies and counseling centers. Novice counselors and psychotherapists may find examples of ways to generate and adapt their own creative interventions in the therapy room. More seasoned therapists may find ways to incorporate ideas in therapy or new ways to use a theory. This book can also be used as a resource in practicum or supervision courses. Because of the wide range of interventions, theory bases, and background of the contributors, this book has wide applicability for those who want to use the interventions as they are, but they are also flexible enough to be adjusted to fit a specific couple, family, or presenting problem.

A Theme of Connection

Many of these interventions, distinct and individual in their own ways, appear to show a common theme—a theme of *connection.* Readers will notice that many of these interventions provide ways for members of families or couples to connect with one another. In our fast-paced lives, couples and families can lose touch with one another. This book provides many ideas for how to reconnect couples and families so they once again have bonds and separate identities as family or couple units.

Acknowledgments

We would like to take this opportunity to acknowledge the remarkable people who have been instrumental in helping us to get this book off the ground. First, we would like to thank our families, specifically Eric Hertlein and Brian Yaun, for putting up with our schedules, proofreading, and otherwise offering their support in this endeavor. We would also like to thank the staff at The Haworth Press for their excitement, interest, and guidance in this project. We would like to thank Dr. Lorna Hecker, Series Editor, for her continual support of this project and for offering this wonderful opportunity to be involved in an enterprise that benefits the workers on the "front lines" and their clients. Howard "Bud" Protinsky has provided a wonderful foreword, and we thank him for coming out of retirement just briefly enough to do so. We also would like to thank our numerous authors who have contributed to this book and who have made this project a success. Their commitment to this project has been extraordinary, and we consider ourselves extremely lucky to have worked with such a talented pool of clinicians and authors.

SECTION I: INTERVENTIONS FOR COUPLES

– 1 –

The Aesthetics of Communication

Wan-Juo Cheng
Rudy Buckman

Type of Contribution: Activity

Objective

Many couples, concerned about the damaging effects of frequent arguments on their relationship, come into therapy to improve their communication skills. Depending upon their unique experiences, couples usually enter therapy with their own ideologies and discourses about relationships. Similarly, depending on their unique experiences and professional training, therapists also have ideologies and discourses about relationships. Most professional ideologies and therapeutic discourses have specific ideas about the causes of relationship problems and their proper treatment. However, treatment difficulties may arise when these professional ideologies and therapeutic discourses marginalize the couple's voices and undermine the collaboration between the therapist and couple. Although the intended effect of these professional ideologies and discourses is to improve the couple's relationship, we have frequently found that as these professional ideologies/discourses (e.g., "I" statements, communication exercises, time-outs) are introduced into therapy, many couples become frustrated. They frequently tell us that it is hard for them to consistently practice and perform the therapeutic ideology, especially when an issue is heated. Consequently, their frustration with each other, combined with a sense of failure over not mastering the therapeutic ideology, often leads to more frequent and desperate arguments. The purpose of this chapter is to present a way of working with couples as a co-author rather than working on them as an expert. To accomplish this, a metaphor (i.e., communication as an art form) is constructed that encourages collaboration between the therapist and couple by inviting them to participate in developing their own unique way of communicating.

Rationale for Use

Therapeutic models/paradigms may be viewed as metaphors that help therapists make sense of their experiences. Since the 1980s, a paradigm shift has occurred in marriage and family therapy from a mechanistic cybernetic analogy of therapy toward an aesthetic one of therapy as an art of ongoing dialogues (Anderson & Goolishian, 1988, 1990; Atkinson & Heath, 1990).

In the cybernetic model tradition, the therapist determines the cause of and intervenes in the couple's dysfunctional pattern of communication. For example, the therapist discerns a pursue-withdrawal pattern in a couple's relationship and intervenes to disrupt this dysfunctional pattern. The therapist takes a leadership position as an expert (Haley, 1976; Minuchin, 1974; Watzlawick, Weakland, & Fisch, 1974) or a coach (Bowen, 1978) to change the pattern, to deal with power struggles between the couple, or to manage an individual's anxiety and levels of differentiation. However, any of these patterns or differentiation levels of family members that the therapist identifies based on his or her theoretical model is a metaphor for the therapist to picture and punctuate the health or normalcy of the couple. In this context, the couple's points of view may be silenced.

Alternately, from a social constructionist perspective, a behavior or pattern that has occurred at one time no longer exists in the present; however, the meaning assigned to the behavior or pattern remains across time (White & Epston, 1990). Hoffman (1990) also suggests that problems that bring clients into therapy can be viewed as stories that the clients tell themselves. The meanings of the stories inevitably change as the client renarrates in different contexts. The therapist takes a stance as a co-author with the client to construct an alternative story (Anderson & Goolishian, 1992; White & Epston, 1990).

From the social constructionist perspective, presenting concerns and solutions that clients have attempted to resolve issues may be viewed as metaphors, reflecting clients' beliefs and values about relationships and life struggles. As Wittgenstein (1958) suggests, "knowing what is right/wrong and how to go on" (p. 40) is constructed knowledge gained through communal language rather than individual processes. Dominant discourses as cultural tales that frame what people think or how they behave may work for clients in some circumstances yet not in others. What needs to be kept in mind is that all discourses are metaphors and multiple meanings are possible. For instance, one spouse walking away from the other when arguing may be taken as a rejection. However, it could also be considered protection against an escalation.

Metaphor provides an avenue for the therapist to gather information indirectly (Combs & Freedman, 1990) as well as to intervene in a playful, imaginative, and nonthreatening way (Linzey, 1994). Consequently, therapy provides a context in which both the therapist and the couple weigh different discourses or cultural metaphors, speculate on the possibility of other points of view, and engage as artists in creating alternative metaphors that may provide a better fit for them. This activity invites couples who come into therapy for their communication difficulties or frequent fights to cocreate other unique stories of communication.

Instructions

Prior to cocreating a metaphor, a therapist must learn a couple's communication stories, their ideas about communication, what they have tried to do differently to move in the right direction, and the results of their attempts. In therapy it is likely that the couple will start to argue with each other. The therapist may stop them by asking, "Where did the conversation lead the two of you?" or "Is this way of communicating getting you closer or farther away from your preferred way of talking?" The therapist also should acknowledge the frustration of both partners.

At this point, the therapist may introduce the metaphor of communication as an art form. The brief opening can begin as follows:

> Well, I have another idea about communication, which I have learned from other couples I've worked with. Many of them have been through the same issue that you are working on, and they tell me that communication is an art. Similar to artists learning their own unique way of communicating through the medium of art, couples have to learn how to communicate with each other in their own unique way. Also, just as painting by the numbers may frustrate the creativity of artists, communication exercises may frustrate and block a couple from developing their own unique and meaningful communication styles. However, creating a unique way of communicating does not just involve one of the people in a relationship. As you know, the art of communication, parenting, or intimacy requires a couple to work together.

The therapist may then ask the couple what they think about couples working together to develop their own unique way of communicating, just as artists work to discover their own unique artistic vision. If they agree and are willing to work together to develop their own unique way of communicating, the therapist continues to extend the metaphor by explaining that some couples find it helpful to actually work on an art project together. Again, if the couple agrees, the therapist extends the metaphor by including discussions of how the couple would like to proceed (e.g., when is a good time to work together, in which art media), what aesthetics already guide them in the art of communication, what has influenced their aesthetics (e.g., personal experiences), how similar or different are their aesthetics, how open or closed are they to each other's aesthetics, and what are their hopes and dreams for their relationship. It is also important to prepare the couple for possible difficulties in the journey; for example, the therapist might muse aloud,

> I wonder if it might be tough for the two of you to work on an art project together, since you have different styles. As you know, an artist may be very insistent on colors, shapes, or compositions for certain aesthetic reasons. They may not easily give up on their principles. This would be an interesting but challenging experience for the two of you.

In addition, the therapist may ask the couple to think of their beliefs and values about intimate relationships in the following way:

> Art consists of skills and aesthetics. Whereas skills can be improved from time to time, aesthetics are more difficult to change, since they involve an individual's beliefs and values. Yet beliefs and values may evolve. I believe that we all have learned many communication skills from schools, families, and society. However, I am more curious about your own personal beliefs and values when you work on the artwork.

Brief Vignette

Tim, twenty-eight years old, and Ann, twenty-three years old, had been together for three years and planned to get married. Tim had a long-term relationship before dating Ann, whereas she had only several dating relationships. He worked at a maintenance store as a manager, and she was a college student and worked part-time at the store with him. They were referred to me (W.C.) by a therapist who had worked with them for a year. Because they constantly argued over trivialities, such as the remote control, the toilet seat, and so on, they were concerned that their relationship was damaged by seemingly never-ending arguments. They had begun to wonder if they were suited for each other. After a big argument, they decided to postpone the wedding and to seek couples' therapy to improve their communication skills and relationship.

During the year of therapy with the previous therapist, who worked primarily from a Bowenian perspective, both worked hard to understand the positive and negative heritages from their families of origin. The therapist analyzed their communication problems and relationship issues, and prescribed specific strategies to correct the problems. Tim's family of origin was determined to be an "ideal" family in which all family members stayed calm and talked things through when dealing with conflicts. In contrast, Ann's family constantly fought yet never resolved issues. She described her family members as more hostile and/or avoidant toward one another. The previous therapist implied that Ann had to work on her communication style and suggested that Tim assist her with this task, especially in remaining calm. Homework assignments were given each week, and the couple was expected to practice these strategies between sessions. Both tried to practice different communication strategies such as time-outs and "I" statements, but they continued to argue. In fact, they reported that the harder they worked, the more frustrated and demoralized they became when the strategies failed to reduce their arguments. At this point the couple was referred to me (W.C.).

In the first meeting, I started by exploring what they had learned about their communication problems from the previous therapy experience. Tim seemed to believe that he was a rational communicator, whereas Ann had to learn how to control her anger and improve her communication skills. Ann agreed with Tim that she had much to learn but was uncomfortable with the previous therapist's analysis of the communication style in her family of origin. In reference to the homework assignments, they both thought that, overall, the homework assignments helped a little. Furthermore, Tim revealed that Ann was reluctant to practice and that her reluctance had impeded their progress. Ann indicated that she did not practice much and explained that she loathed doing homework of all kinds and did not appreciate being the "target" of interventions by the previous therapist.

After reviewing their previous therapy sessions, Tim sighed heavily and Ann remained silent. The air in the therapy room seemed frozen, as if the arguments and the resulting frustrations over not being able to improve their relationship had become an oppressive "monster" that was determined to render them hopeless and destroy their relationship. In the face of this oppression, we began to discuss whether more training in communication skills would be helpful.

As the discussion continued, I became curious about their definitions of "better communication" and how they had come to believe and value these definitions. Tim stated that remaining calm and talking things through during conflicts was crucial for better communication. Further explaining his position, he described the environment in which he grew up, where rationality, calmness, strength, and toughness were highly valued. In fact, in his family, emotions were viewed as impediments to resolving issues. Thus, in his relationship with Ann, he found it difficult to communicate when Ann, for example, raised her voice. Ann believed that even though emotions might get in the way of resolving issues, the free expression of emotions was to be valued. She believed that emotions were not only reactions to events but were also key to being understood as a person and helpful in showing affection.

As our conversations continued, similarities and differences about their values and beliefs concerning communication and their definitions about "better communication" became more explicit. With their differences and similarities in mind, I tentatively introduced the metaphor of communication as an art and gradually extended the metaphor to include the possibility of them working together on an artwork. They became enthusiastic about the metaphor and stated that they would like to work on a painting representing their communication. The following excerpt is from the second interview:

WAN-JUO: Let's see what you brought me.

[Tim and Ann show the painting.]

WAN-JUO: Wow! It is fantastic. Tell me a story about this painting.

ANN: This is what happened the other day. I was very mad at a colleague of mine. So, I called him [Tim] at work. He didn't say anything so I hung up the phone.

TIM: I was teaching. . . .

WAN-JUO: You answered the phone while you were teaching?

TIM: Yes.

ANN: So, I called him later to apologize. Still, he didn't say anything. I feel, whatever. I hung up again.

TIM: I was still with students. [To Ann] But I was listening to you. I really want to know what made you so upset so I can help you.

ANN: Sometimes, I feel . . . he doesn't understand what I say. If he doesn't, just leave me alone . . . I just wanted him to leave me alone. . . . [To Tim] You know I wasn't mad at you. Just leave me alone. I was trying to calm myself down. Sometimes, just leave me alone for a while to think about what's going on. I know I'll be okay.

WAN-JUO: So, when you say, "leave me alone," you really mean it.

ANN: Yes.

WAN-JUO: Tim, how do you interpret "leave me alone"?

TIM: I can't leave her alone. She was extremely mad. . . .

ANN: like a crazy . . .

TIM: I can't. I've got to know what happened and figure out how I can fix the problem for her. I want to be there for her.

ANN: [To Tim] You don't have to fix every problem for me. Just give me some time to think. I'll be okay.

WAN-JUO: Tim, what might happen if you really leave Ann alone?

TIM: I am afraid that she would just run away from me . . .

WAN-JUO: Okay, where's this idea from?

TIM: I don't know . . . I am just afraid of it. I love her. I don't want her to just walk away from me. So, I really want to be there for her.

ANN: [To Tim] I love you too. I won't run away from you. I just need time to figure out what's going on by myself.

WAN-JUO: So, Tim, it sounds like "being there for Ann" is crucial for you in your relationship.

TIM: Yes, that is what I'm supposed to do in an intimate relationship.

ANN: Yeah, sometimes you have got to leave me alone.

WAN-JUO: Sounds like both "leave me alone" and "being there for each other" are in the picture. It is not either/or but both/and. How do you do both . . . umm . . . I mean, you leave the other alone while still being there for her/him?

TIM: I don't know.

[Pause]

ANN: You don't have to fix every problem for me. This puts me in a bad position. It made me feel bad about myself. You could just tell me it is okay to hate her [the colleague] or she sucks. I would feel a whole lot better.

We continued to talk about their arguments through metaphors and found differences between the metaphor of argument as a monster and the one of argument as an artwork of communication. In the next session, Tim and Ann reported that they fought again over a little thing during the week. Tim was angry and yelled at Ann to stay while she was walking away. Ann stayed, remained calm, and listened to what Tim had to say. Half an hour later, they laughed together and went out for dinner. They felt good about their relationship, even though they still argued. The couple has since taken a break from therapy.

Suggestions for Follow-Up

The therapist may amplify the couple's experience of doing the artwork together by recognizing the type of artists they are, their skills and the aesthetics they possess as strengths, and process how they negotiated with each other in terms of composition, colors, or shapes. In the future, the therapist may explore with them how this painting would be different in three months, one year, three years, and so on, and how their story would change over time.

Contraindications

Because this activity represents a collaborative effort between the therapist and couple, it is inappropriate to use this activity when a couple is not open to cocreating a communication metaphor unique to their relationship. Also, it is contraindicated for couples when abuse and violence are present. Situations of abuse and violence create an environment filled with emotional pain and interpersonal toxicity, which undermines the necessary interpersonal safety and respect needed to support this activity. It is typically more fruitful for therapists to focus on stopping the abuse, developing interpersonal safety, and encouraging the perpetrator to take responsibility for the abuse and violence. Once this is accomplished and the perpetrator is interested in learning how to have a relationship based on safety, trust, respect, and equality, activities such as this one may be appropriate.

Readings and Resources for the Professional

Combs, G. & Freedman, J. (1990). *Symbol, story and ceremony—Using metaphor in individual and family therapy.* New York: W.W. Norton & Co.

Gergen, K. (1999). *An invitation to social construction.* Thousand Oaks, CA: Sage.

Linzey, T. (1994). Ironic metaphors and ironic professional education. *Australia and New Zealand Journal of Family Therapy, 15,* 27-32.

White, M. & Epston, D. (1990). *Narrative means to therapeutic ends.* New York: W.W. Norton & Co.

Zimmerman, J.L. & Dickerson, V.C. (1993). Bringing forth the restraining influence of pattern in couples therapy. In S. Gilligan & R. Price (Eds.), *Therapeutic conversations* (pp. 197-214). New York: W.W. Norton & Co.

Zimmerman, J.L. & Dickerson, V.C. (1996). *If problems talked: Narrative therapy in action.* New York: Guilford Press.

Bibliotherapy Source for the Client

Zimmerman, J.L. & Dickerson, V.C. (1996). *If problems talked: Narrative therapy in action.* New York: Guilford Press.

References

Anderson, H. & Goolishian, H. (1988). Human systems as linguistic systems: Preliminary and evolving ideas about the implications for clinical theory. *Family Process, 27,* 371-393.

Anderson, H. & Goolishian, H. (1990). Beyond cybernetics. *Family Process, 29,* 157-163.

Anderson, H. & Goolishian, H. (1992). The client is the expert. In S. McNamee & K.J. Gergen (Eds.), *Therapy as social construction* (pp. 25-39). Newbury Park, CA: Sage.

Atkinson, B. & Heath, A. (1990). Further thoughts on second order family therapy. *Family Process, 29,* 145-155.

Bowen, M. (1978). *Family therapy in clinical practice.* New York: Jason Aronson.

Combs, G. & Freedman, J. (1990). *Symbol, story and ceremony—Using metaphor in individual and family therapy.* New York: W.W. Norton & Co.

Haley, J. (1976). *Problem-solving therapy.* New York: W.W. Norton & Co.

Hoffman, L. (1990). Constructing realities: An art of lenses. *Family Process, 29,* 1-12.

Linzey, T. (1994). Ironic metaphors and ironic professional education. *Australia and New Zealand Journal of Family Therapy, 15,* 27-32.

Minuchin, S. (1974). *Family and family change.* Cambridge, MA: Harvard University Press.

Watzlawick, P., Weakland, J., & Fisch, R. (1974). *Change: Principles of problem formation and problem resolution.* New York: W.W. Norton & Co.

White, M. & Epston, D. (1990). *Narrative means to therapeutic ends.* New York: W.W. Norton & Co.

Wittgenstein, L. (1958). *Philosophical investigations.* Oxford: Blackwell.

– 2 –

Needful Things: Fostering Communication in Couples

Megan J. Murphy

Type of Contribution: Activity

Objective

The purpose of this activity is to help couples list and prioritize the complaints they have about their relationship. More important, they learn to recognize the fears and feelings that prevent them from directly addressing their concerns with their partner.

Rationale for Use

This activity is useful for therapists working with couples who present in therapy with few or no complaints, yet the therapist may receive indications that the partners do have some concerns about the other that they are reluctant to address in session. By having couples participate in this activity, the therapist is validating each partner's concerns while helping them "go deeper" with their complaints—opening them up to the tender feelings behind their complaints about each other.

This activity is informed both by an intergenerational approach and emotionally focused therapy. It is particularly important for the therapist to remove himself or herself from the position of fielding complaints from one or both members of a couple, and to encourage differentiation via direct communication between two people whose anxiety level is moderate (Kerr & Bowen, 1988). The therapist recognizes that clients who have complaints about a partner yet have difficulty sharing complaints with that partner may need some guidance in emotionally reconnecting. Thus the therapist detriangulates himself or herself, while encouraging partners to directly communicate the feelings behind the complaints they have about each other. The therapist assists couples in accessing emotions that accompany the initial complaint. Focusing on emotions helps the couple work through issues while maintaining and strengthening the couple's bond (Johnson, 1996).

Focusing on primary emotions such as fear can help clients reconnect with their partners by "creat[ing] new levels of emotional engagement" (Johnson, 1996, p. 41). Therapists can assist clients in addressing partners from a safe place using primary emotions, which are healthy responses to stressful situations. Discussing fears can open up new ways of communicating and interacting within the relationship. As a result of highlighting primary emotions, secondary emotions, such as anger, are avoided; responding habitually with secondary emotions is often indicative of a couple attempting to return to old interaction patterns. Couples who can spontaneously and tenderly address primary emotions reap the benefits of a closer, more intimate relationship.

Instructions

The therapist should introduce this activity either at the beginning of a session or shortly thereafter to allow for enough time to process clients' lists and responses. The therapist introduces this activity by saying to the couple that he or she would like to try something different that will help them connect with each other while also being honest; couples might find this task difficult yet ultimately rewarding. By reassuring clients that he or she will be there as a guide through the session, the therapist takes responsibility for creating a safe environment for processing emotions in session.

The therapist brings two pads of paper to the session—giving one pad to each partner. The therapist tells the partners to write down, on the left side of the paper, a list of all the issues they would like to address with their partner at some point in therapy. On the right side, clients list their corresponding fears (to each issue) of what will happen if they address the issue with their partner. They are not to discuss or share their lists with each other, and are to be reassured that only the therapist will see the lists. Once they are finished, the therapist reviews the lists, and then returns them. The therapist asks each partner to rank his or her concerns and then select one to talk about with his or her partner. The therapist guides the discussion, ensuring that couples discuss the fears and feelings associated with the original complaint. This way, the therapist helps couples focus on softer primary feelings, such as fears, rather than more harsh secondary feelings, such as anger (Johnson, 1996). For example, the therapist would have one person begin by introducing a complaint, then describing his or her fear in talking about the complaint with his or her partner. The therapist then would ask the listening partner to respond to the complainant's fear of talking about the issue in their relationship. It is possible for the couple to continue the conversation without much guidance, especially if they are able to remain in the "emotional realm." Couples who attempt to address other concerns on their lists are redirected to either share their fears or to inquire about their partner's feelings. At the end of the session, the therapist collects the lists to keep in the file for future reference.

Brief Vignette

Brenda, twenty-six, and John, twenty-seven, both Caucasian, had been attending therapy for approximately six months. Married for four years, they came to therapy to increase communication in their marriage and to feel closer as a couple. They had no children but were planning to start a family once Brenda finished her undergraduate education. Brenda expressed a desire to feel closer to John before they took on the responsibility of having children. John thought Brenda was overly close to her family. He felt isolated when Brenda made plans each weekend for her and John to participate in one of her family's activities.

Partly influenced by the stoic culture of the Midwest, they often insisted that things were "fine" in session, despite their body language, affect, and phone communications. When I would call to set up or confirm an appointment, one partner would inevitably share some complaint about the other that he or she would not bring up in session, despite my encouragement to do so. Over the phone, John would tell me he was afraid to bring up difficult issues with Brenda out of fear of hurting her feelings. John would say Brenda was always nagging him to talk, and he believed he could not ask for time alone for himself without upsetting her. Despite these persistent problems and resulting arguments, both appeared extremely anxious about addressing these concerns with each other in therapy.

By the sixth month of therapy, we had met many small goals. Brenda and John both reported feeling closer and were spending more time together, yet some larger issues had not been addressed. For example, Brenda would say John was reluctant to share his feelings or even initiate conversation. John expressed that he was unsure how to start a conversation with Brenda. It was apparent that Brenda was quite upset about various issues, as she would save her complaints for therapy sessions. When she and John talked about these issues in therapy, they seemed to stifle their emotions—agreeing to a compromise—yet disagreement and conflict were apparent in their body language and conversational tone. Their reports of conflicts at home were very different from how they presented in sessions; arguments at home were likely to be heated, with yelling, crying, and one person leaving—usually John—whereas arguments in session were relatively muted and tame. It was apparent to me that they each cared very much about each other, sometimes so much so that they were fearful of hurting each other. It was this place of caring that I chose to emphasize through this activity, while detriangulating myself in an effort to help the couple grow closer.

After they made their lists of issues and corresponding fears, I discovered how long their lists actually were; each had at least ten issues that were important to them. Interestingly, their fears both centered on Brenda's feelings. John was very afraid of hurting Brenda's feelings, and indeed, Brenda often felt isolated and unloved by John. Given this information, I asked John to go first in sharing a concern with Brenda.

John actually combined two concerns on his list (another benefit to this activity was for each to realize that they did not actually have a long litany of complaints that were overwhelming to deal with—complaints were often different forms of a few core concerns). He described his concern about lack of time together because of their conflicting schedules. He immediately, without prompting from me, began to account how difficult it was for him to talk to her because he did not want to hurt her feelings. He told her how much he loved her and was at a loss as to how to find more time to spend with her—part of that time he would like to spend talking with her about his feelings.

In sharing one of his concerns with Brenda, he inadvertently and very successfully attended to one of her primary concerns about the relationship—that he was emotionally unavailable to her. While he was talking, she was able to listen to him without getting defensive or going on the attack. When it was Brenda's turn, she quite naturally began sharing with him her deep hurt over being shut out of his emotional life. He was then able to emotionally connect with her and soothe her. The power of this session was evident in their embrace at the end of the session. They were finally able to physically demonstrate their affections, whereas previously they sat stiffly in their chairs.

Suggestions for Follow-Up

Depending on the initial impact of the activity, the therapist may wish to revisit the lists at a later date. The therapist can return the lists to the partners and have them either reprioritize their lists and practice talking about another issue and fear and feelings with each other or, if significant therapeutic progress has been made, they could more openly discuss their lists. Therapeutic questions can emphasize the benefits of this activity. Questions can include the following:

- How would you change your list now?
- Have the fears you initially wrote about changed or disappeared?
- What have you done to reduce the fears and/or openly talk about your concerns with your partner?

- What has your partner done to reduce your fears?
- Have you been able to talk with your partner about an issue you have at home, like you have in therapy?

Contraindications

This activity is not recommended for clients with a history of domestic violence, or sexual or emotional abuse. Therapists should ensure that both members of the couple feel safe with their partner before pursuing this activity. Appropriate rapport with the therapist must be established for partners to trust the therapist to guide the process of the activity and their conversation.

Readings and Resources for the Professional

Johnson, S. M. (1996). *The practice of emotionally focused therapy: Creating connection.* New York: Brunner/Mazel.

Johnson, S. M. (2002). *Emotionally focused couple therapy with trauma survivors.* New York: Guilford Press.

Kerr, M. E. & Bowen, M. (1988). *Family evaluation: An approach based on Bowen theory.* New York: W. W. Norton & Co.

Bibliotherapy Sources for the Client

Christensen, A. & Jacobsen, N. S. (1999). *Reconcilable differences.* New York: Guilford Press.

Coleman, J. W. (2002). *How to say it for couples: Communicating with tenderness, openness, and honesty.* Englewood Cliffs, NJ: Prentice Hall.

References

Johnson, S. M. (1996). *The practice of emotionally focused therapy: Creating connection.* New York: Brunner/Mazel.

Kerr, M. E. & Bowen, M. (1988). *Family evaluation: An approach based on Bowen theory.* New York: W. W. Norton & Co.

– 3 –

Altering the Abyss: Externalizing Negative Interaction Cycles

Andrew S. Brimhall
Brandt C. Gardner

Type of Contribution: Intervention/Activity

Objective

The purpose of this chapter is to introduce a clinical intervention that helps clinicians understand not only a couple's negative interaction, but also how to use that information in a therapeutic manner. The intervention builds on the strengths of three field-tested theoretical concepts and demonstrates how they can be integrated into one powerful intervention. Three objectives exist for this intervention: (1) to help couples identify destructive patterns that exist within their relationship, (2) to help couples see and understand each person's role in maintaining that pattern, and (3) to help couples replace negative interaction cycles with more positive, healthy interactions.

Rationale for Use

Circular patterns are an integral part of any relationship (Watzlawick, Beavin, & Jackson, 1967). Although these patterns can be positive or negative in nature, researchers agree that negative interaction cycles have detrimental effects on relationships (Carrere, Buehlman, Gottman, Coan, & Ruckstuhl, 2000; Noller & Feeney, 1998). Both distressed and nondistressed couples are likely to engage in negative interactions; however, research indicates that distressed couples typically assign more negative intent to their partner's behavior, react more negatively to that behavior, and respond less positively to negative and positive stimuli than their nondistressed counterparts (Carrere et al., 2000). As clinicians, it is important to understand these cycles and determine what effect they are having on clients' relationships.

Role of Emotion

An essential aspect of helping couples redefine their relationship is helping them to uncover underlying emotions (Johnson, 1996). These emotions can be differentiated into four different categories: primary, secondary, instrumental, and maladaptive responses (Greenberg & Safran, 1987). Of these four, primary and secondary emotions have received the most clinical attention (Marston, 1927; Wetchler, 1999). Primary emotion is classified as the direct response to a situation, while secondary emotion is the reaction to or attempt to cope with that initial response (Johnson, 1996). For example, the primary emotion of hurt or fear is often masked by angry defensiveness—a secondary emotion. This angry defensiveness has the potential to trigger a negative interaction, because rather than responding to hurt or pain, the waiting spouse senses anger and responds accordingly. Therefore, each spouse formulates emotions and reactions based on his or her perceptions of the other's behavior, rather than the underlying emotions, thus exacerbating the negative interaction pattern (Johnson, 1996; Notarius, Lashley, & Sullivan, 1997; Prado & Markman, 1999).

Negative Interaction Cycles

Geist and Gilbert (1996) provide a description of how negative interactions can escalate. They write, "the less one feels heard, the more anger, whining and sadness one expresses; and the more anger, whining and sadness one expresses, the less one is able to listen effectively" (pp. 57-58). As these patterns occur over time they often become entrenched and turn into negative interaction cycles that predict divorce (Gottman & Notarius, 2000). Sensing the detrimental effects of these cycles, clinicians look for ways to raise couples' awareness of what is happening—one such tactic is circular pattern diagrams (CPDs).

Circular pattern diagrams. Based on the idea that a couple's behavior may be incongruent with their underlying beliefs, circular pattern diagrams were developed as a way to assess a couple's interaction (Wright & Leahey, 1994). Clinicians use these diagrams to slow the couple down and help them explore alternate meanings. This is accomplished by linking a specific behavior to an underlying cognition/emotion. For example, a wife who is being critical may feel sadness, but rather than expressing this sadness, she decides to use criticism (Gaelick, Bodenhausen, & Wyer, 1985; Geist & Gilbert, 1996). Upon hearing her criticism, the husband may feel hurt, but rather than sharing that with his wife, he responds by withdrawing from her. This response may engender more sadness, leading to more criticism and heightening his desire to leave.

Diagramming every step of this interaction helps the couple visualize that each person plays a vital role in maintaining the negative interaction—a primary goal of circular pattern diagramming (Wright & Leahey, 1994). The theory behind this form of assessment is that couples begin to realize that the behavior they experience from their partner does not match his or her underlying intentions (Prado & Markman, 1999). This process helps the other spouse realize that the underlying emotion his or her partner was experiencing was hurt or fear, even though he or she was showing angry defensiveness.

A CPD helps couples in three specific ways:

1. It helps them identify the negative pattern.
2. It helps them gain a better understanding of their partner's underlying emotions and cognitions.
3. It helps them realize that each person contributes to maintaining the cycle (Johnson, 1996; Wright & Leahey, 1994).

Emotionally focused therapy (EFT). To extend this information into more than just assessment, one might look to emotionally focused therapy. Based on the same principles and assumptions of circular pattern diagrams, Step 2 of EFT identifies the negative interaction cycle. However, rather than limiting that information to the role of assessment, it extends into the actual process of therapy. Throughout EFT, a clinician will refer back to the negative interaction cycle gathered during initial assessments and discuss how that cycle is being displayed within therapy (Johnson, 1996; Greenberg & Johnson, 1988). This is similar to White and Epston's (1990) concept of externalization. Johnson (1996) makes this link when she writes, "The identification and continuing elaboration of the negative cycle of interaction throughout therapy externalizes the problem in a manner not unlike the narrative approaches to therapy" (p. 55).

Although the process of identifying and discussing the negative interaction cycle is similar to externalization, it loses some of its power by not having a tangible representation of the negative interaction. The tangible representation helps the couple, as well as the clinician, to visualize the pattern and see it as something outside of the relationship—a process facilitated by the use of externalization.

Externalization. In 1990, White and Epston introduced externalization, a process that helps couples to objectify and/or personify a problem that they are experiencing as oppressive. Although these problems were often presented as internal, clinicians noticed that they were affecting the entire family. Families feel overwhelmed and discouraged, and experience the ongoing existence of the problem as a personal, relational, and familial failure. Rather than attribute the problem to the problem itself, families internalize it and see it as a reflection on their inability to control their own lives. As the problem persists, families begin to define their lives through the lens of the problem and thus present in therapy what White and Epston have labeled a problem-saturated description of their dominant story.

In an attempt to help couples separate themselves from their problem-saturated stories, White and Epston (1990) experimented with the concept of externalization. This style of intervention allows couples and families to explore new descriptions of themselves, one another, and their relationships. No longer dominated by their problems, they are free to explore other possibilities. This newfound freedom allows them to reevaluate their lives and discover a perspective not built around the problem (White & Epston, 1990). This new perspective helps them realize that their relationships are more meaningful than they were experiencing. Based on these experiences, White and Epston listed the following six items as positive aspects of using externalization. Externalization

1. decreases unproductive conflict between persons, including disputes over who is responsible for the problem;
2. undermines the sense of failure that many persons develop in response to the continuing existence of the problem despite attempts to resolve it;
3. paves the way for persons to cooperate with each other, to unite in a struggle against the problem, and to escape its influence in their lives and relationships;
4. opens up new possibilities for persons to reclaim their lives and relationships from the problem and its influence;
5. frees persons to take a lighter, more effective, and less stressed approach to "deadly serious" problems; and
6. presents options for dialogue, rather than monologue, regarding the problem (pp. 39-40).

Based on these six principles, neither the person nor the relationship is seen as the problem. Instead, the problem is seen as a separate entity, with the couple either sustaining it or nurturing it. Once the couple sees the problem as external, the clinician can process their experience through a series of relative influence questioning (White & Epston, 1990).

Using relative influence questioning, a clinician introduces questions that help the couple map the influence of the problem on their relationship as well as map the influence of the couple on the problem. Through these questions, a couple is able to understand the role of the problem and begin to undermine its power, rendering it less effective. This allows the couple to regain control of their lives and redefine their relationship without the pervasive influence of the problem.

Integrating the approaches. In conclusion, the most powerful contribution of the circular pattern diagram is the ability to help couples visualize their negative interactions. However, the power of the circular pattern diagram is limited because it is primarily used as an assessment tool and not extended into the realm of intervention. Understanding the power of implementing a couple's negative interaction cycle into the course of therapy, emotionally focused therapists constantly refer to the couple's cycle and how it affects their relationship. Although this technique is powerful, it fails to capitalize on the visual characteristics of the circular pattern diagram. Although the negative interaction cycle has been compared to externalization, the lack of using a visual diagram has the potential of lessening its possible effects on the couple. Based on these critiques, it is necessary to develop an intervention that integrates the strengths of all three approaches.

By using circular pattern diagrams and externalization, a clinician can not only assess a couple's negative interaction cycle, but also map the influence of that cycle on the couple's relationship. However, the process does not stop there. Clinicians can also map the influence of each partner on the cycle. This allows the couple to recognize the cycle, to begin to undermine its pervasive influence, and to redefine their relationship in a more healthy and positive manner. The following section outlines how this integration is performed.

Instructions

The following intervention is broken up into three different stages. Stage 1 is based on tracking the actual cycle. In stage 2 the clinician helps the couple externalize the cycle by giving it a name and describing its characteristics. Stage 3 is where the clinician begins to map the influence of the problem on the relationship as well as map how each partner maintains that cycle.

Stage 1

In staying true to the theory behind the circular pattern diagram, within the first couple of sessions the clinician begins to track the couple's negative interactions. The goal of this stage is to help the couple slow down their interactions and uncover any emotions and/or cognitions that may be influencing their behavior. Due to the circular nature of this process, it does not matter where the clinician begins; it is important to remember that cycles tend to escalate, and it might be necessary to go around the diagram a number of times. Most couples will be able to track their cycle to a point when communication is broken and the interaction ends. The clinician begins by labeling a circular pattern diagram, and then inquires about each partner's *thoughts, emotions,* and *behaviors*. Once the couple has had the opportunity to successfully uncover the entire cycle, the clinician is ready to move to stage 2.

Stage 2

The goal of stage 2 is to help the couple view the problem as an external force. This is best accomplished by encouraging them to give the cycle a name. This process is facilitated by exploring the influence the problem has on the couple's relationship. Questions regarding size, shape, color, and other characteristics of the patterns can also be useful in tracking the impact of the cycle on the relationship. Once the pattern has been named and defined, the therapist is then able to move on to stage 3.

Stage 3

Although the clinician already began the process of mapping the cycle's influence in stage 2, stage 3 is dedicated to helping couples explore the prevalence of the cycle in their daily lives. After the diagram has been completed and properly named, the clinician places the paper in a chair with wheels and asks questions regarding its place in the relationship (between the couple, on the other side of the room, etc.). The clinician can also question the prevalence (at night, after work, etc.) and the strength (overwhelming, "I don't even want to try anymore") of the cycle. Clinicians can also track if the couple has ever had the strength to push the cycle away by asking questions such as "tell me about a time when this was not as powerful." By asking questions regarding the couple's ability to stay clear of the cycle, the therapist begins to ascertain ways in which the couple may be influencing the problem.

In order to understand the entire process, the following section will include a fictional vignette of a clinician using this intervention with "Mike" and "Jen." The basis of the negative interaction cycle is a common pattern of pursue/withdraw and, although Mike and Jen are fictional, their comments are based on the reactions of numerous couples who have participated in this intervention.

Brief Vignette

Stage 1

THERAPIST (T): Jen, you mentioned that whenever you and Mike argue, he tends to withdraw. If there were a script running through your head that recorded your exact thoughts, what would it say? [Note: it does not matter which partner you start with.]

JEN (J): Well, it would say, "He makes me so mad." I've even found myself getting so upset that I've thought, "I could just strangle him." I guess I find myself thinking that this just goes to show how much he respects the way I feel. [Note: facilitator begins filling out a circular pattern diagram.]

T: So when these thoughts run through your mind, what kind of emotions do you associate with them?

J: Anger most of all.

T: What do you think is underneath the anger? In your opinion, what is fueling it?

J: I suppose it would be confusion and disappointment. I don't want to have a marriage where we cannot talk about our feelings.

T: So anger, confusion, disappointment . . . anything else?

J: I imagine I feel some resentment as well.

T: All right then. Now Mike, how do you know when Jen is experiencing these emotions? What things do you notice her doing and/or saying?

MIKE (M): Well, she starts in on how I never want to talk and how I'm the reason we have problems. I try to get away, but she just follows me wherever I go.

T: Which triggers what thoughts for you?

M: I wish she'd just go away and leave me alone.

T: And when you want her to leave, what feelings are you experiencing?

M: I feel trapped. It's almost as if I'm suffocating. I just want to get away, get a little bit of space so I can breathe, but there she is constantly on my back.

T: So we have trapped, a sense of suffocation, a feeling that you can't breathe. I assume then that these emotions usually lead you to withdraw even further, is that right?

M: Yeah, that's usually how it goes. I try to escape and she follows right behind, until both of us get so angry we don't want to talk anymore.

The clinician would continue this type of questioning, trying to uncover underlying emotions and cognitions, until the extent of the pattern was explored. Once the couple feels it is complete, the therapist could then move to stage 2.

Stage 2

T: So here is the pattern you've described. Jen feels angry, confused, and disappointed because she thinks you don't respect her. These feelings usually lead her to try harder to get your attention. And Mike, you say this attempt makes you feel trapped, as if you're suffocating and you're just thinking, "Leave me alone." Feeling trapped, you try to escape which just reinforces Jen's fear and causes her to try even harder, until you reach a point where both go their separate ways. Does that sound right?

M AND J TOGETHER: That sums it up pretty well.

T: It sounds like this is a scary process for each of you. If you were to give it a name what name would you call it?

M: That's a tough one. It just sucks energy from both of us and neither of us ends up feeling very close to the other.

J: I see it almost as an abyss. It's this dark chasm that just keeps us apart. When we are arguing and fighting I feel like Mike is so far away. All I want to do is reach out to him, but I just don't know if I can reach.

T: An abyss. Does that fit how you've been experiencing this cycle, Mike?

M: Yeah, that is a pretty good description of how I feel.

T: So when this abyss is at its peak, how big would you say it is?

M AND J TOGETHER: It engulfs both of us.

T: Does it have a color?

J: It's dark black. It feels like I am alone and I can't even see my hand in front of my face.

Questions regarding the size, shape, and other characteristics about the cycle would continue until the couple was able to see it as an external entity that was affecting their relationship. Once that occurred they would be ready for the final stage.

Stage 3

T: [Placing the diagram on the chair.] From what I hear you saying, this cycle is like an abyss that wedges itself in between you [wheeling the chair over and placing it between the couple] and then escalates until you feel engulfed and overwhelmed. Does that seem to capture it?

M: I'd never thought of it that way before, but yeah it seems to fit. It seems like we are always separated by something. Whether it is work, or the kids, or whatever, we start to argue and then we are further apart than when we started.

T: Jen, tell me of a time when it wasn't that way. Tell me about when you and Mike were able to get the best of the abyss rather than letting the abyss control the relationship.

J: Well, there have been plenty of times. When we were first married, we were able to sit down and discuss our goals, our dreams, and even our disappointments without attacking each other. It seems like this has gotten worse over the past couple of years.

T: What has changed, in your opinion?

J: I don't know. We just don't seem to care about each other as much as we used to. It seems like instead of being there for each other we want to tear each other down.

T: [After several minutes of mapping the influence of the problem.] So we've seen that this abyss has a pretty strong hold on your relationship. But it seems like you've been able to keep it at bay in the past. Mike, what is one thing you think you could do this week to move the abyss even an inch away from you and Jen?

M: I guess that I could let her know when I'm feeling trapped, let her know that I want some space.

Mapping the influence of the problem on the relationship, as well as the influence of each partner on the problem, is a process that occurs throughout therapy. The clinician helps the couple understand that the problem is the problem, that they have power to overcome this problem, and that a united front against this enemy is their best line of defense. It is also important to note that some clinicians may be uncomfortable with the negative focus of this intervention because their particular mode of therapy may rely on a strengths-based model. Although the focus of this chapter is externalizing the negative interaction cycle, the same principles hold true for positive interactions or virtuous cycles. Externalizing the positive interaction cycle follows the exact same format and only heightens the usefulness of the intervention. Armed with this intervention, clinicians can successfully track the effect of negative interaction cycles, positive interaction cycles, or a combination of both.

Suggestions for Follow-Up

This intervention can be used throughout the entire process of therapy. For example, at the first session after discussing the abyss it would be very easy for the therapist to start the session by asking, "Where was the abyss this week?" This intervention also lends itself to helping the couple track the influence of the cycle over the course of therapy (e.g., When you arrived it was this big and it was between the two of you; now as therapy progresses it is getting smaller and less prominent). As an extension of this intervention, clinicians can simultaneously track the couple's positive interactions—help the couple compare and contrast their relationship based on which external force is present. While this information helps the clients track their progress, it also helps the clinician account for change. Although it is not a formal way of collecting data for outcome research, it does provide the clinician with a way to quantify the change that has happened in therapy.

Contraindications

This intervention is not recommended for couples for whom violence exists and/or one or both partners are unsafe. The process of uncovering underlying emotions is a difficult endeavor and at many times leaves participants feeling vulnerable. This intervention is based on the underlying assumption that these primary emotions will be met with respect. It does not assume that everyone will be accepting of those emotions, but it does assume that those within the relationship still have some form of emotional investment and are willing to learn how they can contribute to making their relationship work. Because this intervention is theoretically tied to EFT and narrative couple therapy, readers are directed to follow any additional guidelines regarding contraindications espoused by those two models. For a comprehensive discussion of these contraindications, please refer to Johnson (1996, Chapter 9) and White and Epston (1990).

Readings and Resources for the Professional

Johnson, S. M. (1996). *The practice of emotionally focused marital therapy: Creating connection.* Florence, KY: Brunner/Mazel.

White, M. & Epston, D. (1990). *Narrative means to therapeutic ends.* New York: W.W. Norton & Co.

Wright, L. M. & Leahey, M. (1994). *Nurses and families: A guide to family assessment and intervention.* Philadelphia: F. A. Davis.

Bibliotherapy Sources for the Client

Gottman, J. M. (2001). *The relationship cure.* New York: Crown.
Gottman, J. M. & Silver, N. (1999). *The seven principles for making marriage work.* New York: Crown.
Notarius, C. I., Lashley, S. L., & Sullivan, D. J. (1997). Angry at your partner? Think again. In R. J. Sternberg and M. Hojjat (Eds.), *Satisfaction in close relationships* (pp. 219-248). New York: Guilford Press.

References

Carrere, S., Buehlman, K. T., Gottman, J. M., Coan, J. A., & Ruckstuhl, L. (2000). Predicting marital stability and divorce in newlywed couples. *Journal of Family Psychology, 14,* 42-58.
Gaelick, L., Bodenhausen, G. V., & Wyer, R. S., Jr. (1985). Emotional communication in close relationships. *Journal of Personality and Social Psychology, 49,* 1246-1265.
Geist, R. L. & Gilbert, D. G. (1996). Correlates of expressed and felt emotion during marital conflict: Satisfaction, personality, process, and outcome. *Personality and Individual Differences, 21,* 49-60.
Gottman, J. M. & Notarius, C. I. (2000). Decade review: Observing marital interaction. *Journal of Marriage and the Family, 62,* 927-947.
Greenberg, L. S. & Johnson, S. M. (1988). *Emotionally focused therapy for couples.* New York: Guilford Press.
Greenberg, L. S. & Safran, J. D. (1987). *Emotion in psychotherapy: Affect and cognition in the process of change.* New York: Guilford Press.
Johnson, S. M. (1996). *The practice of emotionally focused marital therapy: Creating connection.* Florence, KY: Brunner/Mazel.
Marston, W. M. (1927). Primary emotions. *Psychological Review, 34,* 336-363.
Noller, P. & Feeney, J. A. (1998). Communication in early marriage: Responses to conflict, nonverbal accuracy, and conversation patterns. In T. N. Bradbury (Ed.), *The developmental course of marital dysfunction* (pp. 11-43). New York: Cambridge University Press.
Notarius, C. I., Lashley, S. L., & Sullivan, D. J. (1997). Angry at your partner? Think again. In R. J. Sternberg and M. Hojjat (Eds.), *Satisfaction in close relationships* (pp. 219-248). New York: Guilford Press.
Prado, L. M. & Markman, H. J. (1999). Unearthing the seeds of marital distress: What we have learned from married and remarried couples. In M. J. Cox (Ed.), *Conflict and cohesion in families: Causes and consequences* (pp. 51-85). The advances in family research series. Mahwah, NJ: Lawrence Erlbaum Associates, Inc.
Watzlawick, P., Beavin, J., & Jackson, D. (1967). *Pragmatics of human communication.* New York: W. W. Norton & Co.
Wetchler, J. L. (1999). Integrating primary emotion into family therapy supervision. *Journal of Family Psychotherapy, 10,* 71-76.
White, M. & Epston, D. (1990). *Narrative means to therapeutic ends.* New York: W.W. Norton & Co.
Wright, L. M. & Leahey, M. (1994). *Nurses and families: A guide to family assessment and intervention.* Philadelphia: F. A. Davis.

CIRCULAR PATTERN DIAGRAMS

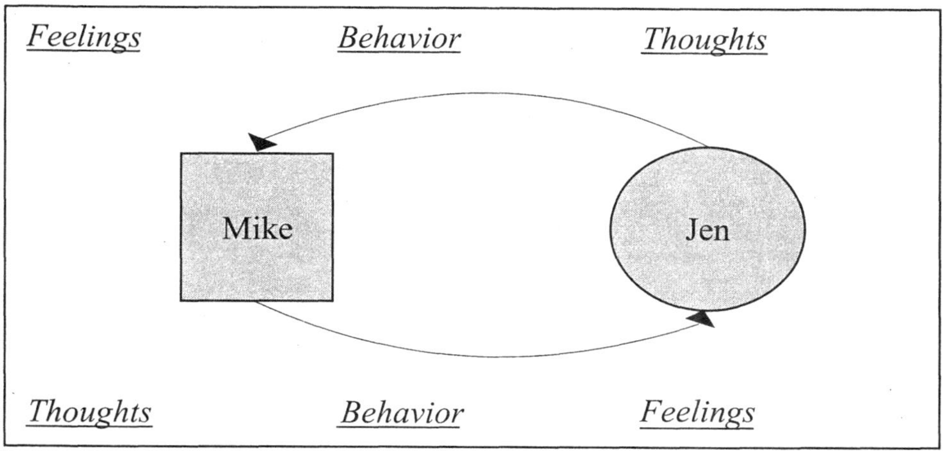

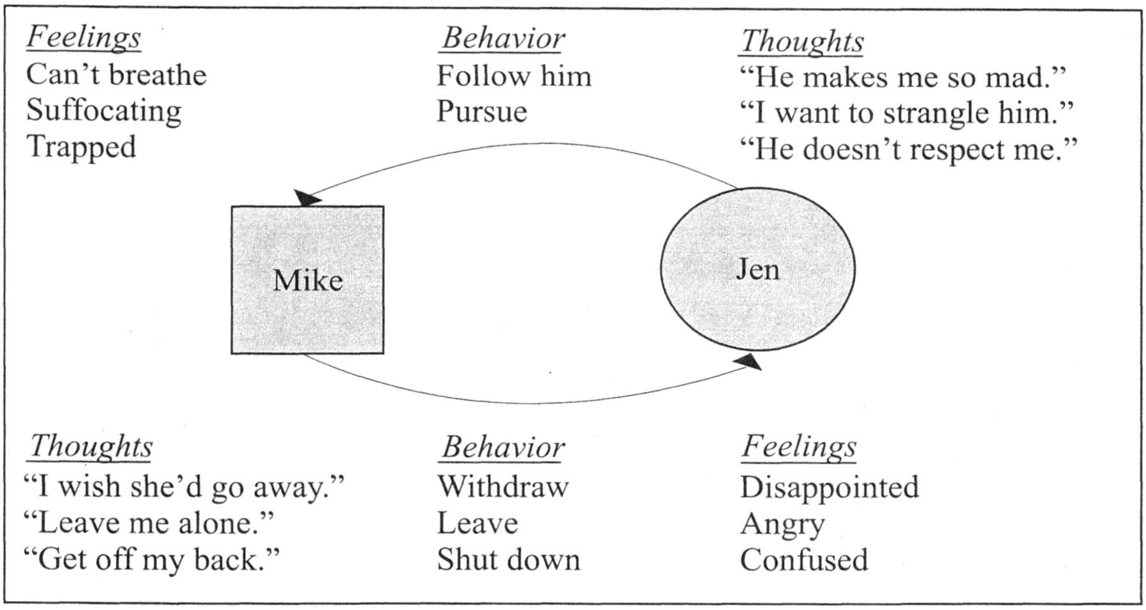

– 4 –

Money Talks

Margaret Shapiro

Type of Contribution: Activity

Objective

The purpose of the activity is to assist couples in discussing financial issues directly and effectively by improving communication and negotiation skills. By talking more directly, couples also recognize the symbolic aspects of money and how finances can have a profound impact on their emotional relationship.

Rationale for Use

Exploring a new place is much easier with a map, and getting where you want to go is less confusing and more efficient with a plan. Exploring relationships is also easier with a map or plan. Genograms serve as a map of families (McGoldrick, Gerson, & Schellenberger, 1999); developmental schemas are a map of growth and change. Theorists such as Freud (1905), Gesell (1940), Piaget (1950), Erikson (1963), and Kohlberg (1984) offer schema based on different aspects of a (male) individual's growth and development. Each psychologist proposes a theme or point of focus, which is then divided into stages. Broad expectations are delineated in each stage or age group for evolving development in different areas of sexuality, physical growth and coordination, intellectual development, mastery of psychosocial tasks, and moral awareness. More recently, Gilligan (1982) differentiated important developmental differences between genders. Carter and McGoldrick (1999) have written extensively about stages in the family life cycle, while Wallerstein and Blakeslee (1995) have written about stages and tasks of marriage. Awareness of these perspectives helps therapists refine goals, hone expectations, and explore themes while also pursuing the client's specific conflicts and concerns.

Some research indicates that the most frequent as well as most destructive conflicts among couples concern money (Stanley, Markman, & Whitton, 2002). How much or how little money a couple possesses has little bearing on the conflict, because money is both a reality and a metaphor. It is an emotionally loaded subject and metaphorically means different things to different people. Money can symbolize power, self-esteem, competence, acknowledgment, security, commitment, protection, control, independence, and love. Discussions ostensibly about money are usually also about other more submerged or hidden issues. For example, couples may feel it is easier to argue about the amount of life insurance than to be vulnerable to each other and reveal how one partner does not feel loved or protected if the other is not willing to provide more life insurance. Similarly, it is easier to argue about a bill or a new purchase than to reveal how one partner feels powerless, incompetent, or scared of not adequately providing for the family financially.

The following schema, Money Talks, is based on choosing a financial icon or symbol for each stage of a couple's life together and discussing in depth the issues this particular symbol may raise. This schema is based loosely on the stages of the family life cycle as described by Carter and McGoldrick (1999). The stages of a relationship are

- dating seriously;
- engagement;
- getting married;
- early marriage;
- family with young children, with teenagers, and with older children;
- grandparenting; and
- retirement.

Divorce, stepfamilies, and same-sex couples are included in this framework. These stages are meant only as a loose guide, as many couples do not have children or may choose alternative family-like arrangements.

By recognizing and emphasizing the importance of Money Talks early in a relationship, a therapist can help couples become more accustomed to discussing controversial issues, learn specific skills to communicate and negotiate, and understand that differences are often rooted in family-of-origin learning. By including questions of meaning, such as "What does this mean to you?" or "Why is this so important to you?" a therapist helps the couple understand and appreciate differentiation, attachment, and loyalty issues. Each person can begin to incorporate the importance of understanding, but not agreeing with, the other. As a result, there is less chance of minimizing, misinterpreting, or invalidating each other's position. Two prominent marriage research groups (Gottman, 1999; Markman, Stanley, & Blumberg, 1994) maintain that eliminating these destructive attitudes, which quickly become a pattern of communication, help a relationship stay vital, connected, and respectful.

Instructions

In working with couples it is necessary to first teach specific communication skills. Many communication techniques are described in the literature, and most emphasize clear articulation, unimpeded listening, and feeling understood. Slowing the dialogue down is essential so that each partner in the relationship feels understood. Couples are reassured when they realize that understanding the other does not mean agreeing with their partner. The Speaker-Listener Technique, spelled out by Markman et al. (1994) in *Fighting for Your Marriage* is clear, simple, and easy to teach:

> *Rules for the Speaker:* Speak for yourself; Don't go on and on; Stop and let the listener paraphrase
>
> *Rules for the Listener:* Paraphrase what you hear; Focus on the speaker's message; Don't rebut
>
> *Rules for Both:* The speaker has the floor; Share the floor; No problem solving (pp. 63-66).

The impact of the Money Talks exercise is increased if these communication techniques are taught and practiced with the couple in advance.

There are ten Money Talks, with specific conversations in each stage. In the early stages couples are asked to assess financial matters in the early part of their committed couplehood. In the middle stages couples are asked to discuss the meaning of money as they become a family and deal with their own and their children's evolving needs. In the last stages couples are asked to discuss financial matters as they relate to their later needs and priorities. The tenth Money Talk relates specifically to stepfamilies, same-sex couples, and unmarried couples with children.

Many of the talks can be repeated or revisited at different stages, such as the checkbook, insurance, retirement planning, who shall work more, and gifts. The topics have different implications at different ages, as well as when financial circumstances change.

Early Stages

Money Talk 1. The icon for seriously dating is a credit card. The couple at this stage may be living with each other. Couples rarely talk about their credit card use or debt at this stage of their relationship because it may be viewed as rude or inappropriate to ask about their partner's bills or charging habits. However, if the couple is considering a long-term commitment, this is an important discussion. It is essential that couples in a serious relationship begin to discuss financial issues and have some recognition of both the origin and impact of their own behavior, thoughts, and feelings. These guided discussions help couples articulate their individual priorities and begin to think about the importance of negotiation as their relationship progresses.

Questions at this stage include the following:

What does debt mean to each of them?
How did their family of origin think of and handle debt?
What are their thoughts about paying off the other's preaccumulated debt once they get married?
How do they each think of using credit cards?
How many cards does each have?
Do they pay the minimum or do they try to get it all paid off?
What other differences do they have regarding finances at this point?

Talking about these issues with a therapist allows for clear communication and gives each person a chance to both fully verbalize and hear concerns, questions, and thoughts.

Money Talk 2. The icon for the engagement stage is a ring. Couples should discuss the following questions:

What does a ring mean to each of them?
How important is the price?
Does an expensive ring mean one is loved or more committed?
Should it be picked out together or should it be a surprise?
Should it be financed by borrowing money or a savings account?
Should the payment of the ring be a joint decision?
Should either set of parents be involved?
What does having a family ring or gem mean to each of them?
What would it mean to not have a ring?
How else could the couple symbolize their engagement and commitment?
How did each set of parents signify their engagement to each other?
Does this have an impact on each partner?
What does it feel like to talk about finances in connection with this important event?
What is the hardest part of talking about the financial aspect of buying a ring?

This discussion never fails to bring up surprising issues for the couple, and it is the rare couple who can discuss this alone and in depth without conflict.

Money Talk 3. The icon for marriage is the wedding invitation. The following issues should be discussed at this stage:

Who will pay for the wedding celebration?
How much will it cost?
What should absolutely be included, and what is extra?
How shall the couple make decisions with two sets of involved parents?
How much can they do on their own, and disagree with one family or the other?
How did each set of parents celebrate their own wedding?
What is the impact of this on each partner?
What is the hardest part of talking about finances in connection with the wedding?
How does it feel? How is the couple dealing with their differences?

This often brings to the fore the difficulty and confusion of being both a member of a couple and a member of a family. It is hard to please both sets of parents and a partner, and loyalty issues can be very disturbing at this stage.

This stage is more complicated if the partners come from different ethnic, religious, or economic backgrounds. It is essential that the therapist encourages the couple to discuss these differences and how they impact the wedding and family expectations. The following questions are important to consider:

Does one family expect the other to contribute half of the expenses?
Does one family expect the other to host the rehearsal dinner, while the other family never heard of a rehearsal dinner?
Does one family have specific cultural or religious customs that they want observed while the other family has no way of knowing these customs?
If the bride and groom are from different countries, does one family expect the whole village to be invited to the celebration while the other family is thinking this will be a small family celebration?

Discussing these questions and expectations in advance prevents many misunderstandings later.

Money Talk 4. The icon or symbol for the early stage of marriage is the checkbook. The questions center on how to manage finances:

Shall we have one checkbook or two or three, and what does that all mean?
How much privacy shall each person have in regard to saving, spending, and organizing finances?
What shall be separate and what shall be a joint decision?
Is there a way to have both some autonomy and some mutuality?
Does it make sense for there to be a certain purchase price at which the couple agrees to discuss the advisability of the purchase?
How shall decisions be made if there is a fairly big disparity between their incomes?
If one partner has inherited money, how shall that be managed?

At this stage, family-of-origin influence becomes more explicit and is often a surprise for each partner. For example, one person is often amazed that his or her partner would even think of having a separate checkbook or, on the flip side, would ever need to consult with the other when considering an investment. The relationship will be in for a rough journey if financial discussions are not frequent, clear, respectful, and focused by this stage. Discussions about conflictual subjects only become more difficult if the couple has not yet developed skills to communicate, problem solve, and negotiate before moving on to the middle stages of life with children.

Middle Stages

Money Talk 5. The icon for the young family stage is a crib. There are some significant financial decisions at this point:

Shall one parent stay home with the baby or work part-time?
Shall both parents work full-time, and what does that mean in terms of child care?
Who stays home if the child care arrangements fall through?
What are the implications in terms of spending and saving?
Does the person who makes more money think he or she has, or deserves, more power in deciding how it is spent?
How can some balance be maintained?
How are the finances arranged so that the one making less does not feel he or she needs to beg or ask permission for each purchase or expense?
If one parent is working part-time or staying home, what are the expectations of each about who does the errands, cooks, shops, and cleans?
What is shared and what is the sole responsibility of one partner?
If work schedules change at this point, how will these responsibilities be shifted and balances maintained?
Shall they buy a bigger house to accommodate more children?
Shall they start saving for college education, or for private school if that is part of their plan?
Shall they think about life or disability insurance in case of some unforeseen catastrophe?

Many couples are also starting to save for retirement at this stage, even though it is a long way off. Each of these decisions involves extensive thinking, discussion, and change from their previous lifestyle of having to be responsible only for themselves. For the conversation of saving for college education the questions continue:

Can they expect or ask either set of grandparents for help with college tuition?
What does that mean for each partner?
How soon and how much shall they save each month or each year?
Do they expect to take out loans or have the child work?
How much should they sacrifice for each child's education or is it also the child's responsibility?
How did their families finance each partner's education and what was the expectation?

This is a conversation that gets repeated with the child as he or she approaches college age but is often a worthwhile discussion between parents when the child is very young.

The purchase of a house can be very complicated, and the following issues should be discussed:

Where do they want to live, in the suburbs or the city?
What does that mean in terms of public or private school?
Should the house be near either family of origin or at a distance?
Do they want to buy a house with the idea of moving in a few years or with the idea of staying in one place while they raise a family?
Can they expect any help from either set of parents?
What does that mean to each partner?
Do they want to do a lot of work on a house which may cost less to purchase?

Do they want to stay within their present means or buy something with the hope that their income will increase significantly in the next few years?
How much of a risk are they each willing to take on location, on incomes rising, or on the repairs that may be needed?
How will the decision of one of them working less or not working at all impact the price of the house?

A third essential conversation is the purchase of life and disability insurance. Thinking about this is often very difficult for young couples, as it implies that unforeseen events can happen and things can go very wrong despite the best laid plans. It may evoke painful memories if either partner has experienced a death or serious injury of a parent which affected the finances of his or her family. Life insurance is usually more frequently thought of than disability insurance, while the reality is disability insurance is just as, if not more, essential. The questions would include the following:

How much money is needed for this family if either parent should die or become disabled?
How do they go about finding insurance policies if they are not available through work?
What is it like to talk about this together?
What does it bring up for each person?
What is it like to feel responsible for the financial future of others—spouse and children?
What is it like to think and talk about not being totally in control of what happens with your family?

Money Talk 6. The icon for the stage of parenting adolescents is a car. Discussions about money with adolescents are provocative and difficult. The parents need to function as a team and privately discuss their expectations of this stage before dealing with the teen directly:

Do they expect the adolescent to have a job and, if so, what will the money cover?
Are parents expected to cover the adolescent's expenses?
Is the teen entitled to an allowance and what should it be expected to cover?
Is the teen expected to do certain jobs in the house to earn the allowance?
What was each of their experiences with money as a teen?
What is the reaction if the adolescent wants a car or his or her own computer, phone, or TV?
Should the teen have a credit card and how should it be used?
What are the penalties for misuse?
How can the parents avoid being split by the teen if they disagree on what should be provided and what is appropriate?
How are they planning for college tuition costs at this point and should the teen be included in these plans?
Is he or she expected to contribute toward educational expenses?
What is it like to set financial boundaries and expectations with a teenager?
How does it feel to talk about money with teens?
What is the hardest part and the most surprising part of these money discussions, both with a spouse and with the teen?

Later Stages

Money Talk 7. The icon for the stage with older children is a quiet phone. Although having children in college is not quite like having an empty nest, parents often experience the house as quieter and begin to anticipate what life will be like without the phone ringing constantly and not competing with the child for the car. Questions for this stage focus on redefining intimacy, couplehood, and reorganizing priorities:

Now that the couple is entering a new phase, what do they want to do together?
If college is almost paid for, can they save toward traveling or a second home?
Is moving to smaller living accommodations a comfortable option?
How do they want to save money or pay off debt at this point?
How long do they each plan to work?
Is this a time to think about changing vocations or doing something one has always dreamed of (e.g., teaching or landscaping or starting a small creative business)?
Can they think about changing roles and having the other partner take on more economic responsibilities if this has been uneven?
Are there any immediate health concerns that impact financial plans?
Do they have a viable retirement plan and long-term care plan?
Do either of their aging parents need help financially or in other ways?
What are each of their thoughts about helping their children financially after college?
What was their own experience with financial help after college or for graduate school?

Money Talk 8. The icon for the stage of grandchildren is a photo brag book. Becoming a grandparent brings up a whole new set of financial questions:

What is expected and what do they each want to do financially as grandparents?
Do they want to and do they have the means to contribute to an education fund for grandchildren?
What kind of gift giving do they want to do at holiday and birthday times?
What feels appropriate to each partner?
Is it appropriate to buy things frequently for grandchildren, and is that setting up a custom that is acceptable to each grandparent and parent?
How does it feel if grandchildren forget to say thank you or do not like or appreciate the gift?
How do they decide how much to spend or save for themselves and how much for grandchildren?
Should they help with a down payment on a house and, if so, will this be a loan or a gift?
What if their grown children have very different economic circumstances?
For example, how do they determine what is fair if one adult child is very well-off and another is struggling?
How do they talk to grown children about financial decisions?
What was the role of grandparents in financial matters in each of their families?

It is essential for the couple to have a discussion and not just assume that they agree on these sensitive issues. One partner may feel their financial responsibilities are completely over toward their grown children, while the other may want to make things easier or feel they have continued financial obligations to their adult children. This issue is even more complicated if stepchildren are involved.

Money Talk 9. The icon for retirement is a rocking chair. The discussion between the couple focuses on financial priorities for the last phase of their life together:

Is philanthropy, even a small amount, something that is important to one or both of them?
How and how much shall they give or leave to a cause or institution?

How shall they arrange their will and estate at this point in their lives?
How shall they take care of each other?
If there are imminent health concerns, how can they be sure there is enough health insurance and that each partner knows how to access it?
Are financial records and information readily accessible and understandable to each partner?
What is most important for each of them to do and accomplish at this stage, both individually and together?
How can they do this with the available financial resources?

Money Talk 10. The icon for stepfamilies is a big calendar to plan, so expectations of who is where and when are congruent among members of postdivorce families. With the divorce rate close to 50 percent, and more people choosing alternative lifestyles, it is important to consider financial discussions for different kinds of families. Stepfamilies face a complicated set of additional financial issues:

What are the financial arrangements that have been set up with former spouses?
What is expected of the stepparent and the former spouse financially?
What feelings does the stepparent and the biological parent have about the financial arrangements?
What are the most difficult parts of this arrangement for each partner?
How can each partner reassure the other of being a priority?
How can the couple set boundaries and be sure each partner feels as if he or she belongs when finances, which can symbolize commitment and love, are so complicated?
What do the adults need from each other when and if things feel chaotic, and how does money enter into this?

Sometimes a separate account to be used just for the couple helps both partners feel more secure.

For same-sex couples or unmarried heterosexual couples, the Money Talks need to include discussions about the legal documents at every phase and be explicit about wishes and expectations if one of them should die or become disabled. Is there life, disability, and health insurance for the partner? In other aspects, however, the Money Talks are similar for committed but not legally married couples at each stage of family development.

Brief Vignette

Rachel and Doug came to therapy to talk about their unending struggle about money. They were in their middle forties, had been married sixteen years, and had three boys who were all in school. Both of them were lawyers, although Rachel had chosen to work part-time since the boys were born. The couple's struggle focused on Doug's desire to save for retirement and Rachel's desire to renovate the house, specifically the family room. Their discussions always ended up in long, loud battles with no resolution. Both felt unappreciated and alone, and felt the other partner did not understand and was insulting.

Both Doug and Rachel agreed that communication techniques would be helpful before the Money Talks exercise. First, the therapist and couple practiced with "I" statements and feeling understood while discussing a less emotional matter. The couple initially had difficulty repeating what each said without rebutting, interpreting, or asking questions. After some practice, they were able to demonstrate these skills on a consistent basis. The therapist emphasized these techniques were meant to be used only when the discussion was not moving forward or when the couple felt stymied, not for general or everyday conversation.

After Rachel and Doug mastered the communication techniques, the therapist initiated a Money Talk based on stage five. She asked Rachel to talk to Doug about what the family room meant to her, using the technique they had just practiced. Rachel said she wanted the boys to have a comfortable place to be with their friends at home, as well as how important it was for her to know they were safe. She also wanted to enjoy their family life together and felt it was worth spending money to make that happen. Rachel identified some items that she would like to purchase, such as a bigger TV, a DVD player, music equipment, a comfortable couch, and some armchairs. Doug understood her concern and acknowledged the importance of enjoying family life and knowing the kids were safe. Then Doug shared that he wanted to be sure the couple had enough money to retire. With the therapist's encouragement, Doug talked about how he did not want to work as hard for the next twenty or twenty-five years. He hoped to retire at fifty-five and do something more meaningful. He did not want to be too old to enjoy life when he stopped working, but that meant socking away as much money as possible now.

The therapist asked about each of their parents' retirement. Doug's father had worked hard until he was over seventy and then had died soon after he retired. His mother had been left with adequate money but no time with her husband. Rachel's father had retired at age sixty-two with an adequate pension, but he and her mother had to be very careful financially. Neither of the couple's mothers had worked. Doug did not want to repeat either of their parents' scenarios. He said he did not want to be worrying about which brand of laundry detergent to buy when he was seventy, like Rachel's parents, and he wanted both some time and money to spend with his wife and family after retirement, unlike his father. Rachel agreed.

After hearing them both, the therapist pointed out how they each valued their family and wanted to enjoy time with them, but they had different timelines. Rachel wanted to be sure it happened now, and Doug wanted to be sure it happened in the future. In fact, when the two of them heard the therapist say that, they agreed they each wanted both. The emotion and tension in the room seemed to visibly diminish as they realized their goals were not so different. With some help the couple was able to talk about options and began to feel like more of a team making plans together. They no longer felt so personally attacked and unappreciated for what they were each trying to do. Doug had felt unappreciated for working so hard and for his careful planning. Rachel had felt criticized for wanting to spend too much money and guilty for not earning more. With the atmosphere calmer, they were able to understand each other and to feel more acknowledged themselves. Within five sessions of therapy, they had discussed their financial situation and made plans to do what each wanted. Rachel would work on a special project for her firm, some hours of which she could do at home, and earn extra money which would go toward family room equipment and furniture. Doug would help put up bookshelves and lay carpet, which would save some money. They also began to think about her working more once the youngest son was a little older, so that all the responsibility for saving for retirement was not on Doug's shoulders. Her firm had a good retirement plan, so even if they spent the money she earned, they would still profit from her retirement plan.

Suggestions for Follow-Up

These Money Talks can be used both with and without a therapist present. It is most effective to begin the talks with a therapist and continue them as homework, with a specific amount of time agreed on, for example, not to talk for longer than one hour. Couples can also develop their own icons to represent specific financial conversations, such as a piggy bank or picture of a new couch. The questions focus on the layers of meaning of the particular topic and also need to include how each of their families dealt with similar issues. Brainstorming options together, after the couple has had a few structured conversations, often helps them to negotiate some resolution. Sometimes just acknowledging and understanding each other is enough; and slowed down, more structured conversations help.

Conclusion

By recognizing the importance of money discussions throughout a relationship, a therapist can help couples discuss underlying themes such as

- setting priorities;
- negotiating the I and the we, i.e., how to hold onto both self and couplehood or maintaining both autonomy and intimacy;
- recognizing differences in family-of-origin styles and their influence on the couple;
- avoiding triangulation, particularly with adolescents;
- redefining intimacy once the children leave;
- rethinking priorities in retirement; and
- understanding stepfamily issues of belonging and expectations.

Money conflicts between couples both impact and are impacted by these themes. There is much less chance of distortion and misunderstanding when one person understands, both emotionally and cognitively, the significance of a particular financial concern or event to the other person. Money Talks support each partner in being clear to himself or herself and to each other in deciding what role money will have in their life together. In the long run, couples will realize that sharing difficult conversations about money—its complications, implications, and consequences—is the currency of intimacy and trust.

Contraindications

Money Talks will not be useful with couples for whom money disorders are a concern. These include excessive gambling, shopping addiction, or excessive hoarding of money. The topics suggested will be less useful for couples who are struggling with economic survival, although the communication techniques would be useful. The specific topics will be more useful to middle-class couples who feel they can plan and predict at least some of their financial future. Coparenting, divorced couples should have these conversations with a therapist and should avoid involving the child in the discussions. If couples cannot manage to have structured conversations and use the techniques on their own, the therapist should be present. These couples should be cautioned to not have extensive financial conversations on their own. Finally, it is important that the therapist *not* see himself or herself as a financial planner or investment counselor while talking about financial matters with couples. The point of these talks is not to offer financial advice. A referral to a financial planner or advisor is appropriate for specific financial concerns about investment, retirement, education planning, bankruptcy concerns, divorce, or tax planning. The therapist is useful for processing the underlying meaning of the financial discussion, while the financial advisor is useful for the factual content involving money.

Readings and Resources for the Professional

Barth, D. (2001). Money as a tool for negotiating separateness and connectedness in the therapeutic relationship. *Clinical Social Work Journal, 29,* 79-93.
Gallagher, N. (1992). Feeling the squeeze. *Family Therapy Networker, 16,* 17-29.
Gallen, R. (2002). *The money trap.* New York: Harper Resource.
Mellan, O. (1992). The last taboo. *Family Therapy Networker, 16,* 41-47.

Trachtman, R. (1999). The money taboo: Its effects in everyday life and in the practice of psychotherapy. *Clinical Social Work Journal, 27,* 275-288.
Turkel, R. (1988). Money as a mirror of marriage. *Journal of the American Academy of Psychoanalysis, 16,* 525-535.

Bibliotherapy Sources for the Client

Bach, D. (2001). *Smart couples finish rich.* New York: Broadway Books.
Hayden, R. (1999). *For richer, not poorer: The money book for couples.* Deerfield Beach, FL: Health Communications, Inc.
Markman, H., Stanley, S., & Blumberg, S. (1994). *Fighting for your marriage.* San Francisco: Jossey-Bass, Inc.
Mellan, O. (1994). *Money harmony: Resolving money conflicts in your life and relationships.* New York: Walker and Company.

References

Carter, B. & McGoldrick, M. (Eds.). (1999). *The expanded family life cycle: Individual, family, and social perspectives.* Boston: Allyn & Bacon.
Erikson, E. H. (1963). *Childhood and society* (2nd ed.). New York: W. W. Norton & Co.
Freud, S. (1905). *Three essays on the theory of sexuality.* English translation by A. A. Brill. New York: Nervous and Mental Diseases Monograph.
Gesell, A. (1940). *The first five years of life: The preschool years.* New York: Harper & Brothers.
Gilligan, C. (1982). *In a different voice: Psychological theory and women's development.* Cambridge, MA: Harvard University Press.
Gottman, J. (1999). *The marriage clinic: A scientifically based marital therapy.* New York: W. W. Norton & Co.
Kohlberg, L. (1984). *Essays on moral development,* Vol. 2: *The psychology of moral development.* New York: Harper & Row.
Markman, H., Stanley, S., & Blumberg, S. (1994). *Fighting for your marriage.* San Francisco: Jossey-Bass, Inc.
McGoldrick, M., Gerson, R., & Shellenberger, S. (1999). *Genograms: Assessment and intervention.* New York: W. W. Norton & Co.
Piaget, J. (1950). *The psychology of intelligence.* New York: Harcourt Brace.
Stanley, S., Markman, H., & Whitton, S. (2002). Communication, conflict and commitment: Insights on the foundations of relationship success from a national survey. *Family Process, 4,* 659-674.
Wallerstein, J. S. & Blakeslee, S. (1995). *The good marriage.* Boston: Houghton Mifflin Co.

– 5 –

How Does Your Garden Grow?

Lisa Jameyfield
Cezanne Elias

Type of Contribution: Activity that incorporates handouts and homework

Objective

This activity has been developed to enhance the emotional awareness of couples by providing psychoeducation relating to couple style. The need for nurturing and strengthening relationships is also a focus. This activity provides the participants with a metaphorical explanation of couple interactions and the need for ongoing evaluation within a relationship. Awareness of interaction style and emotional components of the relationship are also addressed.

Rationale for Use

This activity is intended for use with couples who are currently committed to a relationship and are attempting to enhance communication skills and increase the intensity of intimacy within their relationship. Acceptance and change can also be fostered through the psychoeducational processes directed through the activity. Clients can be provided with the groundwork that can give them the skills that lead to long-term nurturance. This activity is best facilitated through emotionally focused therapy and integrated behavioral couple's therapy.

Emotionally focused therapy for couples (Greenberg & Johnson, 1988) embraces the underlying emotions that formulate the interactions that we have with each other as couples. Emotionally focused therapy attempts to use therapeutic processes that uncover primary emotion that is exhibited by partners as anger, detachment, or other expressions. These emotions make it difficult for the couple to maintain the relationship in a functional way. Through this process, the couple can begin to find meaning in their partner's actions and begin to help heal the relationship. The included planting activity helps the couple to remember what things brought them together in the first place and helped them grow emotionally as a couple. The foundation for emotional groundwork is represented through the soil. Using the elements and seeds as emotional makeup, the couple further rediscovers their emotional ties and are able to express their feelings in a new way (Greenberg & Johnson, 1988).

Integrated behavioral couples' therapy (Jacobson & Christensen, 1998) focuses on acceptance and change. The behavioral component involves challenging clients' cognitions to allow them to become better focused on understanding each other. Maintaining communication is key to strengthening the bond between the couple to allow opportunities to better understand each other. Achieving another level of understanding can increase empathy and compassion, further allowing the couple to develop their relationship. Through the activities of promoting active listening and expressive communication, couples are able to validate each other's feelings and maintain a strong bond. The shared experience of planting a seed represents various concepts in integrated behavioral couples' therapy. The readiness of the soil to accept the seed can be an illustration for the couple to allow the foundation of their relationship to accept each other. The type of seed will dictate what conditions it needs for growing, just as providing the support that one's partner needs will improve the relationship (Jacobson & Christensen, 1998).

The couple is required to complete steps necessary for planting a seed in a pot (garden) and become consciously aware of the growing process necessary to maintain an optimal plant. The use of metaphors is a strong component and may be a consideration in using this activity.

Instructions

Planting of an actual seed is recommended for this activity. The necessary materials for completing this project include the following:

1 small pot
2 cups potting soil
2 plastic forks (rakes)
2 plastic spoons
1 small cup
1 seed packet
address labels
a small amount of water
paper towels

This activity should be planned for two consecutive sessions, allowing for homework between sessions. There are two basic components. The first component focuses on the preparation the couple made in their initial relationship. The therapist should ask questions relating to the couple's first meeting, as well as their family-of-origin relationships. The second component helps the couple determine their interaction style and indicates ways in which they can provide support for the relationship. The first session should include parts one through four. This will allow for soil preparation to begin and the discussion to take a metaphorical stance. Homework can be assigned to determine the couple style. The therapist should direct the couple to observe their own behavior over the coming weeks, paying close attention to their thoughts and feelings about their partner and themselves. The second session will address the couple style, the actual planting of the seed, and the steps necessary for it to grow and be nurtured.

Part 1: Laying the Groundwork for Growth

The therapist instructs the couple to remove the soil from the bag. The couple can do this in any manner they choose. The therapist can provide spoons, but the couple can also use their hands or other objects that represent their relationship. Once the couple decides on the object they will use to remove the soil, the therapist instructs them to place the soil in the planting pot. To process this step, the therapist could ask the following questions:

Like the seed, what and whom did you need to grow?
What in your life is sunlight?
What in your life is water?
Under what conditions does your seed grow best?

The therapist should have the couple respond first as individuals and then as a couple.

Part 2: Planting Your Seed

The therapist instructs the couple to prepare for planting the seed in the soil. The seed can be symbolic of many things:

What kind of seed would you like to plant?
What meaning does that type of seed hold for you and your partner?
Would you like to be the same type of seed or a different seed than your partner?
If you are different seeds, can you both grow in the same soil?
How did you determine what kind of seed to plant?

The therapist should include the feelings of both clients as individuals and as a couple. Discussion should follow, relating the process of acceptance to each relationship as a couple. The therapist asks the couple to address the following questions as individuals and then as partners:

What about your life together has made your relationship grow?
How does your relationship grow in times of conflict?

The therapist may at times ask questions that would help facilitate the thought process:

How did you know that your relationship had developed to the point of being ready for marriage?
What do you learn from confrontations or conflicts?

The therapist will then relate that sometimes factors outside of planting will have an effect on the couple's soil and seed. There can be too much sunlight or not enough sunlight; there can be shadows and rain. The therapist will then instruct the couple to work the seed into the soil while asking the following questions:

What factors affect your soil and the ability for your seed to grow?
What adjustments are made during this time?
What adjustments have you made to allow your relationship with your partner to grow?

Part 3: Watering Your Seeds

The therapist now begins the discussion of watering the seed. The couple may choose to water the seed in any way that reflects their individuality. They might bring a container from home that holds special meaning, such as a vase or bowl. The couple may bring the seed to the source of water, symbolizing their need to move away from family or friends to allow their relationship to grow. Once the couple determines how they will water their seed they should proceed, allowing the following questions to lead discussion:

Like the water, how can each of you, in your relationship, help your love to grow?
When you first met, how did you nurture your partner during times of conflict?
How do you nurture your partner in times of conflict now?
When you first met, how did you nurture your partner when things were calm?
How do you nurture your partner now when things are calm?

The therapist should explain that every plot of soil is unique; it may nurture some seeds and not others. One way to nurture the seed is to know what is needed. Like the seed, not all couples need the same things to grow. There are many typologies of divergent couple relationships. While reading and discussing the types of couples, the therapist should ask the clients to decide which one illustrates their partnership. Clients may find that they fit into more than one category or fit different categories at different times. The following are some examples summarized from Gottman (1988).

Close/Distant: Sometimes one partner wants to be very close to his or her partner while the other partner likes having some distance between them.

Conventional/Unconventional: Sometimes people who lead very conventional lives are attracted to people who are more adventurous and unconventional. Sometimes it is the opposite. This can create problems when one or both partners do not live up to their conventional or unconventional titles.

Artist/Scientist: The artist believes in spontaneity and play. He or she believes that the most important things in life are to be carefree and have fun; the artist finds the day-to-day aspects of life less important. The scientist finds it hard to be spontaneous and is very much a planner. He or she enjoys planning each task and planning for the future.

Control/Responsibility: Some couples argue about who is going to take care of the bills, balance the checkbook, and/or make dinner. Sometimes conflict can arise when both partners want control and responsibility over an area, or when neither partner wants to take control and responsibility over an area. Some partners want their partner to take more responsibility but then have a hard time letting go of that control and responsibility.

The therapist asks the clients to identify the couple styles that best describe their relationship and then to discuss their answers. The therapist may say,

> Sometimes these different styles can look like erosions in the sand, like weeds in the garden. However, weeds are a part of every garden and affect each chunk of soil and every plant regardless of how unique they are. Sometimes the roots of these weeds are so deep that no matter how much you pull them, they grow back.
>
> Because weeds will always exist in your garden, they must be tended to and the plants must be frequently nurtured. Weeds can, in fact, be extremely beneficial to the garden, for they are opportunities to care for and tend to the plant and the soil it is growing from. Similar to tending to your seeds, list some of the best ways you can tend to your relationship.

The therapist should tell the clients to consider the following concepts during their discussion:

> How do we best facilitate communication?
> When do I feel the closest to my partner and why?
> When do I feel the safest sharing my feelings?

The therapist should instruct each partner to write his or her list items on a label. Then, for each to stick his or her label on the pot, combining labels. The therapist should tell the couple to put their plant somewhere they can see it, to serve as a reminder to tend to their weeds during times of conflict and times of calm.

Brief Vignette

Mandy and Joe were coming to therapy following the loss of Joe's job. His job loss created a great deal of stress within the couple's relationship and they were fighting more often. The fighting had escalated and occurred in front of their children at times, further alienating them as a couple. Mandy and Joe had been attending couples therapy for six sessions. They initially found some relief from therapy. They reported a slight decrease in conflict, and Mandy felt that she was not as stressed. After session four, the couple seemed to be at a standstill. Although the conflict had decreased, they did not feel that they were able to make a connection. The therapist suggested that they try an activity that might help reinforce some of the feelings that brought them together in the first place. The couple agreed that a planting activity sounded interesting and thought a change might help.

The therapist instructed the couple to put the soil in the pot. The couple decided to do this with their hands, since they felt as if they were starting their relationship from nothing. Mandy decided that their relationship had too much rain lately and was in need of some sunlight to dry the rain. Joe felt their soil could grow with basic nutrients but thought Mandy needed the richest fertilizers to be satisfied. Mandy and Joe discussed the type of soil needed, and Joe discovered that he had misread Mandy, as she too wanted only the most basic of soils.

The couple selected a sunflower seed to plant in their soil. During this process, Joe and Mandy discussed how their similar choice of soil was reflective of their earlier relationship. They decided that this "sameness" was one of the things that felt good about their relationship. Mandy and Joe had grown up in the same town and had attended the same high school. That was one of the things that initially drew them together. Joe also realized that one of the other things that helped their relationship grow was their ability to spend time together. Before the recent job loss, Mandy and Joe enjoyed eating out every Friday and spending time at a local bar afterward. These weekly outings had stopped since money was an issue. At times, Mandy's mother offered them extra money to go out. This made Joe very uncomfortable and further depressed him, keeping him more firmly at home. Mandy thought that they had not been growing during this conflict but rather pushing away from each other. Joe decided that reconnecting by spending time together might help. He suggested that they go on walks together on Fridays until they were able to afford to go out again.

The couple was instructed to water their seed, choosing something that was meaningful to them as a couple. They chose a glass from their favorite restaurant and remembered some of the fun that they shared. They were careful to give only a little water, remembering that they both felt in need of some sunlight for their seed. Mandy recalled when Joe used to sing her songs if they had a fight. He also had a way of making her laugh during times of conflict. Mandy couldn't remember the last time she had laughed with Joe. Joe recalled his love for humor and did not realize the comfort that Mandy received from him. Joe in turn remembered how close Mandy used to be with him. She frequently held his hand and snuggled by him. Joe missed this closeness and realized he would like to feel special again. The therapist provided additional education on couple style as Mandy and Joe were ready to complete the final phase of their planting activity. Mandy and Joe agreed that they fit perfectly into the category of control/responsibility. Mandy identified with the controlling portion of the couple, while Joe felt he was forced to have most of the responsibility. Realizing this difference, they began to discuss ways to change their thinking and help support each other. Mandy agreed to get a part-time babysitting job until Joe found other employment. Joe agreed to do the weekly bills with Mandy so she did not feel so overwhelmed. When asked to make label stickers to put on their potted plant, Joe and Mandy discussed what they had rediscovered about their relationship. They agreed that the words "basic" and "laughter" were triggers to help them remember each other's needs. They also added "stable" and "time together" as points of reference. Joe also wanted to add "plenty of sunshine" to the labels, reminding him that they needed to recover from his job loss and continue to work on repairing the loss to the relationship.

Suggestions for Follow-Up

The plant should remain in the home with the labels serving as reminders for the couple as to the steps necessary for them to tend their garden. The therapist can refer to the garden as a metaphor for the progress in therapy. The therapist can also suggest that completing a task together can lead to discussion of other ways in which couple time can be developed. The discussion of the experience can be beneficial in determining the need for additional psychoeducation or related activities. The couple may choose to plant a real garden and tend it together. This activity would provide time for the couple to relate to each other while remembering the concepts they learned during their therapeutic planting session.

A similar result could be provided through interaction by working on a project that did not involve gardening. This could relate to a home improvement task, hobby, or sport. Spending time together while completing an enjoyable activity can enhance the concepts illustrated through the planting process.

Another couple activity could include the use of couple style information discovered during the planting session. After determining couple style, they could work together on developing a collage that lists their unique contributions to the relationship and what things allow them to form a partnership. This collage can be made with words, pictures, clippings from magazines, or other materials. Developing a way to illustrate individual strengths and strengths together can help cement the process experienced through the planting activity. An enhancement to this activity could be provided through the use of cartoon paper dolls. Paper dolls could be purchased or the couple could draw themselves or each other and add layers of clothing to represent current feelings. This may provide the couple with another activity that reinforces their ability to relate as a couple.

Contraindications

This activity would not be appropriate for couples who are highly conflictual or experiencing distance in the relationship. Couples who are experiencing physical abuse, or extreme verbal or emotional abuse would not respond well. Any situation where domestic abuse is occurring is not appropriate for this type of activity. The couple needs to be able to discuss topics without shouting or constantly cutting each other off. This activity would not be recommended for clients with cognitive challenges nor recommended for clients who may have difficulty comprehending the concepts described through the use of metaphor.

Readings and Resources for the Professional

Greenberg, L. & Johnson, S. (1988). *Emotionally focused therapy for couples.* New York: Guilford Press.

Gurman, A. S. & Jacobsen, N. S. (2002). *The clinical handbook of couple therapy* (3rd ed.). New York: Guilford Press.

Jacobson, N. & Christensen, A. (1998). *Acceptance and change in couple therapy: A therapist's guide to transforming relationships.* New York: W. W. Norton & Co.

Johnson, S. (2002). *Emotionally focused couple therapy with trauma survivors.* New York: Guilford Press.

Watzlawick, P., Weakland, J., & Fisch, R. (1974). *Change.* New York: W. W. Norton & Co.

Wile, D. B. (1993). *Couples therapy: A nontraditional approach.* New York: John Wiley & Sons.

Bibliotherapy Source for the Client

Gottman, J. S. & Silver, N. (1999). *Seven principles for making marriage work.* New York: Three Rivers Company.

References

Gottman, J. M. (1988). *Why marriages succeed or fail: And how to make yours last.* New York: Bloomsbury.

Greenberg, L. S. & Johnson, S. M. (1988). *Emotionally focused therapy for couples.* New York: Guilford Press.

Jacobson, N. S. & Christensen, A. (1998). *Acceptance and change in couple therapy: A therapist's guide to transforming relationships.* New York: W. W. Norton & Co.

– 6 –

Negotiating Couple Boundaries: The Metaphor of Gardens

Lee Williams

Type of Contribution: Activity

Objective

The objective of the garden metaphor is to help couples draw boundaries between individual versus couple issues.

Rationale for Use

Individuals frequently want to influence the behavior of their partners. Often this is motivated by a concern as to how the partner's behavior will impact the individual's own well-being. Other times, however, it may be motivated out of a concern for the partner's well-being. Although trying to influence a partner's behavior is a natural and ongoing process for all couples, some couples struggle with one or both partners perceiving the other as too controlling. This is particularly true for couples in which one individual tries to influence the other partner's behavior, but the partner perceives the issue as something that should be outside the other's influence. The metaphor of gardens described here helps couples think more clearly about individual versus couple issues, allowing them to better negotiate what should or should not be open to their partner's influence.

From a structural family therapy (Minuchin, 1974) perspective, boundaries between subsystems must be clear for a family or couple to operate effectively. According to Minuchin, "The boundaries of a subsystem are the rules defining who participates, and how" (p. 53). Based on this definition, the metaphor of gardens can aid couples to clarify their boundaries by helping them decide if a particular issue is in the individual or couple domain.

Instructions

When the therapist perceives that the couple is having difficulty negotiating what are individual versus couple issues, the therapist can introduce the idea that relationships have three gardens. Each individual has his or her own garden for which he or she is responsible, making two gardens. Between both of the individual gardens is a third garden, which is the couple garden. Because many individuals are helped by a visual aid, it is recommended that the therapist draw three equally sized circles side by side that are touching, but not overlapping, each other.

The therapist then explains that each partner is responsible for his or her individual garden. The couple garden that grows between them, however, represents the relationship. Both individuals are responsible for taking care of this garden. The couple is then told that they need to be clear in which garden each issue resides. If a decision or issue clearly impacts both individuals, then it is in the couple garden. If an issue predominantly involves just one individual, then it is considered to be in that individual's garden. If an issue is clearly in an individual's garden, then the other partner needs to respect the individual's autonomy by not trying to influence the partner's behavior on this issue. The exception is if the partner asks for advice or guidance. In essence, one must be invited into the partner's individual garden. Otherwise, the partner is instructed to kindly remind the other that this is his or her individual garden.

Describing the garden metaphor with one or two examples may be a sufficient intervention for some couples. These couples simply need a different conceptual map to alter their way of thinking and to possess the skills needed to negotiate whether issues are primarily in the couple or individual gardens.

Other couples, however, may need more guidance or help implementing the model. One way to do this is to actually have the couple work through one or more issues in session, with the therapist helping them negotiate whether an issue is in the individual or couple garden. In some cases, couples may need to strengthen their communication skills to effectively dialogue or negotiate with each other. To prepare the couple for such a conversation, the therapist might ask each partner to write down in advance whether he or she would put certain topics or issues in the couple or individual gardens.

Brief Vignette

Tom and Mary, both Caucasian, had been married for fifteen years. Both were in their late sixties, with neither of them working outside the home. The couple entered therapy because of increased conflict and dissatisfaction in their marriage. Both parties acknowledged, however, that conflict existed in the relationship for the past ten years. In therapy, Mary complained that Tom was too controlling. Upon further exploration of this dynamic, it appeared that Tom was constantly giving Mary advice on everything, which she found to be invasive and demeaning. Tom stated, in his defense, that he was simply trying to be helpful to Mary by sharing his expertise about things. Tom, for example, thought he was more knowledgeable about major appliances and therefore insisted that the couple purchase a certain type of stove and refrigerator.

The couple was introduced to the idea of the three gardens and how to differentiate among them. Mary immediately embraced the idea, claiming that Tom was constantly trampling her garden. Tom again insisted that he did not mean any harm. Tom was then told that although his intent may have been positive, the impact of his actions made his wife feel that she was not qualified to take care of her own garden. Tom admitted he had not thought of it in this way before. Tom was then told that another way he could show caring for his wife was to respect her autonomy on issues in her own garden. Tom worried that his wife might make some mistakes without the benefit of his knowledge. I agreed with Tom that mistakes were probably inevitable, but added that everyone was entitled to make and also learn from their mistakes. Furthermore, Tom was assured that this might be a small price to pay for greater marital harmony. Framed in this manner, Tom seemed receptive to experimenting with this new approach.

In subsequent weeks, Tom reported that he was trying hard to stay out of Mary's garden. Tom began giving Mary less advice, for example, when he recognized that some issues primarily affected her and had little direct impact on him. This, in turn, resulted in fewer conflicts between the couple. Indeed, the conflict over the stove was resolved by the couple on their own when they used the garden metaphor to facilitate their decision making. Tom acknowledged that because Mary did nearly all the cooking, she would be most affected by the decision. As a result, he deferred to her with regards to what stove they bought since he felt it was primarily in her garden.

Suggestions for Follow-Up

Couples can potentially get stuck in trying to decide whether an issue is in a couple or individual garden. One person may argue, for example, that the partner's behavior has some impact on him or her and that this issue should be in the couple garden. In contrast, the partner may argue that the impact on the other is small in comparison to the impact the decision has on himself or herself. Thus the partner argues it should be in an individual garden. In cases like this, the individual who is less affected may need to be encouraged to pick his or her battles. In the previous case example, Tom decided that the kind of stove they bought did not affect him enough to make this a battle worth fighting. It is also possible that one partner may deny or underestimate how much impact his or her behavior has on the other. An individual with a substance abuse problem, for example, may be reluctant to admit how his or her behavior is negatively affecting others. Put a different way, the weeds from the individual's garden could be seen as spreading into the couple garden, creating a relational problem. In cases such as these, the therapist may need to help the individual see how his or her problems are negatively impacting the other partner.

The therapist may also need to explore possible gender issues with the couple. Gottman and Silver (1999) state that one of the seven principles for making marriages work is letting your partner influence you. They state, however, that men generally have more difficulty than women in accepting influence from their partners. Indeed, gender socialization may contribute to the couple having different perceptions regarding what should be individual versus couple issues. Traditional gender socialization may make many men more protective of their autonomy, whereas gender socialization may encourage women to consider the needs of others, perhaps even at the expense of their own needs.

Therapists, like the couples themselves, also need to be careful as to how and when they use their influence. They need to be sensitive to the fact that what is defined as a couple or individual issue in their own relationships might be different for the couple with whom they are working. It is easy to imagine that one couple might decide that buying a stove was a couple issue because both would use it or see it as a large expenditure they both would need to agree upon. For Tom and Mary, however, the fact that one person primarily used the appliance made it an individual issue.

Contraindications

The garden metaphor is not intended for couples in which one partner is trying to dominate or control the other partner through violence and other fear-inducing tactics (Greene & Bogo, 2002). This metaphor also assumes that both individuals are committed to the relationship or to having a couple's garden. This activity would be contraindicated for couples when one or both partners question whether to continue with the relationship.

Readings and Resources for the Professional

Greene, K. & Bogo, M. (2002). The different faces of intimate violence: Implications for assessment and treatment. *Journal of Marital and Family Therapy, 28,* 455-466.

Minuchin, S. (1974). *Families and family therapy*. Cambridge, MA: Harvard University Press.

Bibliotherapy Sources for the Client

Christensen, A. & Jacobson, N. S. (2000). *Reconcilable differences.* New York: Guilford Press.

Gottman, J. M. & Silver, N. (1999). *The seven principles for making marriage work.* New York: Three Rivers Press.

Lerner, H. G. (1985). *The dance of anger.* New York: Harper & Row.

References

Gottman, J. M. & Silver, N. (1999). *The seven principles for making marriage work.* New York: Three Rivers Press.
Greene, K. & Bogo, M. (2002). The different faces of intimate violence: Implications for assessment and treatment. *Journal of Marital and Family Therapy, 28,* 455-466.
Minuchin, S. (1974). *Families and family therapy.* Cambridge, MA: Harvard University Press.

The Three Gardens

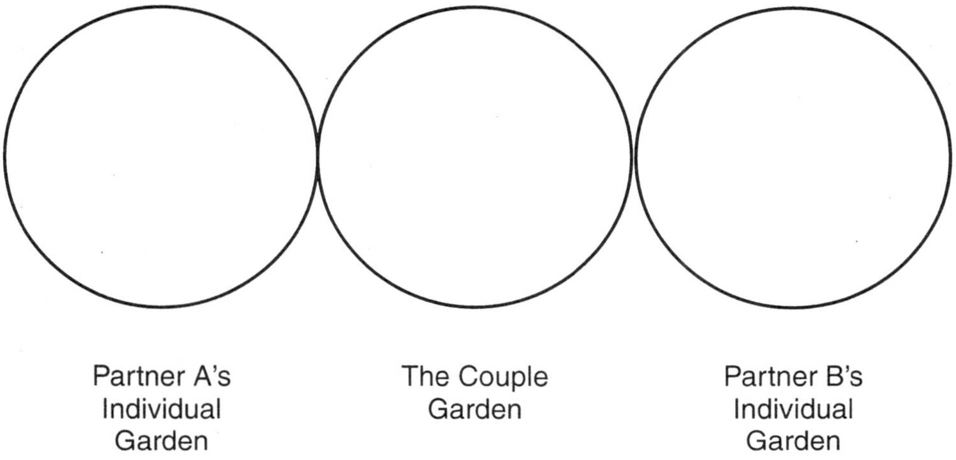

– 7 –

The Coming-Clean Ritual

Jon L. Winek
Patricia A. Craven

Type of Contribution: Activity

Objective

The objective of this activity is to help a couple move past an impasse in therapy that frequently occurs after the disclosure of an extramarital affair. Couples who are appropriate for this intervention have entered into therapy to resolve issues that have given rise to the affair. Typically, the couple is early in their treatment and has reached an impasse on issues involving trust and truthfulness. This ritual is the first of five rituals that are referenced to move the couple to a final stage of rebuilding the relationship (Winek & Craven, 2003). The stages are described as

1. knowing the details,
2. releasing the anger,
3. committing to the relationship,
4. reestablishing trust, and
5. rebuilding the relationship.

The coming-clean ritual is enacted in the first stage of knowing the details.

Rationale for Use

This ritual allows both parties to simultaneously address important issues. The involved partner often has a need to get out of a deceitful lifestyle. This ritual gives the couple an opportunity to stop lying and to "come clean." The uninvolved partner often has a need for the truth. Some clients report becoming obsessed with knowing the truth after they find out that their partner has engaged in an extramarital affair. Often these questions intrude on his or her psyche and lead the client to start pressing his or her partner to answer. This can occur at awkward times and make it difficult for the couple to engage in normal activities. This interaction locks the couple in the past, so they are unable to deal with the current relationship. If the partner answers truthfully in these interactions, emotional outbursts of hurt feelings and anger are likely. If the partner is evasive or dishonest, he or she becomes unable to escape the dishonest lifestyle that coexists in an adulterous lifestyle. The coming-clean ritual disrupts this pattern and allows the healing of the relationship to begin.

Because adultery in a relationship produces a dramatic shift in how the relationship is experienced, our approach is grounded in an experiential/symbolic approach (Whitaker & Bumberry, 1988). From this perspective it is believed that the trauma of an affair is experienced on both individual and systemic levels. The negative emotions associated with the experience can intrude into all levels of a couple's functioning. This in turn impacts the emotions, cognitions, and behaviors of the partners. "From this perspective the couple who is experiencing the trauma of an adulterous relationship must struggle through their experiences with a narrow range of constructs" (Winek & Craven, 2003, p. 249). "Symbolic Therapy, then, is involved in the effort to move directly into the level of living, not settling for the realm of thinking, talking, or reasoning . . . Symbolic therapy is an effort to deal with the representation system underneath what's actually being said" (Whitaker & Bumberry, 1988, p. 78).

Rituals may provide a way for people to find support and containment for strong emotions (Scheff, 1979). The use of ritualized interventions allows for several therapeutic advantages. Therapeutic rituals can create a shared commitment and experience and foster a feeling of connection to one's partner. Rituals become anchor points that facilitate life-cycle transitions and not only mark a transition but also make a transition (Imber-Black, Roberts, & Whiting, 1988).

1. Rituals create a sense of commitment and connection. It is common that early in treatment these couples struggle in reconnecting with their partner.
2. Rituals allow for the grounding of values. Rituals create an emotional connection to the participants' core values. In this situation, values of truthfulness and being informed are brought to the foreground of therapy.
3. Rituals involve moments and acts that are nonverbal in nature. This orientation allows the clients to take direct action to address the problems. The action orientation also encourages the clients to take responsibility for their situation. Rituals combine "doing" with "believing."
4. Rituals are symbolic in nature and, as a result, assist the clients in making emotional shifts. By connecting the actions of the ritual with the symbols we can enter into a client's emotional world. The symbols of the coming-clean ritual provide an opportunity for the betrayer to come clean and become truthful.

Instructions

Implementing the ritual takes several sessions to plan. We have found that the impact of the ritual is a direct function of the planning and preparation. The ritual is set up in three phases: (1) introducing the ritual, (2) designing the ritual, and (3) enacting the ritual. Careful attention to the details of all three phases is essential for the couple to be successful in the enactment of the ritual.

After a couple in therapy finds themselves stuck regarding issues of truth and the details of the affair, it can be useful to introduce the coming-clean ritual. We have found it helpful to talk about rituals in general before a specific ritual is introduced. Rituals are described as a therapeutic tool that allows the clients to do something that in turn can help them change how they feel about some aspect of their lives. The coming-clean ritual is presented as a way the couple could work together to start to heal the trauma of the affair. It is helpful if you provide them with feedback on the nature of the sticking point by describing the couple's interactional pattern.

Designing the ritual involves spelling out the specifics of the ritual. The first step consists of the uninvolved partner generating a list of questions. He or she agrees to control the urge to ask the questions as they come to mind. In exchange for deescalating the conflict, his or her partner agrees, at a predetermined time and place, to sit down and answer all questions honestly and completely.

Prior to enacting the ritual, partners are seen individually to discuss their role in the ritual. The involved partner is encouraged to focus on honesty during this session. He or she is asked to explore the short-term costs of being honest (i.e., hurt, angry partner) against possible gains (escaping a deceitful lifestyle). With the uninvolved partner, two issues need to be addressed in individual sessions. First, he or she must get some degree of control over his or her anger. If this does not occur then the ritual can become emotionally explosive. As Westfall (1995) has described, it can be useful for the therapist to help the clients edit their questions. This is to help the ritual be positive rather than a negative, destructive interrogation. Westfall (1995) describes a question that the uninvolved partner frequently has:

> "Did you like being with your lover more than you liked being with me?" The therapist can reframe the spouse's question in a way that gets at the heart of the question, but without the painful rejection implicated in the spouse's plea. For example, "How were you different when in the company of the affair partner?" or, "What did you like about yourself in this situation?" (p. 157).

After a list of questions has been developed and edited the couple is ready to negotiate the specifics of the ritual. The couple needs to decide where and when the ritual is to take place. Some couples prefer to hold the ritual in their home while others prefer to enact the ritual in another place such as their church or the therapist's office. The clients also need to decide if they will enact the ritual alone or with the support of some other person. For example, a couple could include the therapist as a witness to the ritual. Regardless of who is included, it is important that the therapist meet with them so they will be clear in their roles.

Brief Vignette

Bill and Mary had been married for twenty-two years. Mary was cleaning out Bill's dresser drawer and found unfamiliar movie tickets and restaurant receipts. She remembered Bill making several business trips out of state. Mary became suspicious but said nothing. Their two children were both attending college and came home on the weekends. Mary spent most of her time making sure her family's needs were met. She also cared for her aging mother a few days a week. Bill sought therapy individually because of his obsessive feelings of guilt. He admitted in therapy he had become involved with a younger woman at work and engaged in fictitious business trips to spend time with her. Bill still loved his wife but felt torn between this young woman and his wife of twenty-two years.

Bill agreed that he needed to disclose his affair to his wife. They, in turn, both agreed to come in for couples' therapy to heal their relationship. Bill made the choice to cut off the affair with the younger woman and begin repairing his relationship with his wife. Mary felt betrayed and deeply hurt by Bill's infidelity. Her hurt turned inward to depression, and although she wanted to end the relationship, she felt obligated to try therapy. After a few weeks in therapy she came to realize that she still cared for Bill, but her positive thoughts toward him were intruded upon by questions about the affair.

Some of the questions she had about the affair involved self-blame: "What did I do to drive you to another woman? Aren't you attracted to me anymore?" She also had questions about the details of the actual events: "What did she look like? How old is she? How many times did you sleep with her?" When she asked Bill these questions in an unstructured way an argument ensued and both parties were hurt for several days. It was at this point that the idea for the coming-clean ritual was introduced.

Mary and Bill engaged in daily rituals and were familiar with the concept of rituals and their utility. Both were flexible and open to the process and realized this was a pivotal point in their relationship. Both seemed troubled by the secrecy and wanted to get the truth revealed in a therapeutic environment. The couple, unfamiliar with communicating openly about sensitive issues, was at a point of wanting to both change and repair their relationship.

As the ritual was described, Mary agreed to hold her questions until the enactment of the ritual. She started to write them down in a journal she kept hidden from Bill. This was the first time she had kept anything private from him, and this led to a discussion of boundaries in relationships.

The ritual was designed and scheduled to take place in Mary's office after normal business hours. Bill was to arrive alone and agreed to answer the entire list of questions fully and truthfully. Bill was reluctant, but anxious to relinquish his deceitful lifestyle and answered all questions to reveal them "once and for all." As Mary's questions were answered, she marked them off with a black magic marker. She reported that after most of the questions were answered, understanding became less important to her. After all of the questions were answered, Bill left the office and Mary spent some time with a friend who was supportive and had also survived an affair in her relationship.

A follow-up session was conducted with each partner to process any underlying feelings of anger and hurt, as well as a conjoint session to allow the couple to reconnect. Bill felt a combination of relief and remorse. He was sorry about what he had done but also felt considerably better about his own morals and values having come clean about his actions. Mary's curiosity about Bill's motivations and intentions was exposed. She needed further processing of some of the answers as she was putting the puzzle together. In the conjoint part of the session, it was arranged and mutually decided to leave the questions with the therapist. Bringing the questions home would invite further questions and tempt the couple to revisit the ritual.

Suggestions for Follow-Up

An extended session is scheduled for the couple shortly after the ritual is enacted. Approximately one-third of the session is spent with the individual partners. In each of these interviews they are asked questions about their emotional responses to the ritual. Each is allowed to process his or her feelings in a nonjudgmental environment. The couple can choose to leave the questions for the therapist to dispose of at a designated time.

A final follow-up activity allows for a second ritual, which features destruction of the archived questions. Couples who continue to address these issues in therapy soon face issues of anger. A ritual can be cocreated to destroy the questions by cremation or burial. This can be a powerful symbol for the couple, and engaging in such a ritual results in further facilitating the therapeutic process.

Contraindications

This intervention is appropriate for most clients in the early stages of therapy to resolve issues of trust and betrayal associated with the disclosure or discovery of an affair. However, there are situations in which such an intervention would be inappropriate. Clients engage in rituals in everyday life to some extent; if the clients' use of rituals is rigidly constructed or the couple is "under-ritualized," it may be more difficult for the couple to engage in the ritual. This resistance may interfere with the success of the ritual. If an affair is continuing during therapy, this ritual is not appropriate because the couple is not at a stage of healing the relationship. A commitment to the relationship is essential to the success of the coming-clean ritual.

If the therapist is also treating the couple for domestic violence, this type of ritual may evoke anger and feelings of jealousy. Discussing these questions in a safe haven of therapy may be contraindicated if there has been violence in the past. This session may evoke underlying feelings outside the therapeutic environment. Control of one's anger is essential in engaging in the coming-clean ritual. The couple should be at a level to hear the truth and want to move on in the relationship.

Readings and Resources for Professionals

Rituals

Berg-Cross, L., Daniels, C., & Carr, P. (1992). Marital rituals among divorced and married couples. *Journal of Divorce & Remarriage, 18*(1/2), 1-30.

Coale, H. W. (1992). Costume and pretend identities: A constructivist's uses of experiences to co-create meanings with clients in therapy. *Journal of Strategic and Systemic Therapies, 11*(1), 45-55.

Connell, G. M., Mitten, T. J., & Whitaker, C. A. (1993). Reshaping family symbols: A symbolic experiential perspective. *Journal of Marital and Family Therapy, 19,* 243-251.

Giblin, P. (1995). Identity, change, and family rituals. *Family Journal, 3*(1), 37-42.

Imber-Black, E. (1989). Creating rituals in therapy. *The Family Therapy Networker, 13*(4), 39-46.

Imber-Black, E., Roberts, J., & Whiting, R. (1988). *Rituals in families and family therapy.* New York: W. W. Norton & Co.

Olsen, F. (1993). The development and impact of ritual in couple counseling. *Counseling and Values, 38,* 12-21.

Scheff, T. J. (1979). *Catharsis in healing ritual and drama.* Berkeley: University of California Press.

Selvini-Pazzololi, M. S., Boscolo, L., Cecchin, G. F., & Prata, G. (1977). Family rituals: A powerful tool in family therapy. *Family Process, 16,* 445-453.

Troll, L. E. (1988). Rituals and reunions. *American Behavioral Scientist, 31,* 621-631.

Turner, V. (1969). *The ritual process.* Chicago: Aldine.

Usandivaras, R. (1985). The therapeutic process as a ritual. *Group Analysis, 18*(1), 8-16.

Van der Hart, O. (1983). *Rituals in psychotherapy: Transition and continuity.* New York: Irvington.

Wambolt, F. S. & Reiss, D. (1989). Defining a family heritage and a new relationship identity: Two central tasks in the making of a marriage. *Family Process, 28,* 401-420.

Winek, J. L. & Craven, P. A. (2003). Healing rituals for couples recovering from adultery. *Contemporary Family Therapy, 25,* 249-266.

Wolin, S. J. & Bennett, L. A. (1984). Family rituals. *Family Process, 23,* 401-420.

Wyrostok, N. (1995). The ritual as a psychotherapeutic intervention. *Psychotherapy, 32,* 397-404.

Extramarital Affairs

Boekhout, B. A., Hendrick, S., & Hendrick, C. (1999). Relationship infidelity: A loss perspective. *Journal of Personal & Interpersonal Loss, 4,* 97-124.

Brown, E. M. (1991). *Patterns of infidelity and their treatment.* New York: Brunner/Mazel.

Buunk, B. P. (1987). Conditions that promote breakups as a consequence of extra-dyadic involvements. *Journal of Social and Clinical Psychology, 5,* 271-284.

Cano, A. & O'Leary, K. D. (1997). Romantic jealousy and affairs: Research and implications for couple therapy. *Journal of Sex & Marital Therapy, 23,* 249-270.

Cottone, R. & Mannis, J. (1996). Uncovering secret extramarital affairs in marriage counseling. *Family Journal, 4,* 109-116.

Glass, S. P. & Wright, T. L. (1992). Justifications for extramarital relationships: The association between attitudes, behaviors, and gender. *Journal of Sex Research, 29,* 361-387.

Gottman, J., Coan, J., Carrere, S., & Swanson, C. (1998). Predicting marital happiness and stability from newlywed interactions. *Journal of Marital and Family Therapy, 60,* 5-22.

Greenberg, L. S. (1998). Allowing and accepting painful emotional experiences. *International Journal of Action Methods, 51,* 47-62.

Hargrave, T. D. (1994). Families and forgiveness: A theoretical and therapeutic framework. *Family Journal, 2*(4), 339-349.

Humphrey, F. (1982). Extramarital affairs: Clinical approaches in marital therapy. In M. Goldberg (Ed.), *The psychiatric clinics of North America* (pp. 581-593). Philadelphia: W. B. Saunders Company.

Johnson, S. M., Makinen, J. A., & Millikin, J. W. (2001). Attachment injuries in couple's relationships: A new perspective on impasses in couple's therapy. *Journal of Marital and Family Therapy, 27,* 145-155.

Kell, C. (1992). The internal dynamics of the extramarital relationship: A counseling perspective. *Sexual and Marital Therapy, 7*(2), 157-172.

Pittman, E. (1989). *Private lies: Infidelity and the betrayal of intimacy.* New York: W. W. Norton & Co.

Schnarch, D. M. (1991). *Constructing the sexual crucible: An integration of sexual and marital therapy.* New York: W. W. Norton & Co.

Silverstein, J. L. (1998). Countertransference in marital therapy for infidelity. *Journal of Sex and Marital Therapy, 24,* 293-301.

Smith, T. E. (1991). Lie to me no more: Believable stories and marital affairs. *Family Process, 30,* 215-225.

Sprenkle, D. H. & Weis, D. L. (1978). Extramarital sexuality: Implications for marital therapists. *Journal of Sex and Marital Therapy, 4,* 279-291.

Tiabbi, R. (1983). Handling extramarital affairs in clinical treatment. *The Journal of Contemporary Social Work, 64,* 200-204.

Weil, B. E. (1993). *Adultery: The forgivable sin.* New York: Birch Lane.

Bibliotherapy Sources for the Client

Rituals

Cox, M. (2003). *The book of new family traditions: How to create great rituals for holidays and everyday.* Philadelphia: Running Press Book Publishers.

Doherty, W. (1999). *The intentional family; Simple rituals to strengthen family ties.* New York: Morrow, William, & Co.

Doherty, W. (2001). *Take back your marriage.* New York: Guilford Press.

Lang, V., Nayer, L., & Nayer, L. B. (2000). *How to bury a goldfish: And 113 other family rituals for everyday life.* Emmaus, PA: Rodale Press.

Leach, M. & Borchard, T. J. (2002). *I like being married: Traditions, rituals, and stories.* Garden City, NY: Doubleday & Co.

Nelson, G. M. (1986). *To dance with God: Family ritual and community celebration.* Mahwah, NJ: Paulist Press.

Affairs

Brown, E. M. (1999). *Affairs: A guide to working through the repercussions of infidelity.* Indianapolis, IN: Wiley Publishing Inc.

Gottman, J. (1999). *The seven principles to making marriage work: A practical guide from the country's foremost relationship expert.* New York: Crown Publishers.

Harley, W. F. (2001). *His needs, her needs: Building an affair-proof marriage.* Grand Rapids, MI: Baker Book House, Inc.

Kinnet, L. N. (2001). *Beyond the affair: The healing of a marriage.* Published by Booklocker .com.

Spring, J. A. & Spring, M. (1997). *After the affair: Healing the pain and rebuilding trust when a partner has been unfaithful.* New York: Harper Collins Publishers.

References

Imber-Black, E., Roberts, J., & Whiting, R. (1988). *Rituals in families and family therapy.* New York: W. W. Norton & Co.

Scheff, T. J. (1979). *Catharsis in healing ritual and drama.* Berkeley: University of California Press.

Westfall, A. (1995).Working through the extramarital trauma: An exploration of common themes. In G. R. Weeks, M. Turner, & L. Hoff (Eds.), *Integrative solutions: Treating common problems in couples therapy* (pp. 148-194). New York: Brunner/Mazel.

Whitaker, C. A. & Bumberry, W. M. (1988). *Dancing with the family: A symbolic experiential approach.* New York: Brunner/Mazel.

Winek, J. L. & Craven, P. A. (2003). Healing rituals for couples recovering from adultery. *Contemporary Family Therapy, 25,* 249-266.

– 8 –

Creating Rituals for Couples Coping with Early Pregnancy Loss

R. Valorie Thomas

Type of Contribution: Homework/Activity

Objective

The objective of this homework/activity is to help couples create a ritual to facilitate healing after an early pregnancy loss.

Rationale for Use

Miscarriage or the "inability to carry a pregnancy to term" is often experienced as a "silent sorrow" for many couples. Miscarriage accounts for 95 percent of all early losses up to twenty weeks gestation (Glazer, 1997). Couples experiencing one or more early miscarriages (within the first trimester) often have emotional experiences that include anger, blame, a sense of loss of control, and feelings of helplessness (Cooper-Hilbert, 2001; Diamond, Kezur, Meyers, Scharf, & Weinshel, 1999; Glazer, 1997). They also report symptoms of anxiety, depression, and guilt (Diamond et al., 1999; Glazer, 1997). A miscarriage experience is often unacknowledged by family and friends when they fail to recognize the profound emptiness that is left behind. When a couple loses a child early in their pregnancy, they are faced with grieving the future of their baby and their family together. In an instant, their hopes and dreams of having a child are shattered. Couples may find themselves in a revolving dynamic of blame in addition to having difficulty resolving their intense feelings of loss. For example, one couple reported that after their second early miscarriage, they withdrew from each other, becoming more isolated as each day passed. "It was too painful to talk about; we were devastated and angry at God and every other couple we knew who had a baby. Why us? I blamed my husband; I blamed myself. We both felt we were being punished. Why didn't our genetics make a baby?" Another couple reports, "It was our first baby; we were heartbroken. The more I cried, the more my husband withdrew. He wanted to forget, and I wanted to remember. Finally, we stopped talking altogether." Like these examples, couples often find themselves stuck in their grief and unable to move on in their life. Couples need recognition and validation for their losses and a way to say good-bye to their dream of having this particular baby (Scharf & Weinshel, 2000). "Couples need to be helped to mourn" (Scharf & Weinshel, 2000, p. 110). Avoiding the grieving process can paralyze a couple's ability to communicate effectively, problem solve, and reengage in sexual intimacy and enjoyment. They may also begin to feel disconnected (Glazer, 1997) and withdraw from family and friends. On an individual level, some partners experience symptoms of anxiety and/or depression. Thus the impact of early pregnancy loss (especially multiple losses) profoundly affects couples' relationships.

Drawing from symbolic-experiential therapy, the creation of a ritual experience allows couples to construct a "symbolic [emotional] experience realizing the uniqueness of [each partner's] own perceptions, . . . vulnerabilities, and [own] limits . . ." (Whitaker, as cited in Roberto, 1991, p. 445). In other words, a ritual experience helps couples define their own way of expressing their grief based on their unique values and beliefs as well as assists them in creating new meaning in their lives. It provides couples with an avenue to recognize their loss both personally and publicly (if desired), allowing them to bring closure to their experience and put their baby to rest. For couples who have experienced one or more miscarriages, the following homework assignment is useful to help them mark this important event and say their good-byes.

Instructions

The following guidelines (adapted from *Rituals in Families and Family Therapy,* Imber-Black, Roberts, & Whiting, 1988) can help therapists work with couples to design a meaningful event.

1. The purpose of the ritual should be discussed with the couple. For example, for many couples, the ritual validates the existence of their baby and marks the pregnancy as real. It also serves as a way to mark a passage of their child that allows the couple to move on and put their baby to rest. In addition, the therapist can help the couple to discern what they wish to gain from the ritual experience. Examples include the following: create a forum to grieve the loss of their child, recognize their unborn child, recognize that their baby's spirit has passed to another world, mark closure, and take steps in accepting their loss.
2. The ritual should include symbolic actions or articles relevant to the loss. This may include the act of planting a tree, pouring water out of a vase onto the ground, lighting a candle, playing a special song, reading a letter composed by the parents, or reading a special poem. Items relevant to the loss may include the mother's hospital bracelet, appointment cards, a mother's journal, a sonogram picture, a candle, a blanket, a toy, or any other physical evidence that the couple decides connotes meaning to the loss of their baby.
3. A specific plan needs to be devised. The couple can then decide how the event will take place, when it will occur, where it will be performed, who will be present, what articles will be present, and how it will conclude. The meaning of each aspect of the plan should be thought out. It is important to remember that some couples may choose to involve close family and friends and others may choose to perform the ritual privately as a couple. Counselors can help couples explore their preferences while tenderly encouraging them to gain support from their community of friends and family.

The following case example demonstrates the use of a ritual.

Brief Vignette

Bridget, age thirty-seven, and Miaca, age forty, had been married for five years. Bridget and Miaca entered therapy because of strain on their relationship due to a second early pregnancy loss four weeks earlier. Bridget reported that since the miscarriage, Miaca had been quiet, withdrawn, and did not want to talk about their loss. She stated that he was minimizing the loss of their baby and had told her that she needed to "move on" and stop crying. Bridget felt overwhelmed, depressed, and empty. She said she needed comfort and understanding from Miaca. Miaca reported that he was sad and hurt about the miscarriage and felt helpless in assisting Bridget to move on. He stated that he did not want to dwell on their loss because it was too painful and there was nothing they could do about it anyway. He shared that he had been having difficulty concentrating at work as well as difficulty sleeping. He was worried about Bridget and stated that the miscarriage was taking a toll on their relationship. He shared that he was beginning to question whether they should continue to try to create a family.

The therapist suggested that it may be helpful for them to construct a ritual to say good-bye to their baby. With the assistance of the therapist, Bridget and Miaca identified and explored their feelings in more detail and decided that they wanted to mark the passing of their child by creating a ritual.

Step 1

Both Bridget and Miaca identified feelings of hurt and loss due to the early miscarriage of their baby. They expressed feeling unjustified in their grieving, stating, "After all, we don't have a baby; we don't have anything we can touch." They also expressed a deep sense of emptiness and void. The purpose of their ritual was to recognize and honor their baby and mark the passage of their child. The couple stated that they hoped to gain strength to face their future and a sense of closure as a result of their ritual.

Step 2

Bridget and Miaca created a ritual prayer to mark the passing of their baby. They reviewed Bible passages and books provided by the therapist to create their special ceremony. Each decided to write a letter to their baby expressing his or her hopes and dreams of their life together. The couple decided to share their letters with each other prior to the public ritual they created. The couple found this experience to be both painful and healing.

Step 3

Bridget and Miaca identified several close friends and family members they wanted to include in their ritual ceremony. Bridget agreed to call the family members and friends, while Miaca agreed to invite their church pastor to perform the ritual. They decided to honor their baby by inviting their guests to their home on a Friday evening (dusk) at 6:00 p.m. The ritual would take place in their backyard rose garden, a favorite place for both of them. They decided to include the use of candles for each guest to carry to the garden, after a short prayer in their living room. The candles would then be placed in a pottery dish to burn until the end of the ritual. They also agreed to burn their letters to their baby on a silver dish given to them by a family friend. They had often used the dish to celebrate birthdays and festive occasions. The dish symbolized the celebration of their baby's short life with them. Finally, Bridget and Miaca brought closure to the ritual by receiving a special blessing from their pastor. The couple concluded the event by serving food and coffee and celebrating the support and understanding of their friends and family. The following is the ritual ceremony and prayer created by Bridget and Miaca in honor of their baby.

"Saying Good-Bye to Our Baby Rose"

Begin in the House

We are gathered here today to remember and honor Bridget and Miaca's baby. Our hearts are heavy and saddened for them as we recognize and grieve their future hopes and dreams for their lives together as a family with this child. We ask that God give them strength as individuals and as a couple at this difficult time.

On the Way to the Rose Garden

[Each attending member carries a lit candle in honor of the baby. The candles are placed in a planter made of pottery that had been given to the couple as a congratulation planter to mark their pregnancy.]

In the Rose Garden

We plant this rose bush as a symbol of life that was short-lived in this world. The blossoming of roses will forever be a reminder of their sweet baby. [The couple pours a small pitcher of water on the bush.] The water symbolizes the tears they have shed for their baby. [Bridget and Miaca place their letters on a silver dish.] The letters are burned to symbolize the rising of the letters to heaven where their sweet baby rests.

The Parent's Blessing

[The pastor blesses Bridget and Miaca asking God to be with them in the days ahead.]

Departing from the Rose Garden

[Family and friends quietly follow the couple, led by the pastor, back into the home.]

Suggestions for Follow-Up

Once the couple has carried out their ritual, the impasse has been marked. Couples may find it helpful to process the following questions with their therapist:

1. What is different now? What has changed between the two of you as a result of creating the ritual together?
2. What have you learned about yourself and the way you grieve? What have you learned about your partner and the way your partner grieves?
3. What strengths have you become aware of in yourself and in your partner as a result of this experience?
4. What do you think your baby would say to you now that you have honored and remembered your baby?

Contraindications

It is important to allow couples to decide if and when they would like to partake in the creation of a ritual. This activity can be modified for use with one individual or for couples experiencing multiple losses. In the case of multiple losses, a candle can be used to represent each loss.

Readings and Resources for the Professional

Cooper-Hilbert, B. (1998). *Infertility & involuntary childlessness: Helping couples cope.* New York: W. W. Norton & Co.

Diamond, D., Kezur, D., Meyers, M., Scharf, C. N., & Weinshel, M. (1999). *Couple therapy for infertility.* New York: Guilford Press.

Glazer, E. S. (1997). Miscarriage and its aftermath. In S. R. Leiblum (Ed.), *Infertility: Psychological issues and counseling strategies* (pp. 230-245). New York: John Wiley & Sons.

Imber-Black, E. & Roberts, J. (1993). *Rituals for our times: Celebrating, healing, and changing our lives and our relationships.* New York: W. W. Norton & Co.

Imber-Black, E., Roberts J., & Whiting, R. (1988). *Rituals in families and family therapy.* New York: W. W. Norton & Co.

Keye, W. R., Jr. (1999). Medical aspects of infertility for the counselor. In L. H. Burns & S. N. Covington (Eds.), *Infertility counseling: A comprehensive handbook for clinicians* (pp. 27-46). New York: W. W. Norton & Co.

Leiblum, S. R. (1997). *Infertility: Psychological issues and counseling strategies.* New York: John Wiley & Sons.

Scharf, C. N. & Weinshel, M. (2000). Infertility and late-life pregnancies. In P. Papp (Ed.), *Couples on the fault line: New directions for therapists* (pp. 104-129). New York: Guilford Press.

Videotape for Practitioners

Lerner, S. (Producer). (1995). *Couples and infertility: Moving beyond loss* [Videotape]. Produced in collaboration with the Ackerman Institute for the Family's Infertility Project: Ronny Diamond, MSW, David Kezur, MSW, Mimi Meyers, MSW, Constance N. Scharf, MSW, and Margot Weinshel, MSW, RN. Guilford Publications, Inc. New York, New York.

Support Group

RESOLVE Inc.
The National Infertility Association Since 1974
National Headquarters
7910 Woodmont Avenue
Suite 1350
Bethesda, MD 20814
Phone: 301-652-8585
Fax: 301-652-9375
E-mail: info@resolve.org
www.resolve.org

RESOLVE is a national organization that supports individuals and couples experiencing infertility.

Bibliotherapy Sources for Clients

(Useful for Practitioners As Well)

Eadie, B. J. (1994). *Embraced by the light.* New York: Bantam Books.

Eck Menning, B. (1988). *Infertility: A guide for the childless couple.* New York: Prentice Hall.

Ilse, S. & Burns, L. (1985). *Miscarriage: A shattered dream.* Long Lake, MN: Wintergreen Press.

Kohn, I. & Moffit, P. L. (1992). *A silent sorrow: Pregnancy loss.* New York: Bantam Doubleday Dell Publishing Group, Inc.

Kubler-Ross, E. (1969). *On death and dying.* New York: Macmillan.

Kushner, H. (1981). *When bad things happen to good people.* New York: Avon Books.

Marrs, R., Friedman Bloch, L., & Kirtland Silverman, K. (1997). *Dr. Richard Marrs' fertility book.* New York: Bantam Doubleday Dell Publishing Group, Inc.

Metzger, D. A. (1998). A physician's perspective. In B. Cooper-Hilbert (Ed.), *Infertility and involuntary childlessness: Helping couples cope* (pp. 1-21). New York: W. W. Norton & Co.
Rupp, J. (2002). *Praying our good-byes*. Notre Dame, IN: Ave Maria Press.
Sanders, C. M. (1998). *How to survive the loss of a child.* New York: Prima Publishing.

References

Cooper-Hilbert, B. (2001, January). Helping couples through the crisis of infertility. *AAMFT Clinical Update: Infertility, 3*(1), 1-6.
Diamond, D., Kezur, D., Meyers, M., Scharf, C. N., & Weinshel, M. (1999). *Couple therapy for infertility.* New York: Guilford Press.
Glazer, E. S. (1997). Miscarriage and its aftermath. In S. R. Leiblum (Ed.), *Infertility: Psychological issues and counseling strategies* (pp. 230-245). New York: John Wiley & Sons.
Imber-Black, E., Roberts J., & Whiting, R. (1988). *Rituals in families and family therapy.* New York: W. W. Norton & Co.
Roberto, L. G. (1991). Symbolic-experiential family therapy. In A. S. Gurman & D. P. Kniskern (Eds.), *Handbook of family therapy* (Vol. 2, pp. 444-476). New York: Brunner/Mazel.
Scharf, C. N., & Weinshel, M. (2000). Infertility and late-life pregnancies. In P. Papp (Ed.), *Couples on the fault line: New directions for therapists* (pp. 104-129). New York: Guilford Press.

SECTION II:
INTERVENTIONS FOR FAMILIES

– 9 –

The Four Cs of Parenting

Lee Williams
Erin Cushing

Type of Contribution: Handout

Objective

The objective of the handout is to provide parents with an introduction to four important parenting principles.

Rationale for Use

The Four Cs of Parenting provide a basic framework for conceptualizing important parenting principles. The Four Cs are Consequences, Consistency, Calm, and Charged Batteries. The first two Cs, administering consequences and doing so in a consistent manner, are integral parts of most parent management programs. These concepts are rooted in the behavioral therapy tradition, where positive reinforcement and punishment are used to shape behavior. The third C, remaining calm while administering consequences, encourages parents to be nonreactive, which helps reduce the level of negativity in the parent-child relationship. Finally, the fourth C, maintaining charged batteries, recognizes that effective parenting is difficult if one's personal resources are depleted. The Four Cs provide a simple and easily recalled model of parenting, making it ideally suited for parent psychoeducation. Therapists can also easily use the Four Cs as a checklist for assessing a client's potential strengths or growth areas with regard to parenting.

Instructions

When the therapist perceives a parent would benefit from some basic education about parenting, the Four Cs can be introduced as a way of organizing the key elements of successful parenting. The therapist can introduce the Four Cs either verbally or by using the handout. The advantage of the handout is that it can be used as a reference or reminder for the parent at home, particularly if it is posted in a visible place within the home (e.g., refrigerator). Use of the handout assumes that the parent or parents can read, which may not always be the case. The advantage of the Four Cs, however, is that principles can be easily remembered even if they are not recorded in written form.

In most cases, the therapist should provide a description of all Four Cs in one session. Doing so is helpful because each concept is related to the other, and the Four Cs are most effective when used together. Depending upon the needs of the clients, however, some of the Four Cs might need to be explored in more detail in subsequent sessions to help build their knowledge and skill within that area.

Usually the first C to be introduced is *Consequences*. The therapist explains that in real life our actions carry consequences. As a result, parents need to teach their children that their actions will have consequences. If a child misbehaves by breaking a rule, for example, then the parent is expected to attach a consequence to the behavior. Ideally, the consequence or punishment will fit the crime.

It is important that the therapist explain that attaching consequences to behavior not only happens when a child misbehaves but should also occur when a child does something positive. Parents are encouraged to "catch your child doing well." A parent, for example, might praise a child for an act of honesty or compassion toward others.

One common difficulty that parents encounter is administering consequences that require the cooperation of the child. Asking the child to clean his or her room, for example, may not work as a consequence since it requires the child's cooperation to succeed. In these cases, the parent can become frustrated or believe that consequences are ineffective. Therefore, the therapist can explain that it is best to choose consequences that do not require the cooperation of the child, particularly if the child can be oppositional. Withholding an allowance or restricting privileges (e.g., putting a video game in timeout) might be a more effective alternative. Therapists may need to help parents brainstorm possible consequences that can be enforced without the child's cooperation.

The next C to be introduced is *Consistency.* The therapist explains that the power of attaching consequences to behavior is most effective when done consistently. The therapist can further explain that if a child receives a consequence for breaking a rule only occasionally, then the child may continue to misbehave out of the belief that he or she can get away with it most of the time. Being consistent also reassures the child that the parent can be depended upon, not only for setting limits but also for protecting or ensuring the child's welfare. It is also helpful to remind parents not to threaten consequences that they are not prepared to actually carry out. Otherwise, this can make the parents appear inconsistent and undermine their authority. To the extent possible, both parents (or other caretakers who are in a parenting role in relation to the child) should try to follow the same rules and be consistent in giving consequences. This avoids giving children mixed messages and reduces the likelihood that they will take advantage of the parents not having a united front.

The third C usually introduced is *Calm.* The parent is encouraged as much as possible to deliver the consequence in a calm and nonreactive manner. The therapist explains that this is important for two reasons. First, remaining calm helps the child avoid assuming that he or she is being punished simply because the parent is upset rather than for breaking a rule. In other words, children may focus more on the fact that the parent is upset or angry rather than the lesson to be learned from the consequence. Second, children who sense that they can make their parents upset may enjoy having this kind of power or influence over their parents. As result, the child may continue to act out as a way of maintaining power over the parent. The therapist can also point out that parental power comes from giving consequences, not by becoming upset. Hecker (1998) encourages parents to be like "good cops" to illustrate this concept. Rather than berate a driver for speeding, a good cop will be pleasant and polite while giving the individual a ticket. The officer's power comes from his or her ability to give the individual a ticket or consequence rather than being upset with the driver.

The final C to be introduced is *Charged batteries.* The therapist explains that coming up with consequences, administering them in a consistent manner, and remaining calm are all very difficult if your personal batteries are run down. Therefore, an important aspect of parenting is keeping one's batteries charged. Depending upon the specifics of the case, the therapist can point out possible factors that may contribute to the client having poorly charged batteries, such as struggling with depression, health problems, stress, or limited resources. In addition to treating the problems that are draining the parents' batteries, the therapist should encourage parents to do self-care activities that will help recharge their batteries. Attending a support group, exercising, taking personal time for a recreational activity, starting a hobby, or spending time with friends are some examples of things that individuals might do to charge their batteries.

Brief Vignette

Charlie was a fourteen-year-old Caucasian teenager, and his mother, Linda, was a single mother in her early forties. Linda complained that Charlie was disrespectful, ungrateful, and constantly pushing her limits. Charlie felt his mom was always in a "bad mood" and nagging, yelling, and criticizing him. The dyad was introduced to the Four Cs of parenting. Charlie expressed reluctance to the notion of more rules, while Linda was excited to lay ground rules. During the therapeutic conversation about positive and negative *consequences* Linda revealed that she felt powerless to enforce her rules. She emotionally retold an incident in which Charlie had threatened to "turn her into CPS if she punished him." She explained that she felt Charlie would turn on her again if she set limits. Once this deep-seated fear was revealed, Linda was able to begin setting consequences. The two worked together at home to author clear and concise consequences for both positive and negative behaviors and brought their ideas back to therapy.

Previously Linda had difficulty being *consistent* and following through on her consequences because she would threaten extreme penalties she could not follow through with. Part of her and Charlie's work was finding the proper "consequence to fit the crime" that Linda could enforce without Charlie's cooperation. Linda also began working on delivering consequences in a *calm* manner. Charlie had been acting out to receive negative attention from Linda. By remaining calm, Linda was able to become the parental figure once again. Charlie appreciated the neutral voice and began feeling less blamed and criticized. In return, he was able to show his mom more respect by refraining from name-calling and profanity.

As Linda practiced her new parenting skills she also worked on self-care activities so she would have *charged batteries*. In the past she had found running in the morning to be a helpful stress release and she began practicing it on a regular basis. She also began turning off her cell phone during meals and set aside one hour a night to spend structured quality time with Charlie. This simple change gave Charlie positive attention and gave Linda a much-needed break from work-related stress.

Suggestions for Follow-Up

The presentation of the Four Cs gives an excellent introduction to important principles in parenting. This type of model will be particularly helpful for clients who need some psychoeducation about parenting skills or practices. The therapist, however, should be prepared to explore common difficulties that parents often experience with instituting one or more of the Four Cs.

One difficulty faced by many parents is feeling guilty about some aspect of their child's life, thereby making it difficult for them to set limits with their children. A mother of a seven-year-old admitted that she hated to give her son consequences because she felt guilty about divorcing his father. In these circumstances, the therapist may need to frame setting limits as a means of providing security for the child rather than as a punitive measure. The mother of the seven-year-old was told that her setting limits with her son communicated that she was in charge of the situation and could take care of him. This in turn would make him feel more secure about the family transition.

Another common difficulty is that some parents ignore misbehavior until they can no longer tolerate it. As a result, anger or frustration has built up to the point where it is difficult for the parent to remain calm. In addition, when they finally do step in to correct the behavior, they may give out a more severe consequence because they are angry. Later, after they have calmed down, they may regret the severity of the consequence and not enforce it. This process ultimately undermines the parents' efforts to be both calm and consistent. Parents can be instructed that a more effective approach is to intervene sooner using smaller consequences that are consistently given, rather than waiting until the misbehavior can no longer be tolerated.

Parents often need additional guidance on how to get their batteries charged by recognizing possible stressors or underlying factors. Some parents, for example, may be significantly depressed and have limited energy for parenting. In these cases, a referral for a medical evaluation and possible medication may be appropriate, and/or individual therapy. Some parents may focus too much on taking care of others at the expense of their own needs and may need coaching on how to integrate more self-care. Life stressors such as job stress, marital/couple conflict, or health problems may also drain a parent's batteries. In some of these cases, individual or couples therapy may need to be considered in addition to family therapy.

At times, it is also helpful for the therapist to warn parents that some children may act out more initially as a way of testing a parent's new resolve in setting limits. This may be particularly true for children who have experienced little in the way of limit setting and value the freedom they have had in the past. If parents are forewarned about this possibility, they are less likely to give up at the first bit of resistance. In addition, the therapist might work with the parents to prioritize areas of change so that the child is not overwhelmed with the need to make changes in multiple areas. Helping parents pick their battles will also permit them to focus their energies and reduce the risk of draining their batteries.

Finally, the therapist can add to the list of Four Cs to address other aspects of parenting that the therapist might want to emphasize with a family. Communication skills, for example, could be added as a fifth C for some families. In the case of Linda and Charlie, communication skills were modeled in the therapy room through practicing "I" statements and reflective listening skills to break the dyad out of an emotionally reactive and blaming communication pattern. Cohesion (or Connection) is another possible principle that could be introduced, particularly if the therapist feels the parents and children are somewhat or highly disengaged. A parent and child, for example, might regularly spend one-on-one time doing a fun activity or playing together to strengthen their connection. Or a family could develop a ritual of going out for family dates or activities to build a sense of connection and belonging within the family.

Contraindications

This approach is most effective for parents who have difficulty setting limits, primarily due to a skills or knowledge deficit. The Four Cs assumes that the parent is invested in parenting and the child's welfare. Therefore, discussing the Four Cs would be contraindicated if the therapist believed the individual had little or no commitment to parenting. The Four Cs will be most effective if the parent (or caretaker) has an established relationship with the child. If the individual has not developed this relationship, then it may be difficult for the child to accept limits from this individual.

Finally, the therapist may need to weigh how much effort should be put into developing a parent's ability to nurture his or her children versus setting limits. In some cases, a therapist may need to focus first on helping the parent develop his or her nurturing skills, particularly if neglect or abuse has damaged the relationship. Or a therapist may need to shift a parent's perception of his or her child from a highly negative to a more positive view. In some cases, both nurturing and limit-setting skills can be developed concurrently. A parent might be instructed to catch his or her child doing something good, for example, and then give the child a positive consequence such as praise.

Readings and Resources for the Professional

Bodenhamer, G. (1995). *Parent in control.* New York: Simon & Schuster.
Phelan, T. W. (1995). *1-2-3 Magic: Effective discipline for children 2-12.* Glen Ellyn, IL: Child Management, Inc.

Bibliotherapy Sources for Clients

Bodenhamer, G. (1995). *Parent in control.* New York: Simon & Schuster.
Phelan, T. W. (1995). *1-2-3 Magic: Effective discipline for children 2-12.* Glen Ellyn, IL: Child Management, Inc.

Reference

Hecker, L. L. (1998). Good cops and bad cops in parenting. In L. L. Hecker, S. A. Deacon, & Associates (Eds.), *The therapist's notebook: Homework, handouts, and activities for use in psychotherapy* (pp. 265-267). Binghamton, NY: The Haworth Press.

The Four Cs of Parenting

Consequences

- In real life, our actions carry consequences.
- Parents attach consequences to their child's behavior.
- Consequences are for negative behavior—have the punishment fit the crime.
- Consequences are for positive behavior—catch your child doing well!
- Use consequences that can be enforced without the child's cooperation.

Consistency

- Consequences must be given consistently to be effective.
- If the consequence is inconsistent, it communicates—you can get away with that behavior most of the time.
- Consistent consequences communicate—I am here to protect you and keep you safe no matter what you do.
- Agree on rules and consequences that all parental figures will enforce.

Calm

- Deliver consequences in a calm and nonreactive manner.
- Remaining calm communicates—I am not punishing you simply because I am upset, but because you broke a rule.
- Remaining calm communicates—I am not going to react emotionally so you can gain power/influence over me by breaking rules.
- Parental power comes from the consequence, not from becoming upset.
- Remain calm by intervening before a crisis occurs.

Charged Batteries

- The first 3 Cs are difficult to carry out if your personal batteries are low.
- Engage in self-care activities to keep your batteries charged.
- Structure time each day to take care of yourself.

– 10 –

Identifying Family Rules

Devon J. Palmanteer

Type of Contribution: Activity

Objective

The goal of this activity is to help clients become aware of the implicit rules for communication, interaction, and emotional expression in their families of origin. These are rules that clients follow in their communication with family and in intimate relationships, often without conscious awareness of them. Developing this awareness contributes to a greater differentiation of self for the client, which is a major component in Bowen Theory (Bowen, 1978).

Rationale for Use

Often people are unaware of, or are unable to clearly communicate, the unspoken rules in their families for expressing emotions or communicating with one another. Many times, these rules influence current behavior in the family and in other relationships, but the family has acted according to these rules for such a long time that the rules have become invisible. Clients react in the same way over and over again because they are unable to see another way. The rules may be like an invisible fencing system—it cannot be seen, but a warning alarm sounds when a boundary is about to be crossed. Some of these established patterns may be effective for the family, while others may be ineffective or even destructive. It can be difficult for family members to distinguish what is working from what is not working when they are participating in these familiar patterns of interaction. In this activity, the client explains the rules to the therapist from the position of teaching an outsider the things he or she would need to do to "fit in" with the family. Taking on the role of a teacher can be helpful for making the rules visible to the family. This activity assumes the client is the expert on the family and helps the client use this expert knowledge to make desired changes.

This activity relates to differentiation, a concept Bowen called a cornerstone in his theory (1978). Differentiation of self describes the degree to which a person is able to distinguish between intellectual and emotional processes. In other words, differentiation is how well a person can separate thinking and feeling, and avoid being controlled by his or her emotions. A well-differentiated person is able to filter his or her emotions through his or her intellectual thoughts and respond accordingly. Differentiated people are not cold and distant, but instead are able to be emotionally involved with others in a thoughtful manner (Bowen, 1978). The more differentiated a person is, the less reactive he or she will be in relationships. Reactivity is a term for how much a person's behavior is fueled by his or her emotions in interactions with others. An undifferentiated person is likely to be reactive and respond with strong emotions without thinking through the results of his or her response. Reactivity triggers reactive responses from others resulting in a pattern of established behavior in the family (Papero, 1990). Bowen referred to this reactivity in families as emotional fusion.

One of the characteristics of a differentiated person is that he or she has an awareness of his or her role in the family. Bowen (1978) writes, "The differentiated person is always aware of others and the relationship system around him" (p. 370). By taking the perspective of an outsider, the client can view the family system and his or her role in it more clearly. This perspective leads to increased differentiation by allowing the client to take an intellectual view of his or her family. Clients are explaining their family to an outsider rather than relaying an experience that may create an emotional or reactive response. This will ultimately allow the client to better communicate with his or her family, and in other intimate relationships.

Instructions

Tell the client you want him or her to imagine something a little strange—that you are about to move in with their family. You would like him or her to help you by teaching you everything you need to know to fit in with the family. Explain that you want to be thought of as "one of them" and not behave like an outsider. You want the family to feel comfortable around you. The imaginary role that you assume in the family should be the same role as the client's, including the client's gender. For example, if the client is a male child in the family he should explain to you how you would need to behave if you wanted to fit in as a male child. If working with a family, this can be repeated from each family member's perspective, which would allow family members to learn about the others' experiences. With couples this might be a useful way for them to learn more about the rules they bring from their families into their relationship.

Each person in the session should have an opportunity to offer his or her perspective. When working with a family it might be helpful to first ask if there is anything you would need to know that applies to the whole family. These general rules can serve as the springboard for the discussion. For example, the family might tell you that to join their family you would need to have a great sense of humor. You should guide the process by having the family members take turns speaking and not allowing family members to interrupt one another. Family members may disagree or invalidate one another's perspectives, so it might be helpful to set some ground rules for the activity and remind family members that the purpose of the activity is to learn about perspectives that may be quite different from their own. These differences offer insight into the family's interaction.

Use the questions at the end of the chapter as a guide to explore roles and expectations in the family. Continue to ask questions until you feel you have a clear picture of how to "be" the client(s) and of how the family interacts. The amount of time this takes will vary with the number of clients and the complexity of the family. Once you feel as if you have enough information, process the activity with the client. Ask him or her how it felt to take this perspective. What did the client learn about his or her family? Is there anything the clients understand or know now that they didn't know before? Help the client to summarize the rules that he or she identified. It may be helpful to write these down on a whiteboard or some place where the client can see them. Ask about areas that seem especially significant, such as rules limiting the expression of emotions such as anger or sadness. If multiple family members are present, ask for their perspectives on what the other members said. Did there seem to be a consensus about the rules or did everyone report a different experience?

It is possible, even likely, that family members will have different perceptions of what it takes to fill a certain role in their family. For instance, what a father might tell you is important to know to be the father in the family might be quite different from what a child in the family describes as the important aspects of being a father. The goal of this activity is not for the family members to come to a consensus about the rules, but rather to make the rules visible in order to help family members better understand their interactions. Identifying the perceived rules, regardless of the level of agreement, is useful for helping family members determine how they may want to adjust their behaviors in relation to the presenting problem.

It is also likely that despite different perceptions, themes may emerge. For example, family members may describe behaviors that are consistent with a theme of avoiding conflict. In this case, it would be useful for the therapist to point out these themes and explore them further with the family.

Variation

This activity could also be used as a homework assignment. Family members could be given the list of questions to answer individually and compare in the next session. Another possibility would be for family members to pair up and interview each other using the list of questions. In the next session after the interview, the interviewers would report back to the rest of the family about what they have learned. For a more hands-on activity, family members could develop trading cards that feature an image or picture that is symbolic of the family member on one side and their "family stats" on the other. The questions could still be used as a guide to help the family determine which facts are most important to include. Family members would present and trade their cards at the next session.

Brief Vignette

Carl, twenty-three, and Josie, twenty, were a brother and sister who came to therapy hoping to improve their relationship with their parents, mainly their alcoholic father. There were two other children in the family, one younger and one older. The only family members that were seen for therapy were Carl and Josie. During the genogram interview they reported all the relationships in their family as being "good" or "fine," yet they were unable to recognize any patterns of behavior in the family. When asked about what things they learned from their family that they wanted to keep, and which things they would like to leave behind, they said "I don't know." Carl and Josie seemed to be struggling to talk about complex emotions and to describe interactions in their family in explicit ways. When specifically asked about what they hoped to improve in the family relationships, they couldn't identify any concrete changes they desired. Both Josie and Carl tended to use vague descriptions of just wanting things to be "better," despite the seeming contradiction that they described everything as "fine."

I suspected that Josie and Carl were fairly enmeshed with their family and therefore tended to respond in reactive ways and according to rules for communication of which they were not aware. Although they had a sense these ways of responding were not effective for them, they were unable to identify what they and other family members were doing to contribute to the dissatisfaction. They were stuck inside the "invisible fence."

After five sessions during which they struggled to talk about interactions in their family, I introduced this activity. First, I asked them to describe what I would need to do to be a kid in their family. They told me to expect many family activities, but that I should try to avoid chores at all costs. In family disagreements I should always side with the kids. They were able to tell me who I should talk to when I was experiencing different emotions and why this family member was the best choice. They were also able to discuss which emotions were not okay to express and what I should do when I was feeling them. After they gave me a general description of what a kid should do, I asked them more about their individual roles, such as the differences between being a male and a female child in their family. Josie told me that to be her, I would need to be concerned with keeping peace in the family, and Carl told me that if I were him, I would leave the house when I was upset. When asked to take this perspective, they were able to develop insightful responses about family interactions and rules. This initial discussion took one session. I ended the session by summarizing what they had told me and asked them to think about how what they had described might be influencing their current interactions with their parents.

In the next session, we discussed what rules were implied in the previous session and how those rules affected their current interactions in the family and with others. They were able to talk about what rules they would like to keep and what they would like to change. Both said they would like to keep the affection they felt from their parents, but wanted the family to communicate more directly. They also were able to identify ways in which they might be able to change their behavior in order to make changes in their relationships that would lead to the improvement that they desired. Josie decided she would talk with her father and explain that she enjoyed spending time with him but could not spend time with him if he had been drinking. Carl thought that letting other family members know when he was upset rather than leaving the house would lead to improvement in the family. Carl and Josie's responses showed they were able to look at their family experiences intellectually, rather than from an emotional perspective, which contributed to an increased level of differentiation. Through the activity, their patterns of emotional expression, and therefore, the areas they wanted to improve, became clearer to them. The activity also created movement in the therapy process which had become stuck on the issue of describing family rules and identifying what needed to change.

This activity made room for more dialogue in the therapy session by asking concrete questions related to the individuals. Some clients, similar to Carl and Josie, find it difficult to describe relationships but are able to describe their own behavior. Instead of asking "describe your relationship with your father," I asked questions such as "How should I act around your father? Is it okay to tell him if I am mad?" Carl and Josie seemed able to better express themselves in response to this type of specific questioning which grew into an understanding of family interaction processes.

Suggestions for Follow-Up

This activity can be built upon in a number of ways. If clients gain insight into their family of origin's communication patterns they may have a more specific vision of their therapy goals or how they want to change. You can choose to follow the client's lead, or try one of the following:

- Ask clients about which of the identified rules they wish to keep for themselves and their own family, and which ones they would like to change or discard. Are there certain ones they especially like or dislike?
- How are these rules influencing current interactions in and outside of their family of origin?
- Can they change the rules of interaction now to make relationships with their family members more fulfilling?
- If a genogram was constructed, revisit the genogram in light of the new information. Can any additional patterns be identified?

In addition, this activity can be adapted for use with individuals as well as couples. When working with an individual client, it might be useful to ask him or her to take the perspective of another family member and repeat the exercise. This may lead clients to insight about other family members' behaviors or motivations and to a greater awareness of their own role. Changing perspectives in this way could also be used when working with a family. Family members may gain a better understanding of their influence on the family system by listening to what others see as the essential components of their roles. For example, you could ask a child what you would need to know to be a parent in the family. Couples could describe to each other how to survive in each of their families, which would serve two purposes. First, it would help each member of the couple understand what to expect when interacting with the in-laws, and second, it could help the couple discover how expectations from their families of origin may be influencing their current relationship system.

Contraindications

If a therapist decides to use this activity with a client who has been abused, he or she should proceed carefully. Although it may be useful to explore how the rules of communication in the abusive family influence the client's current interactions, part of this activity explores the client's own role in the family system. The therapist must avoid blaming the victim or implying that the victim's role somehow caused the abuse. The therapist may also want to consider developing an alternate set of questions for working with clients who have been abused.

Another consideration for this activity is that it should be used only after a therapeutic alliance has been established. All three aspects of the Working Alliance (Bordin, 1994)—goals, tasks, and bonds—should be considered, or this activity may seem odd to the client, who may not understand the purpose. From the perspective of goals, the client and the therapist should have developed goals that are consistent with Bowen Theory (1978), or a better understanding of family interactions. For example, this activity may not be relevant to a client with the goal of managing stress in his or her work life. The tasks aspect of therapeutic alliance has to do with the behaviors and cognitions during therapy. This aspect could be affected if the client does not understand the goals and thinks the activity is silly or pointless. Last, the bond between client and therapist needs to be established in order for the client to be forthcoming about the details of his or her family life.

Finally, some clients come to therapy having already identified rules and roles in their family that are troubling to them. If a client demonstrates understanding and is able to clearly articulate the rules for communication in his or her family of origin without much difficulty, this activity might not be necessary as it would not provide new information to the therapist or client.

Readings and Resources for the Professional

Bowen, M. (1978). *Family therapy in clinical practice.* New York: Jason Aronson.

Bowen Center for the Study of the Family. http://www.thebowencenter.org.

Bowenian Family Therapy on Psychpage.com. http://www.psychpage.com/learning/library/counseling/bowen.html.

Kerr, M. E. & Bowen, M. (1988). *Family evaluation.* New York: W. W. Norton & Co.

Papero, D.V. (1990). *Bowen family systems theory.* Boston: Allyn & Bacon.

Bibliotherapy Sources for the Client

Gilbert, R. M. (1992). *Extraordinary relationships: A new way of thinking about human interactions.* New York: John Wiley & Sons.

McGoldrick, M. (1997). *You can go home again: Reconnecting with your family.* New York: W. W. Norton & Co.

Richardson, R. (1999). *Family ties that bind: A self-help guide to change through family of origin therapy.* Victoria, BC: Self Counsel Press.

References

Bordin, E. S. (1994). Theory and research on the therapeutic working alliance: New directions. In A. O. Horvath & L. S. Greenberg (Eds.), *The working alliance: Theory, research, and practice* (pp. 13-37). New York: John Wiley & Sons.

Bowen, M. (1978). *Family therapy in clinical practice*. New York: Jason Aronson.

Papero, D.V. (1990). *Bowen family systems theory*. Boston: Allyn & Bacon.

Potential Activity Questions

1. What should my overall behavior be like? Describe me.
2. Who could I talk to if I was really excited about something?
3. Who could I talk to if I was sad? What reaction should I expect?
4. What should I do if I get mad at someone in the family?
5. How will I know if someone is mad at me?
6. How can I tell if someone is sad?
7. Who would greet me when I got home at the end of the day? Describe what it will be like.
8. What should I expect at meal times?
9. Does one person in the family tend to start conversations? Who is that?
10. How would I know if someone in the family was sad? Happy?
11. What sorts of rituals can I expect?
12. If I had really great news, who is the first person I would tell?
13. How do I treat (other family members)?
14. Is it okay for me to bring other people over to the house?
15. What are my responsibilities? What happens if I don't fulfill them?
16. How would I know if a family member was disappointed in me?
17. How could I tell if I hurt someone's feelings? What if my feelings are hurt?
18. If I get mad at someone in the family, how do I let them know? What sort of response can I expect?
19. Who can I confide in? Is there anyone whom I shouldn't confide in?
20. What would happen if I wanted time to myself?
21. If I needed permission to do something, who would I ask?
22. If I had a problem I wanted advice on, who should I talk to?
23. Who could I go to if I needed a shoulder to cry on?
24. What should I do if other family members are arguing?
25. If someone tells me a secret, what should I do?
26. If I am afraid about something, who might make me feel better?
27. Are there certain things I shouldn't do as a male/female in the family?
28. Are there any special things about your culture I should know?
29. Is religion important in your family?
30. Am I allowed to challenge others' beliefs?
31. Who are the important people outside of your immediate family?

– 11 –

"Jump, Jump, King Me": The Systemic Kvebaek Technique

Katherine M. Hertlein

Type of Contribution: Activity

Objective

At times, discussing how close family members are to one another can be difficult in the presence of the family; it is often easier for family members to represent how they feel in a family through games, pictures, and other means. The purpose of this activity is to provide family members with the chance to visually represent how they view the closeness and power of the members in their family.

Rationale for Use

The purpose of this activity is for each family member to be able to express how he or she views the family structure in terms of closeness and distance through a checkerboard and its pieces. This project stems from symbolic-experiential therapy, the purpose of which is to integrate symbols and experiences of clients (Connell, Mitten, & Whitaker, 1993). Using symbols in therapy to represent experience provides a way for therapists to help clients link their experience with something tangible, resulting in a better ability to express themselves.

Specifically, this activity is based on the Kvebaek Family Sculpture Technique. The Kvebaek Technique is a family sculpture technique that has family members depict emotional closeness and distance with one another. Family members arrange blocks representing themselves on a standard grid as a method to depict the emotional distance or closeness between themselves and other family members (Berry, Hurley, & Worthington, 1990; Hernandez, 1999). The therapist uses a checkerboard (or the grid at the end of the chapter) and its accompanying checkers and asks the family to construct themselves spatially on the board.

Family members depict emotional distance between themselves and other family members through the symbolic representation of the checkers on the board. This may help the family reframe the problem and see it in a different light, as well as change the way they think about themselves. (This activity is similar to some of the principles of sculpting. In sculpting, the family depicts the family structure through body movements and placement in relation to one another.)

Once the symbol is selected, the family and therapist can use it as a metaphor of interaction between the couple and/or family members (Connell et al., 1993). Symbolic-experiential therapists believe, for the most part, that experiences are filtered through a number of constructs. The less functional a family is, the less variety in constructs they have available to them. The task of the symbolic-experiential therapist is to provide experiences that will provide a variety of constructs to the family members. This will, in turn, reshape family symbols and families will be able to generate more meanings (Connell et al., 1993). One similar technique within the experiential clinical literature is symbolic drawing of family life space (Piercy, Sprenkle, & Wetchler, 1996). In this activity, members of a family depict their emotional distance and communication patterns with one another on a blackboard in a nonthreatening, symbolic manner (Piercy et al., 1996).

Instructions

For this activity, the therapist will need a checkerboard and its accompanying checkers (if no checkerboard is available, the grid at the end of the chapter can be photocopied and enlarged). The board should be large enough so that family members will be able to sit around the board and see the location of the checkers on the board. The therapist will also need copies of the Kvebaek board for each member of the family to record his or her guesses about who each checker represents. This activity may take one to two sessions, depending on the size of the family. The board and its checkers represent spatial relationships between the family members and overall society. The therapist instructs the family of the following parameters:

1. The boundaries around the edge of the checkerboard represent larger society and a family's social network. If a family feels connected to the outside world, they can represent this by putting their checker pieces on squares that are near the outer rim of the board. If a family member feels isolated from the outside world, he or she can place his or her checker pieces toward the middle of the board.
2. Clients can demonstrate who has power in a family by stacking checkers to represent a person as opposed to using just one checker.
3. As a family member is engaging in the activity and visually representing where he or she perceives people in the family to be, other family members are not allowed to comment on the location of the checkers.
4. Family members should also refrain from making verbal guesses about who is represented by what checker until the member engaged in the activity has completed his or her representation. Instead, the family should use their copy of the board to write down their guesses.
5. Family members can use any color checkers they see fit, and can even use colored checkers to reflect certain characteristics of the person the checker is representing.

The therapist makes copies of the board from the end of the chapter for the family members and distributes them. Each family member will need one copy of the board for each time they participate in the activity as a large group. For example, if the family has five members and each person participates in the activity, each member will need four copies of the board. No copy is needed for the individual arranging the checkers.

The therapist then instructs one of the family members to place checkers around the board to visually represent closeness and distance between the family members, according to his or her perception. The therapist can allow the family to determine who will do the activity first. The therapist may also choose a family member to go first, if there is a therapeutic reason to do so.

While the person engaging in the activity arranges the checkers, the therapist asks the other family members to make guesses about who each of the checkers represent from that member's point of view and to write down those guesses on their copy of the board. For example, mom will make her guesses about who each checker represents as her daughter is completing the activity. Mom will record her guesses on her copy of the board—if her daughter puts a checker in the center, Mom will write a family member's name in the corresponding square on her board. Family members are also asked not to show one another what their guesses are until the activity is complete and then reveal their responses verbally.

The member who did the activity will not disclose the answers until all family members have had a chance to make their guesses, one at a time. Once all members have made their guesses, then the individual who put together the representation on the board reveals who is represented where and for what reasons. The therapist and other family members are encouraged to ask questions regarding the location of the checker pieces, as long as the therapist can ensure the safety of the client.

Brief Vignette

Linda phoned requesting counseling for her family after her daughter Jamie's most recent suicide attempt. Linda, fifty-five, had three children: Jamie (thirty-three), Donna (thirty-one), and Belinda (twenty-five). Donna was married, but spent five days of the week at her family's house because her husband traveled during the week. Both Jamie and Belinda still resided in the family home. Belinda had a two-year-old daughter, Maggie, who also lived in the house. All family members, with the exception of the daughters' father, were unemployed and on disability. The father, Ron, did not agree to come to sessions, so the therapist saw the family without him.

Jamie had a history of suicide attempts. In the most recent attempt, she ingested several over-the-counter pain relievers, crashed her car, and became unconscious. She could not remember the details of the accident, and the family was concerned that she would make another attempt. Belinda stated that she was typically the one in the family who felt responsible for taking care of Jamie, and that she and Jamie used to be close to each other but had not been close since Maggie's birth. Belinda stated that she had often felt responsible for holding the family together in the early years of the family's life and was uncomfortable in this role. Once Maggie was born, Belinda said that she was concerned that Maggie would take over this role. Linda agreed that Maggie was a focal point in the family and that Belinda experienced a great deal of stress over the role.

The therapist introduced the Kvebaek activity and explained the parameters to the family. The family seemed excited but somewhat apprehensive about the experiential activity. The therapist selected Jamie to begin the activity. Jamie took the checkers and began to place them around the board. She placed one checker approximately two squares away from the center of the board. The other family members each began writing their guesses on their copies of the board. Jamie placed one checker on each side of the center checker, making sure that both checkers touched the middle checker. Approximately two rows of squares behind the center piece she placed two other checker pieces about one inch apart from each other. Finally, she placed one checker about one square behind the other two pieces. Jamie looked at her arrangement and finally added two checker pieces on top of the first piece placed toward the center.

Jamie indicated that she had completed the activity. The therapist then looked around to the family members, who were studying Jamie's representation. The therapist encouraged someone to start making guesses about who the pieces represented. Donna was the first to offer guesses as to whom she thought the pieces represented. Donna thought the three pieces in the center, from Jamie's perspective, were the three sisters: Belinda in the middle, with Donna and Jamie on either side of her. She said that the baby, Maggie, and Linda were the two pieces two squares removed from the center, and that the father, Ron, was at the farthest point out. Linda guessed that Maggie was in the middle of the center group, with Belinda and Jamie as the checkers on either side of her; she predicted that she was on the outer rim with Donna, and Ron was on the outside. Belinda thought that Linda and Ron were on the outside of the center piece, which was baby

Maggie; Donna and Belinda were the two pieces behind the center three, and Jamie, she supposed, was the outside checker piece.

After all guesses were announced, the therapist asked Jamie to reveal which checkers represented which family members. Jamie stated that she had put Maggie as the center checker, with Belinda and Linda on either side. She stated that at times Linda mothered Maggie, and often Belinda and Linda would quarrel over Maggie's care. As a result, Maggie had the most power in the family, as represented by the stack of three checkers. Jamie put herself next to Donna, two squares removed from Linda, Belinda, and Maggie. She stated that although she and Belinda used to have a good relationship, they were no longer close. The therapist asked Jamie if she wanted some of that closeness again, and Jamie stated that she did. She said that she felt closer to Donna, who, although she was still in the family, had a separate life with her husband. The single checker most removed from the family represented Ron, her father. Jamie stated that Ron was pretty uninvolved with the family as a whole.

At this point, the therapist asked Jamie to explain what past events, if any, led her to put the pieces where she did. The therapist also invited other family members to ask Jamie about why she placed the checkers where she did. Belinda found that Jamie's placement of Maggie in the center validated her concerns about Maggie being the focus in the family and having the implicit responsibility of keeping the family together. She was glad she was not the only person who felt that way about Maggie and now she could bring it up as a valid concern for discussion in therapy.

After Jamie's turn, Linda moved the checkers to represent the family. When she moved them around and made her own picture, the therapist took guesses from the family about which checkers represented which family members. The therapist again asked the family members to record their individual guesses before Linda revealed her intentions. The therapist and family repeated this until every person had a turn to reflect their view of the family closeness on the Kvebaek.

This session was important in this case for several reasons. First, it provided the therapist an opportunity to assess the relationships among the family members and also provided valuable information regarding how members perceived one another. For example, many members in this family indicated that they did not feel close to their father. As a result, the therapist encouraged the family members to invite their father to session. This activity also served as an intervention. For example, when Jamie indicated that she did not feel as close to Belinda as she once did, the sisters processed this event and decided to spend some time together over the week.

Suggestions for Follow-Up

There are several suggestions for follow-up of this activity. First, this activity may be used as an assessment tool as well as an activity. At the outset of the therapy, this activity might give the therapist some idea of how close the family members feel to one another. Toward the end of therapy, the therapist could administer this activity again and see how the closeness and distancing changed for each member of the family. Did some members grow closer while others grew farther apart? Are some of these moves appropriate? For example, a mother and daughter who appeared extremely close at the beginning may be farther from each other at the end of therapy, but this might be the result of a less enmeshed and perhaps better-functioning relationship between mother and daughter. The daughter may listen to mother now and see her as an authority figure where before she viewed her as a peer, limiting mom's effectiveness in parenting.

Another follow-up suggestion is to add a homework component to this activity. After the activity, family members are likely to view the family differently. The therapist can assign each family member to journal between sessions about his or her experiences in the therapy room. For example, in the vignette, if the father in the family, Ron, came to session, he might be saddened at the idea that his children and wife thought that he was on the outskirts of the family.

Journaling about this experience might provide some relief and something to bring up at the next session. For those who need more structure, some questions the therapist might pose as prompts include the following:

What was difficult about this activity? What was rewarding for you?
Were you surprised by any of the representations that your family members made? Why or why not?
What things do you want to be different in your family? What things do you want to see the same?
Who determined who went first? Why?
Did you learn anything you did not know before about your mother? Father? Daughter? Son? If so, what?

Contraindications

This activity would not be indicated for clinical situations in which the therapist was not able to maintain safety within the therapy room. Because of the nature of this activity, it may make clients vulnerable to being open to or otherwise feel attacked by other family members who may disagree with the checker arrangement. It is imperative that the therapist ensures safety and encourages members who disagree with one person's representation to include those components in their own representation.

Readings and Resources for the Professional

Kaduson, H. G. & Schaefer, C. E. (2001). *101 more favorite play therapy techniques.* Northvale, NJ: Jason Aronson, Inc.
Marston, D. C. & Szeles-Szecsei, H. (2001). Using "play therapy" techniques with older adults. *Clinical Gerontologist, 22*(3-4), 122-124.
Mitten, T. & Piercy, F. P. (1993). Learning symbolic-experiential therapy: One approach. *Contemporary Family Therapy, 15*(2), 149-168.

Bibliotherapy Source for Clients

Faber, A. & Mazlish, E. (1980). *How to talk so kids will listen and listen so kids will talk.* New York: Avon Books.

References

Berry, J. T., Hurley, J. H., & Worthington, E. L. (1990). Empirical validity of the Kvebaek Family Sculpture Technique. *American Journal of Family Therapy, 18*(1), 19-31.
Connell, G. M., Mitten, T. J., & Whitaker, C. A. (1993). Reshaping family symbols: A symbolic experiential perspective. *Journal of Marital & Family Therapy, 19*(3), 243-251.
Hernandez, S. (1998). The emotional thermometer: Using family sculpting for emotional assessment. *Family Therapy, 25*(2), 121-128.
Piercy, F. P., Sprenkle, D. H., & Wetchler, J. L. (Eds.). (1996). *Family therapy sourcebook.* New York: Guilford Press.

Family System Checkerboard

Instructions: Record your guesses about who each checker represents on the copy of the board below.

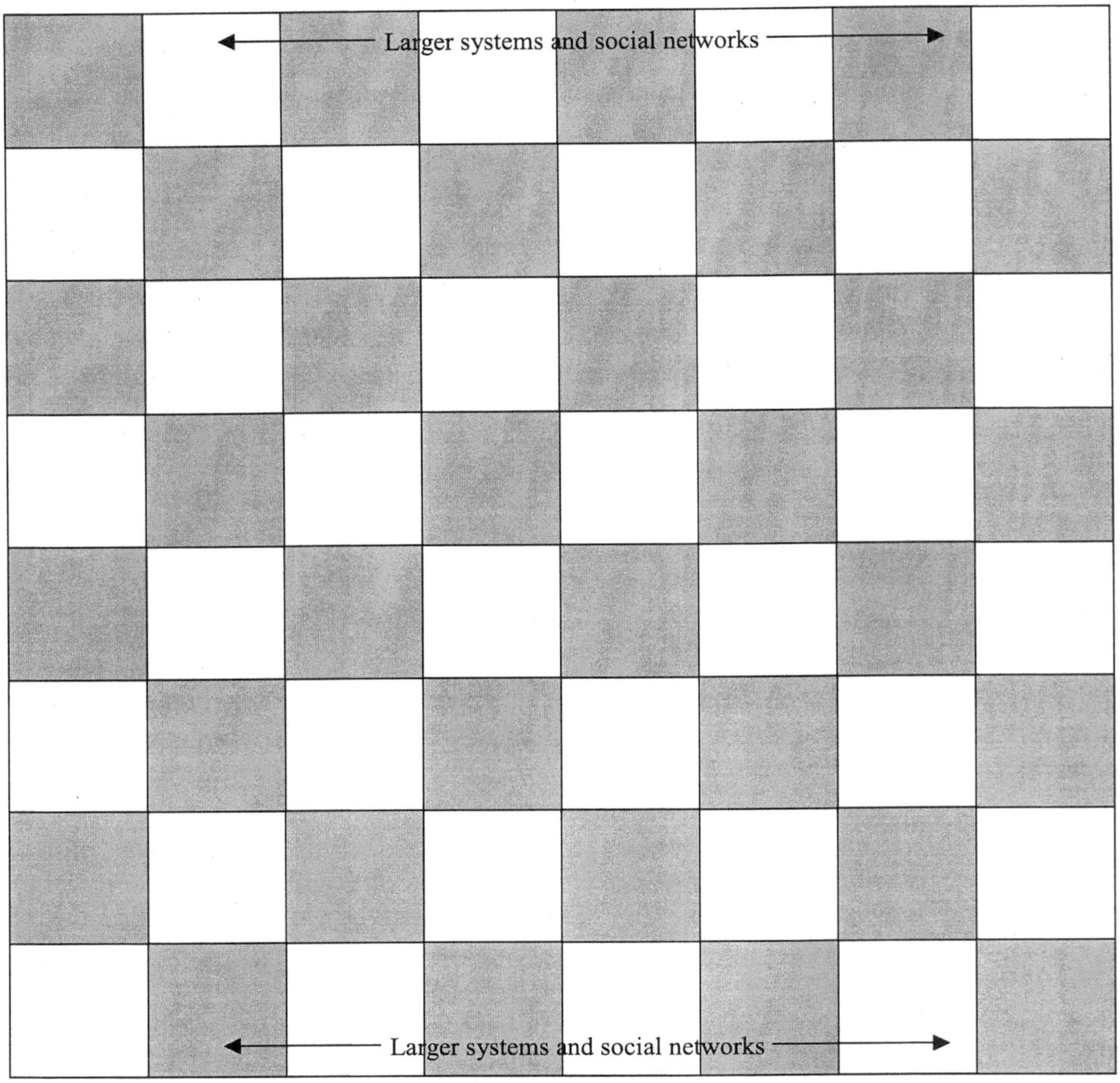

– 12 –

Beginning Body Dialogue: An Introduction to Physical Acting Techniques in Family Counseling

Kevin A. Harris
Paul W. Wilson II
Z. Vance Jackson

Type of Contribution: Activity

Objective

Beginning Body Dialogue is a useful introductory technique to the many physical acting techniques that a counselor may use in family counseling. This activity serves as a tool the counselor can use to familiarize the family with participatory physical activities in counseling, such as family sculpting (Bitter & Corey, 2001). It provides a structured and practically tested exercise the counselor can use for this purpose.

Rationale for Use

Dialogue is the crux of counseling and the basis of the majority of counseling techniques. At times, however, dialogue is insufficient to create therapeutic change. Family members may not communicate well, or they may use verbal techniques to manipulate or undermine the therapeutic process (either consciously or unconsciously). A family counselor may find that the therapeutic process is stagnating and want something to get the process moving again. At times like these, physical activities such as family sculpting can be useful interventions to promote dialogue and get the therapeutic process on track (see Bitter & Corey, 2001).

Although family sculpting and related physical acting techniques are widely used activities in family counseling, some clients may be initially uncomfortable with the extent of group physical activity. The activity in this chapter can help to develop a comfort level among the family members, and between the family members and the counseling professional. The activity can also help family members to express their emotional states both inside and outside counseling sessions.

This activity is based on the Theatre of the Oppressed techniques of Brazilian theatre director Augusto Boal (1979, 1995, 1992/2002). Boal's Theatre of the Oppressed is a form of revolutionary theatre that breaks down the boundaries between actors and spectators. These techniques use audience participation to create a dialogue for the purpose of liberating both actor and spectator from oppression: political oppression such as an oppressive dictatorship, interpersonal oppression such as family conflict, or personal oppression such as depression. Boal's

The authors wish to acknowledge Trent Barstad, MEd, Dr. Theresa Kruczek, PhD, and the Grissom family (not their real name) for their assistance with the Brief Vignette.

techniques have been widely tested and used in the world of theatre performance, and to a lesser degree have found their way into counseling. They bear a striking resemblance to many of the Gestalt techniques of Fritz Perls (Corey, 2001), and they are useful in group and family counseling. Here, a sequence of Theatre of the Oppressed techniques has been adapted for use in family counseling.

Instructions

These instructions are simple to carry out but require a fair degree of familiarity and comfort from the counselor. Before beginning, the counselor should perhaps practice individually before attempting the activity with the family present. Once the counselor has used this activity a few times it can easily be done from memory, but if the counselor prefers, the transcript from the later vignette can also be used as a script.

This activity works best with at least three family members present, although it can be done with as few as two persons (in addition to the therapist). It also works best with slow, wordless music playing in the background. The therapist can bring in a tape or CD player and start the music when indicated in the activity. The total time for this exercise is approximately forty to fifty minutes, allowing five minutes for introduction and ten minutes for a follow-up discussion.

Before beginning the activity with the family, the counselor should spend a few minutes explaining the purpose of the activity and the procedures. Of course, the counselor should also obtain the family's permission to proceed. Many clients are used to sitting for entire counseling sessions and may find it strange, confusing, or uncomfortable to do an exercise in counseling that gets them up out of their seats. With an appropriate introduction, most people can overcome their initial discomfort and will find this activity to be both fun and useful.

The counselor should explain that the participants will be asked to get up out of their chairs and move around the room. They will

familiarize themselves with the room;
familiarize themselves with their bodies;
move things around in the room; and
physically interact with one another.

The counselor should explain that this activity is different from what they may be used to or expect in counseling, but that it can be a lot of fun. The counselor should also explain that the activity will help the family learn to cooperate, interact, and communicate with one another in an honest and genuine way, and will be a learning experience they can later discuss.

There are four steps to this activity: (1) familiarizing with the space, (2) familiarizing with the body, (3) manipulating the space, and (4) physically interacting with others. The counselor should do these steps with the family, modeling for the family how they should be done.

Step 1: Familiarizing with the Space

This is the first and perhaps most essential step to ensure the family's comfort and success with this activity. Central to this step is that each member of the family unit feels he or she has permission to move in the therapeutic space.

First, start the music (if available). Have each individual stand at a comfortable distance from one another (as much as space permits), encouraging them to "find their own space in the room." When they have done so, encourage them to walk around the room at their own pace, exploring with their eyes every inch of the room. Have them pay attention to the music, with each person walking to the beat of the music until he or she feels comfortable walking at his or her own pace.

Encourage the individuals to look at the room, noticing things to which they would not regularly pay attention. What are the qualities of the room, in terms of size, color, temperature, texture, etc.? Answers should not be given verbally, but instead noted silently.

Allow the family to spend at least five minutes on this step. You should do this activity with the family to show them how it is done. If the room is small, a family member may finish exploring the space quickly and indicate he or she is done. If this happens, simply ask him or her to continue exploring the room, looking for details he or she may have missed. It is okay to tell them that you would like them to spend the entire five minutes on this step. Most clients, however, will continue to explore for as long as you do.

Step 2: Familiarizing with the Body

Next, ask the individuals to pay attention to and relax each part of their body. This exercise should be done standing, although if preferred, this step can also be done sitting down. Start with the bottoms of the feet, rising from and touching the floor, then move upward, through the ankles, lower legs, knees, upper legs, hips, stomach and chest, spine, and so on. Encourage them to feel the shoulders connected loosely to the spine, and the arms, hands, and fingers hanging relaxed from the shoulders. Move up the neck and into the head, feeling each part of the face relax. If any part of the body is tense, instruct them to tense it even more, and then relax it. You may also encourage them to "breathe into it"—to breathe in and imagine their breath filling up the tense body part, relaxing it.

Alternately, this exercise can be replaced by a progressive muscle relaxation or another relaxation activity, which may be done with the family seated. Allow the family to spend at least five minutes on this step. Again, do this exercise with the family.

Step 3: Manipulating the Space

Give the individuals permission to manipulate the therapeutic space in creative ways. Have them continue to walk, but in walking, allow them to move obstacles and change and move objects so that they are no longer performing traditional functions. For example, a chair may be gently turned upside down, in a position where it would not usually be found or used. Let the individuals know of any limitations—for example, if windows or doors should not be opened. Also emphasize that an object can be moved only once; one person cannot "correct" another's manipulation of the space. Allow the family to spend at least five minutes on this step. Again, do this exercise with the family.

Step 4: Physically Interacting with Others ("The Mirror Image")

This exercise is done in pairs. If an even number of family members is present, they should pair off and the therapist will observe; if there is an odd number, the therapist should pair off with one of the family members and participate. One person in each pair will be the "mirror." Moving in slow motion, the "mirror" will imitate each movement the other person does. Three rules apply:

1. The person being mirrored must move in slow motion.
2. The person being mirrored should not try to trick the mirror or move unpredictably. The point is for the pair to cooperate—to be so synchronized that an onlooker could not distinguish between person and mirror.
3. The pair should maintain eye contact with each other at all times.

The pairs will gradually develop a sense of give and take—how slow one must move to accommodate the imitation skills of the other, the mirror adjusting speed to match the person and vice versa. When the pairs are comfortable moving in this way, have them switch roles so that the person becomes the mirror, while the mirror becomes the person.

Next, have each pair alternate roles, switching between mirror and person without communicating verbally. Give and take between person and mirror should flow smoothly, so that no "transfer of power" is noticeable to an observer. Remind the partners to keep their movements in slow motion, and that give and take is a skill for both partners to learn—each person is responsible for being both a follower and a leader.

Finally, assuming there is more than one pair, have the pairs switch members so that each person gets a chance to pair up with every other family member. Allow the family to spend at least ten to fifteen minutes on this step, or until the therapist has noted a change in the dynamic of leadership, e.g., when the partners are comfortable taking on both leader and mirror roles.

After completing this activity, the therapist should have the family spend a few minutes discussing the exercise.

How did it feel?
How comfortable was the exercise?
What was difficult about the exercise?
What was easiest?
How challenging was it to mirror someone else?
What was it like to develop a give and take within each pair?
Were there any parallels between the family members' interactions during the activity and their interactions at home?

The therapist should pay particular attention to the family's comfort level with the exercise. If they found it initially uncomfortable and were subsequently never able to overcome their discomfort, additional physical acting techniques are not recommended for the family. Most families, however, will adjust well to the activity, and it can serve as a useful segue into other physical acting techniques the counselor wishes to use.

Brief Vignette

The following vignette provides an example of how the exercise of Beginning Body Dialogue can be useful in the counseling process, especially with families. The transcript that follows can also be used as a script which a therapist can use in session to explain the exercise to a family. This particular vignette is an actual excerpt from a one-time consultation conducted with a family which appeared to be "stuck" in counseling. (Names have been changed and identifying information has been removed for the sake of confidentiality.) The family was having difficulty in communicating with one another, and this exercise was implemented in an attempt to help them develop new ways of communicating.

The Grissom family was comprised of a thirty-eight-year-old mother named Jean, an eighteen-year-old son named Billy, a fifteen-year-old daughter named Jill, and a twenty-year-old daughter named Jane. The oldest daughter, Jane, was not able to attend the session. The family had come to therapy because they were concerned about family communication problems. Jean reported that she felt her family did not respect one another and that they frequently argued. She wanted them to respect one another more. The children also stated that they felt they fought with one another too much. The family wanted to learn how to communicate more effectively and learn to be a "better" family.

The family's therapist, Toby (not his real name), thought that using Beginning Body Dialogue in session might help make some of the family's presenting concerns more salient to the family. Toby allowed one of this chapter's authors (Z. V. J.) to join to the family's third session and use Beginning Body Dialogue with the family. In the transcript that follows, the *therapist* refers to Jackson, the guest therapist for this one-time consultation. Toby was also present but spent most of the session observing.

THERAPIST: I would like to try something a bit different today. It's not exactly what you might expect counseling to be like, but I think it can be very helpful and fun as well. The reason I think this exercise will be positive is because it will help you all learn to cooperate, interact, and communicate with one another in a way that is honest and genuine. This exercise is broken up into four parts. In the first part, I am going to have you all become more familiar with your surroundings. In the second part I am going to have you all become more familiar with your own bodies. In the third part, I would like you all to change some things about the way the room looks. Finally, I would like for you all to interact with one another. I know this might feel a little strange at first and it might even make you laugh a little bit, but these exercises can be powerful tools to help us further explore the concerns that you all have with one another. What do you all think? Would you like to try it?

JEAN: Yeah, sure.

BILLY: Sounds weird, but I'll try it.

JILL: I guess so.

THERAPIST: Okay, it sounds like everybody is willing to give it a shot. That's a start. Again, I know this may seem a little weird to you all at first, but give it a try and let's see what happens. First, I would like everybody to stand up and stretch out a little bit. [*Everybody stands up.*] Okay, now I want you all to walk around the room and try to take notice of some things about the room that you normally wouldn't notice. For instance, you might look at the color of the walls or carpet, the temperature of the room, pictures on the wall, or objects around the room. Try to get a feel for your surroundings and really become familiar with the room. Pay attention to any detail that you can think of. Think about these things and keep the things that you notice to yourself. The most important thing for you to remember during this part is that you all have permission to move around the room. So take about five minutes and walk around the room and get a feel for the room. [*All the clients walk around the room observing their surroundings.*]

THERAPIST: Okay, you can sit down now. [*The counselor chose to do this step with the family seated because of space limitations.*] Now that you have become familiar with the room, I want you to familiarize yourselves with your bodies and relax your bodies. I want you to start at the bottoms of your feet, rising from and touching the floor. Then move upward, through the ankles and your lower legs. Notice how your lower legs are connected to your knees. Now feel your upper legs, hips, stomach, chest, and spine. Try to feel how your shoulders are connected to the spine. Feel how your arms come down from your shoulders and how your hands are attached to your arms at your wrist. Now feel your fingers and wiggle them around a little bit. I want you to move up to the neck and into the head. Feel each part of your face and try to relax the muscles in your face. If any specific parts of your body are tense, make them even tenser and then try to relax them. Let's take about five minutes and try to relax your bodies. [*The family spends about five minutes sitting, becoming familiar and comfortable with their own bodies.*]

THERAPIST: Okay, how did that feel?

BILLY: My back feels a little better.

JEAN: Yeah, my neck was killing me, but now it's a little better.

THERAPIST: That's great! Now that we have become familiar with our own space and bodies, let's try to change some things about them. What I would like for you to do is to stand up and walk around the room again. This time, however, try to move any obstacles in the room, and change and move objects so that they are no longer performing their traditional functions. Take this chair for instance. You could turn it over or flip it on its side. You could take this book and put it under the desk. Try to change the objects around so that they are not performing the functions they usually would. But there are also a few ground rules for this exercise. First, please leave the door closed. Second, each object can be moved only once. If someone changes an object, you cannot move it again. This way hopefully you will begin to get a sense of respect for the rest of your family. Sound good?

BILLY: Yeah sure.

JEAN: Yep.

JILL: I'm not sure why we are doing this, but okay.

THERAPIST: Let's try to take five minutes and do this activity. [*The clients walk around the room and move obstacles and objects around the room. While walking around the room, Jill was about to flip something over and Billy rushed in and flipped it over before Jill could.*]

JILL: I was going to do that!

BILLY: You were too slow.

JILL: I can't believe you did that.

THERAPIST: Let's keep walking around the room, but when we talk about the exercises I want to come back to this.

JILL: Fine. [*Jill scowls at Billy.*]

[*The clients complete the exercise.*]

THERAPIST: Now what I want to do is to take all of the stuff that we have worked on so far and try to put it together. The goal of this exercise is to learn how to interact with one another and to communicate without using your voices. This exercise is done in pairs, so Jean and Jill, why don't you pair up, and Toby and Billy, you pair up. (Since there was an odd number of family members, the guest therapist paired Billy with the family's regular therapist.) What we are going to do in this exercise is have one person be the person being mirrored and the other person will be the "mirror." I want each of you to move in slow motion and I would like for the "mirror" to imitate each movement that the other person does. There are, however, just a few rules to this exercise. First, the person being mirrored must move in slow motion. Second, the person who is being mirrored in this exercise should not try to trick the mirror or move in any unpredictable way. The point of this exercise is for the two to be synchronized and to cooperate. Finally, both people need to maintain eye contact throughout the entire exercise. I want you to work with your partner for three to four minutes and then switch roles. Then after you have both had a chance to be the mirror, I would like for you to try to switch back and forth between roles and try to communicate with each other with your bodies when you want to switch. Then we are going to change partners so everyone gets a chance to work together. Sound good? Go for it.

[*First, Jean and Jill work together while Billy and Toby work together. Then they switch, with Jean working with Billy, and Jill working with Toby. Finally, they switch once more, with Jean working with Toby, and Billy working with Jill. As the pairs are working together on this exercise, several patterns emerge. Both Billy and Jill appear to be comfortable working with Jean, but Billy and Jill do not seem to be working well together. Also, Jean and Jill appear to be enjoying the exercise and laughing a lot. Jean and Billy, however, do not appear to be having fun and there is very little laughter.*]

THERAPIST: Okay, now that we have completed this exercise, I want to know how you are all feeling right now and what each of you noticed during the exercise.

JEAN: Well, I'm feeling pretty good right now. That was kind of fun. I noticed that Jill and I were able to communicate with each other pretty well and we were having a good time. That's how it always is though. She and I get along pretty good most of the time. I noticed it was kind of hard to work with Billy. It felt kind of weird looking into his eyes and doing this. Sometimes we have trouble talking to each other.

JILL: Yeah, it was pretty easy to work with Mom, but it was hard working with Billy. It just felt really weird.

THERAPIST: What do you think about that, Billy? Do you think you were able to work with them?

BILLY: Yeah, it's like they said. Just kind of weird. If Jane had been here, I might have been able to work with her a little better. We all seem to have a pretty good relationship with Jane.

JILL: Yeah, Jane and I pretty much laugh all the time. Well, we fight, but it's usually pretty good.

THERAPIST: I noticed you all were laughing a lot. Is that how your family deals with emotions?

JEAN: Yeah, whenever something comes up, we usually laugh. It's better than crying, you know.

THERAPIST: It sounds like this exercise was able to help bring out some of the communication concerns that all of you have been having. I want all of you to try to do this exercise with Jane at some point during the week. Hopefully this exercise has opened some doors and brought up some things that each of you can talk about with Toby next week.

Suggestions for Follow-Up

In the family therapy session following the Beginning Body Dialogue exercise, the therapist can again have the family discuss their reactions to and impressions of the exercise. If the exercise brought up something particularly meaningful or significant to the family, some time should be spent processing this, particularly if there was not sufficient time to process it the previous week, immediately after the exercise. If, on the other hand, the activity did not bring up any significant issues, but the family still seems receptive to using physical acting techniques in counseling, the therapist might introduce another physical acting technique at this point, such as family sculpting. This technique may simply be introduced as prescribed, or it may be prefaced by an element of Beginning Body Dialogue if the therapist feels this is appropriate. For example, the therapist might choose to introduce family sculpting by first having the family manipulate the space around them prior to having them manipulate each other in family sculpting. At any time, if the therapist suspects that one or more of the family members are uncomfortable with any of the techniques, this discomfort should be addressed in session.

Contraindications

There may be some initial concern about using this activity with family members who have histrionic, narcissistic, or megalomaniacal personality traits or are otherwise overly attention-seeking, as they may try to use this activity to show off or monopolize therapy further. This activity, however, may actually be helpful for these clients. It is primarily introspective, but it also requires cooperation with another person and can help to equalize power dynamics between family members. There may also be some concern about using this activity with those who have physical limitations, such as the physically disabled or the elderly. This activity can be appropriate for these clients, though, if it is done slowly and the amount of time spent standing is minimized. In fact, this activity could be done from a wheelchair, provided there is room to navigate a wheelchair around the room for the purposes of exploring the space.

There are some clients, however, whose physical limitations would cause them to become exhausted were they to move around the room, even with assistance. This activity is not recommended for their use. Also, some clients will never be comfortable using physical techniques in counseling sessions. This activity is not recommended for their use.

Readings and Resources for the Professional

Bitter, J. R. & Corey, G. (2001). Family systems therapy. In G. Corey (Ed.), *Theory and practice of counseling and psychotherapy* (6th ed., pp. 382-453). Belmont, CA: Wadsworth.

Boal, A. (1979). *Theatre of the Oppressed* (C. A. McBride & M.-O. L. McBride, Trans.). New York: Urizen.

Boal, A. (1992/2002). *Games for actors and non-actors* (2nd ed.) (A. Jackson, Trans.). London: Routledge.

Boal, A. (1995). *The Rainbow of desire: The Boal method of theatre and therapy* (A. Jackson, Trans.). New York: Routledge.

Corey, G. (2001). Gestalt therapy. In G. Corey (Ed.), *Theory and practice of counseling and psychotherapy* (6th ed., pp. 192-227). Belmont, CA: Wadsworth.

Bibliotherapy Sources for the Client

Boal, A. (1992/2002). *Games for actors and non-actors* (2nd ed.) (A. Jackson, Trans.). London: Routledge.

Dayton, T. (1990). *Drama games: Techniques for self-development.* Deerfield Beach, FL: Health Communications, Inc.

References

Bitter, J. R. & Corey, G. (2001). Family systems therapy. In G. Corey (Ed.), *Theory and practice of counseling and psychotherapy* (6th ed., pp. 382-453). Belmont, CA: Wadsworth.

Boal, A. (1979). *Theatre of the Oppressed* (C. A. McBride & M.-O. L. McBride, Trans.). New York: Urizen.

Boal, A. (1992/2002). *Games for actors and non-actors* (2nd ed.) (A. Jackson, Trans.). London: Routledge.

Boal, A. (1995). *The Rainbow of desire: The Boal method of theatre and therapy* (A. Jackson, Trans.). New York: Routledge.

Corey, G. (2001). Gestalt therapy. In G. Corey (Ed.), *Theory and practice of counseling and psychotherapy* (6th ed., pp. 192-227). Belmont, CA: Wadsworth.

– 13 –

Communicating with Children: Feelings Game

Shari Sias
Glenn W. Lambie

Type of Contribution: Activity

Objective

The objective of this activity is to help children identify and express a full range of feelings while encouraging parental support of such expressions through parental modeling of healthy emotional expression. The activity is directed toward families who want to increase open communication and trust and become more emotionally expressive. The Feelings Game can also be used as an assessment tool for the therapist to gauge the family's ability to tolerate or allow for emotional expression.

Rationale for Use

Emotional expression is necessary for good mental health (Smyth, 1998; Pennebaker, 1995). Emotional expression includes identifying, labeling, and sharing feelings. Families provide the foundation for sharing feelings (Brody, 1999). Difficulties or conflicts in emotional expression may be a precipitant for families entering counseling. For example, families often come to therapy due to a child's acting-out behavior. The child's behavior may be due to difficulty in verbal expression. Feelings, such as anger or sadness, may take the form of acting out or withdrawing. Family therapy can assist the child in identifying and appropriately expressing his or her feelings, as well as educate parents about developmental issues that may impact the child's ability to verbally communicate his or her feelings. In some cases, the child's reluctance to share feelings verbally is developmentally appropriate. For example, preschoolers lack the vocabulary and the ability to think abstractly, which limits their verbal expression. Through increased understanding of age-appropriate emotional expression, parents are less likely to misconstrue developmental issues as major problems and are better equipped to respond to their children's emotional needs.

To educate parents about the various stages of emotional development, therapists may want to share information such as the following: preschoolers tend to have a limited vocabulary, often express their feelings behaviorally, and have difficulty understanding that it is possible to have many different emotions about a given event (Harter & Buddlin, 1987). Children in middle childhood, ages six to eleven years, are likely to experience and understand more complex emotions (e.g., pride or guilt), understand that it is possible to experience more than one emotion at a given time, and begin to hide their emotions to avoid hurting others (Borich & Tombari, 1995). During early adolescence, ages eleven to fourteen years, children may experience emotional ups and downs, sometimes leading to emotional outbursts, and they may experience an increase in negative emotions, such as anxiety and anger. When feeling overwhelmed by negative emotions, adolescents may hide or mask their true feelings and push parents and other adults away. It is important for parents to look past some of the "masking" to explore the adolescent's true feelings (Vernon, 1993). Adolescents, children ages fifteen to eighteen years, achieve formal operational thinking, which enables individuals to think abstractly and hypothetically (Reimer, Paolitto, & Hersh, 1983). As a result, most adolescents are able to manage their emotions and express them more fully. Common areas of concern for adolescents include relationships and choosing a career or postsecondary education.

Just as the parents need to consider developmental issues when parenting their children, therapists need to take into account their client's developmental level when selecting counseling interventions. When working with families, interventions need to be directed at both adults and children. Traditional counseling interventions focusing on verbal expression are effective with adults, but these same techniques are not particularly effective with children (Vernon, 1999). Children have limited attention spans and tend to learn best by doing rather than by talking. Therefore, it is recommended that therapists use visual, kinesthetic, and auditory methods when working with children (Stith, Rosen, McCollum, Coleman, & Herman, 1996; Vernon, 1993, 1999). The Feelings Game incorporates all of these methods.

Gender is another factor that may influence emotional expression (Brody, 1999; Pollack, 1998). Pollack suggests that in American culture, the socialization process continues to perpetuate gender differences in emotional expression. That is, girls continue to be encouraged to express a full range of emotions, whereas boys are encouraged to express only tough, action-oriented emotions such as anger and rage. Feelings such as sadness or caring are not commonly encouraged in boys. In addition, Pollack found that boys often have their own "emotional schedule" and may take longer to share their feelings than girls. He suggests that it is best for therapists, teachers, and parents to connect with boys through activities such as game playing or by sharing their own experiences to normalize and model emotional expression. Again, the Feelings Game can assist parents in connecting with their children in action-oriented activities and storytelling.

During the therapeutic process, therapists may encourage clients to release or express a variety of emotions. The use of emotional expression in therapy is often guided by the therapist's theoretical orientation. For example, a therapist practicing from a psychoanalytic perspective may see emotional expression as a means of catharsis—the release of unexpressed or unconscious feelings which leads to insight. From a cognitive-behavioral perspective, the goal is to identify and replace irrational beliefs with rational ones, thus better managing one's emotions (Artz, 1994). A couples' or family therapy approach that focuses on the emotional expression of family members is termed emotionally focused therapy (EFT). The goal in EFT is "to restructure a couples interactional pattern by accessing the validating the emotions underlying the position taken by each partner" (Dankoski, 2001, p. 177). When working with families, EFT concentrates on the importance of a secure emotional attachment among family members.

Emotionally focused therapy is one means of exploring gender and power differences in couples' therapy. Research has found that females exhibit better emotional support skills than males (Goldsmith & Dun, 1997; Kunkel & Burleson, 1998), and females tend to place a higher value on providing emotional support than do males (Burleson, Kunkel, Samter, & Werking, 1996). These gender differences are frequently found among couples seeking counseling. Often couples begin therapy with the chief complaint being an "inexpressive" husband and an "overly expressive" wife. EFT helps validate both partners' experience by highlighting the importance of males experiencing their emotions fully as well as supporting the female need for more emotional support from their partner (Dankoski, 2001). As previously stated, emotional expression is an important component of good mental health. This is true for both males and females. When addressing the issue of emotional expression in family therapy, it is important that parents or caregivers, regardless of their gender, be able to model healthy emotional expression. If parents are having difficulty expressing themselves, then couples' therapy may be necessary before focusing on this issue in family sessions.

The Feelings Game is an activity that can be used in family sessions to assist children in identifying and expressing emotions. In addition, it can provide the needed structure for adult family members to model healthy emotional expression. When playing the Feelings Game, family members increase their awareness of emotional expression in themselves and in other family members. Being intentional with identifying and expressing feelings in the counseling session, as well as providing a safe place for sharing, increases the likelihood of open expression. The therapist may also choose to play the game with the family to model the sharing of feelings.

Instructions

Prior to the counseling session, the therapist will need to create pairs of "feelings squares" (see example at end of chapter). A feelings square is a picture that clearly displays a particular emotion (e.g., sad face, angry face, scared face, etc.). Two matching squares are needed for each emotion. When playing the game, clients will try to uncover matching pairs of emotions. It is helpful if the squares are about the size of a playing card. This size is easy for children of all ages to grasp.

Another option is to have the family create the feelings squares in session or as a homework assignment. By having family members create the cards as part of a session, the therapist can observe their interaction patterns (e.g., Who talks to whom and who helps whom?) and evaluate issues of family structure and power (e.g., Who takes the leadership role, and are all family members included in the activity?).

In session, the therapist discusses with the family that a variety of activities will be used in the counseling process including games, art projects, as well as talking with one another. As mentioned, it is helpful to briefly discuss developmental issues with parents or caregivers to increase their understanding and participation in the activity. Next, the topic of feelings is introduced. This can be done by showing some of the feelings squares and asking family members to identify the feeling being expressed.

Finally, the rules of the Feelings Game are presented. The Feelings Game is similar to the Memory Game in that the feelings squares are mixed up, turned face down, and placed in rows. Family members then take turns finding matches. When someone has a match, he or she removes the cards and shares a time when he or she experienced the emotion represented on the card. Other family members are encouraged to listen without correcting or negating the story. If the cards do not match, they are returned face down and the next family member takes a turn. The Feelings Game can be used with a variety of ages. Because reading skills are not required, children as young as four years of age can participate. The Feelings Game has been effective with a variety of family configurations.

Brief Vignette

The following case study includes a grandmother (Susan), a grandfather (Joe), and their grandson (Jay). The identified client was Jay, a ten-year-old boy who was referred to family therapy with his grandparents by his fifth-grade teacher due to "problems getting along with classmates." Jay had recently moved in with his grandparents after living briefly with his father and stepmother. Until the age of nine, Jay had lived with his mother, her boyfriend, and his two sisters, but he had been sent to live with his father due to "fighting with his sisters and not going to school." After approximately three months of living with his father, Jay began to "argue" with his stepmother. It was then decided by the family (Jay's parents and grandparents) that Jay would go to live with his paternal grandparents.

Similar to many ten-year-olds, Jay did not respond well to talk therapy. He only answered direct questions and his responses were brief. Susan reported that Jay was a "kind and caring child" who seemed to have difficulty expressing himself, particularly when he was "upset or angry." Susan and Joe were concerned about how Jay was adjusting to living with "older folks," as well as how he felt about "being moved from family member to family member." In addition, Susan reported that both of Jay's parents had a history of drug addiction and that "Jay hasn't had much structure in the past."

Following the initial assessment period, the therapy goals were established as (a) increasing family communication, including the healthy expression of feelings and emotions, and (b) establishing family rules and roles. After developing rapport with the family, the Feelings Game was introduced as a possible technique to improve emotional expression and communication.

Developmental issues (i.e., differences in learning styles and attention spans of adults versus children and the need for various counseling-related activities) had previously been discussed, so only a brief review was needed. Reviewing developmental issues commonly found in middle childhood supported the use of game playing as a therapeutic technique, as well as assisting the grandparents in determining appropriate rules and behavior expectations for Jay outside of the counseling sessions.

The family was shown several feelings squares and asked to identify the feelings being expressed. Cards relating to positive or playful feelings were introduced first, followed by the rules of the Feelings Game. Jay responded positively to the idea of playing the game, commenting that he enjoyed playing games and was usually good at them. Susan and Joe were open to the idea of playing, and Susan joked about the game improving her memory.

At the beginning of the game, the stories concerning the various feelings were brief and often humorous. As the game progressed, the stories became more detailed and more serious in nature. At the close of the session, each person spoke about his or her experience playing the game (e.g., favorite story, likes, dislikes). Over the course of therapy, Jay would ask to play the Feelings Game. When asked what he liked about the game, he stated, "I like that I get a turn to talk and that makes me feel better."

Suggestions for Follow-Up

This activity assesses a client's ability to identify, express, and communicate emotions. Some individuals, particularly children, may need assistance in first identifying feelings. Once feelings are identified, it may be necessary to help the client develop healthy ways of expressing feelings. Over time, patterns may begin to emerge (e.g., "It's okay to be angry but not sad"). Other techniques, such as teaching the ABCs of rational emotive behavioral therapy (Ellis & Dryden, 1997), may be needed to change identified patterns and support healthy expression of all emotions.

Contraindications

This activity may not be appropriate with families where there are concerns of client safety. It is important that all family members be able to safely express their feelings without the threat of what they say being used against them. This activity may not be appropriate for families with issues of domestic violence and abuse. If safety issues are a concern, the therapist will want to conduct a safety session or sessions. A safety session is "intended to reduce the risk of client violence by opening a forthright dialogue regarding the risk of violent behavior, specifying appropriate behavior, and setting limits and consequences for noncompliance" (McAdams & Foster,

2002, p. 49). For more information concerning how to conduct a safety session see McAdams and Foster.

Furthermore, this activity may not be effective in families where the parents or caregivers are unable to model healthy expression of their own feelings. The therapist may want to spend time with the parents discussing the importance of healthy expression of feelings and work with them on their own emotional expression before having them model this behavior for their children.

Resource for the Professional

Wilde, J. (1997). *Hot stuff to help kids chill out: The anger management book.* Richmond, IN: LGR Publishing.

Bibliotherapy Sources for the Client

Curtis, J. L. & Cornell, L. (1998). *Today I feel silly & other moods that make my day.* New York: Joanna Cotler Books.

Curtis, J. L. & Cornell, L. (2002). *I'm gonna like me: Letting off a little self-esteem.* New York: Joanna Cotler Books.

Moser, A. J. & Pelkey, D. (1988). *Don't pop your cork on Mondays: The children's anti-stress book.* Kansas City, MO: Landmark Editions.

Spelman, C. M. & Cote, N. (2000). *When I feel angry.* Morton Grove, IL: Albert Whitman & Company.

Spelman, C. M. & Parkinson, K. (2002). *When I feel scared: The way I feel.* Morton Grove, IL: Albert Whitman & Company.

Vernon, A. & Al-Mabuk, R. (1995). *What growing up is all about: A parents' guide to child and adolescent development.* Champaign, IL: Research Press.

Whitehouse, E. & Warwick, P. (1996). *A volcano in my tummy: Helping children handle anger: A resource for parents, caregivers, and teachers.* Gabriola Island, BC, Canada: New Society Publishers.

References

Artz, S. (1994). Feeling as a way of knowing. *Guidance & Counseling, 10*(1), 14-17.

Borich, G. D. & Tombari, M. L. (1995). *Educational psychology: A contemporary approach.* New York: Harper Collins.

Brody, L. F. (1999). *Gender, emotion, and the family.* Cambridge, MA: Harvard University Press.

Burleson, B. R., Kunkel, A. W., Samter, W., & Werking, K. J. (1996). Men's and women's evaluations of communication skills in personal relationships: When sex differences make a difference and when they don't. *Journal of Social and Personal Relationships, 13,* 201-224.

Dankoski, M. E. (2001). Pulling on the heart strings: An emotionally focused approach to family cycle transitions. *Journal of Marital and Family Therapy, 27*(2), 177-188.

Ellis, A. & Dryden, W. (1997). *The practice of Rational Emotive Behavior Therapy* (2nd ed.). New York: Springer Publishing.

Goldsmith, D. E. & Dun, S. A. (1997). Sex differences and similarities in the communication of social support. *Journal of Social and Personal Relationships, 14,* 317-337.

Harter, S. & Buddlin, B. J. (1987). Children's understanding of the simultaneity of two emotions: A five-stage developmental acquisition sequence. *Developmental Psychology, 23,* 388-399.

Kunkel, A. W. & Burleson, B. R. (1998). Social support and the emotional lives of men and women: An assessment of the different cultures perspective. In D. J. Canary & K. Dindia (Eds.), *Sex differences and similarities in communication* (pp. 101-125). Mahwah, NJ: Erlbaum.

McAdams, C. R., III & Foster, V. A. (2002). The safety session: A prerequisite to progress in counseling families with physically aggressive children and adolescents. *The Family Journal: Counseling and Therapy for Couples and Families, 10*(1), 49-56.

Pennebaker, J. W. (1995). *Emotion, disclosure, and health.* Washington, DC: American Psychological Association.

Pollack, W. (1998). *Rescuing our sons from the myths of boyhood: Real boys.* New York: Henry Holt and Company.

Reimer, J., Paolitto, D. P., & Hersh, R. H. (1983). *Promoting moral growth: From Piaget to Kohlberg* (2nd ed). Prospect Heights, IL: Waveland Press Inc.

Smyth, J. M. (1998). Written emotional expression: Effect sizes, outcomes types, and moderating variables. *Journal of Consulting and Clinical Psychology, 66*(1), 174-184.

Stith, S. M., Rosen, K. H., McCollum, E. E., Coleman, J. U., & Herman, S. A. (1996). The voices of children: Preadolescent children's experiences in family therapy. *Journal of Marital and Family Therapy, 22,* 69-86

Vernon, A. (1993). *Developmental assessment and intervention with children and adolescents.* Alexandria, VA: American Counseling Association.

Vernon, A. (1999). *Counseling children and adolescents* (2nd ed). Denver, CO: Love Publishing.

FEELINGS SQUARES

(*Source:* Image created by Carolina Viques of Florida State University)

Name Your True Colors: A Card Game for Engaging Families in Problem-Solving Processes

Marta M. Miranda
Pam Black

Type of Contribution: Activity

Objective

The objectives of this activity are fourfold. First, this creative and fun activity assists families by giving them a tool for forming effective working relationships and enhancing family functioning. Second, the described game provides the opportunity for individual family members to self-identify and to appreciate their primary personality characteristics, which in turn identifies the group personality. Third, participation in the activity develops collaborative working relationships based on the strengths and weaknesses of individual members and promotes respectful teamwork. Fourth, it offers an opportunity for improving interpersonal communication skills and for enhancing problem-solving skills, while valuing diversity of styles.

Rationale for Use

Families make decisions on a daily basis regarding their overall psychosocial functioning, the management of the home, and discipline of the children. Many families lack the tools they need when conflict arises, when new developmental challenges emerge that create power struggles within the family unit, and when patterns of dysfunctional behaviors become standard ways of interacting. Families that lack the appropriate tools or engage in disruptive patterns of behavior become rigid and polarized in their roles, which in turn contribute to the loss of confidence and self-esteem in their members. A dysfunctional family atmosphere minimizes creativity and precipitates the members' engagement in a survival struggle that leads to stagnation rather than growth and change (Satir, 1988).

For healthy family functioning to occur and for families to be able to engage in collaborative decision-making processes, they need effective communication skills, problem-solving strategies, and conflict-resolution techniques. This intervention promotes all of these. The activity provides the family with the opportunity to take the time to acknowledge and respect individual differences and similarities. It also encourages the use of strengths to solve family problems. It engages families in the development of a work plan for solving their problems by encouraging communication and collaboration among their members. In choosing this intervention, the worker offers the family a nonthreatening and creative approach to practice new communication skills based on individual personality styles. The use of self-disclosure increases intimacy and trust, which builds rapport and promotes confidence in family members. Finally, this intervention helps families who are stuck in dysfunctional patterns of behavior to move toward adaptation of new roles based on mutual respect for the differences among members. It disrupts rigid and polarized dysfunctional behaviors that prevent the family unit from functioning as a team. Individual characteristics and strengths, which are identified in the card game, are used to accomplish everyday tasks (e.g., chores, helping with homework, preparing meals, etc.) that may otherwise create conflict within the family.

The theories that inform this intervention are family developmental theory, role theory, and symbolic interactionism. These theories validate the stress caused by new developmental tasks, the rigid adherence to roles in order to survive and function in the engagement of family through interaction and relationship (Carter & McGoldrick, 1980; Queralt, 1996; Satir, 1988).

The use of this card game is helpful when family groups are having difficulty communicating and problem solving. It is also appropriate when the family is experiencing internal conflict due to the demands of new family formation. A family worker can use this intervention with newly formed family systems, with families who lack communication and problem-solving skills, and with families who experience distress caused by the challenges of new developmental tasks.

Instructions

Family Worker Preparatory Planning

The use of the True Colors card game is rooted in Myers-Briggs indicator research and was developed by Don Lowry (2001). It has previously been used in corporate and classroom settings to encourage discussion regarding diversity of learning and working styles.

The activity proceeds in two phases. In the first phase, the family worker gathers the family history and explores the presenting problems, forms an assessment, discusses possible intervention with the family, and jointly makes a decision to engage in the use of the color game as a method of intervention. In this phase, the family members are becoming aware of their own personality traits and practicing self-disclosure as each member shares his or her personality palette with the family. In the second phase, the worker engages the family members in the problem-solving process. The family may need to learn and practice basic communication skills, such as "I" statements or reflective listening prior to engaging in the actual problem-solving phase of this activity.

Phase I: Introduction and Self-Awareness

The True Colors booklet provides a list of descriptive qualities and the participant is asked to self-identify from a list of word groups that best describe him or her. The descriptors for each color card are set in clusters. For example, for the color blue the main strength is authenticity, and characteristics include, "I need to feel unique and authentic. I look for meaning and significance in life. I value integrity and unity in relationships. I am a natural romantic. At work I have a strong desire to influence others. I often work in the arts, education, or helping professions, etc." (Lowry, 2001, p. 16). A description of the blue personality style is then given, such as "you seek to express the inner you; authenticity and honesty are valued above all other characteristics" (Lowry, 2001, p. 17). The clusters are arranged in columns, which are totaled, and the participant's color spectrum is revealed with the highest number being the primary style, followed

---

The worker can purchase the *Keys to Personal Success* booklet, which contains the True Colors card game at True Colors Inc. Headquarters, 3605 West MacArthur Boulevard, Suite 702, Santa Ana, CA 92704; www.truecolors.org. If unable to purchase *Keys to Personal Success,* the worker can refer to the book *Gifts Differing* by I.B. Myers and P.B. Myers (1980). Another possible resource is *Follow Your True Colors to the Work You Love* by C. Kalil (1998).

by the second and third highest style, and the fourth total being the lowest style. The participants are then asked to arrange the True Color cards in his or her corresponding spectrum. Participants can use the outcome of their color spectrum to communicate their strengths and needs in order to work and relate successfully in teams with co-workers and/or family members. Following this, participants are given suggestions in order to enhance performance at work and personal relationships, such as expressing feelings, recognizing the need to contribute, having intimate talks, and being open. For green, the primary strength and need is knowledge; orange is skillfulness; and gold is duty. Each of the characteristics, strengths, and keys to personal and work success are explained in detail in the booklet.

The worker briefly introduces the Name Your Colors card game to the members of the family, answering initial questions that they may have about the activity. Each family member is given a *Keys to Personal Success* booklet, which contains a set of True Color cards for identifying and ranking primary personality characteristics.

The worker instructs each member to follow the steps in the booklet to create an individual personality palette. This solo work takes approximately fifteen minutes. After each member completes the individual work with the booklet and cards, the member is asked to share the personality palette with the rest of the family. Three to five minutes are allowed for family members to share information.

Phase II: Problem-Solving Process

The family worker now engages the family in the problem-solving process by asking the family to identify an issue that they wish to solve using the color palette results. The process of identifying the issue can be accomplished in a brainstorming session. The worker instructs the family to take sixty seconds to think about a past or recent issue that has caused conflict within the family. After sixty seconds, the worker calls time and instructs the family to identify some of the issues that came to mind. The worker records them on a large flip chart. Three to five minutes are allowed for the brainstorming session. The worker then asks the family to discuss which issues they choose to process using the color palette results. If there is a tie, the family takes a vote to determine which issue to address. The second issue is to be worked on at the next family session or is to be given as a homework assignment.

After the brainstorming session and discussion, the family unit assigns tasks and chooses a plan of action. The choice is based on the individual strengths and needs of the members reflected in the individual color palettes. The worker records the goals and tasks and then designates who is responsible for the specific action steps. The members select the opportunities to create subsystems within the family to complete specific tasks. Careful communication and close collaboration are necessary among the members. The family is given a copy of the work plan created in the session.

Brief Vignette

The following vignette depicts a family experiencing role stress related to new family formation. New family formation requires renegotiation of family rules, roles, and rituals as this family was in the remarriage stage of the family life cycle (Carter & McGoldrick, 1980). They were also having difficulty negotiating new traditions and developing new alliances.

The Martinez-Smith family was a newly reconstructed unit. Joe (thirty-eight) and Lillian (thirty-five) were recently married and each had a child from a previous marriage. Joe had a ten-year-old daughter named Michelle, and Lillian had a fifteen-year-old son named Adrian. Lillian called the office to request family counseling to address discipline issues regarding Adrian. She reported that Joe and Adrian were having a difficult time negotiating their relationship. Joe perceived Adrian as "lazy," and Adrian perceived Joe as "a sergeant."

Upon gathering the family history and exploring the presenting problem, the family worker decided that one of the possible underlying issues in this newly formed family system was a lack of understanding and respect for individual strengths. A fear of losing control as a result of relating to new family roles and structure appeared to be another probable dynamic. It seemed that the majority of the conflict surfaced around family chores, such as taking out the garbage and doing laundry. The worker took the opportunity to increase awareness of the family members' personality styles and to promote dialogue by suggesting the True Color card game as a way to problem solve.

Prior to the game, the worker exposed the family to five communication skills: "I" statements, reflective listening, clarifying, probing, and feedback. A fishbowl method, using two chairs placed in the center of the room, was used to demonstrate these techniques. With the other members observing the interaction, Lillian and Michelle practiced using the skills while Joe and Adrian observed, then Joe and Lillian practiced while Michelle and Adrian observed. Finally, Joe and Adrian practiced with each other, while Michelle and Lillian observed. After thirty minutes the family worker and the members had a minimal comfort level using the skills. The members set ground rules. Then, the worker and family engaged in a brief discussion of the homework. The family was given the assignment of practicing the newly learned communication skills throughout the week. At the beginning of the next session, the worker reviewed the result of the homework and the members reported that they had used the new skills intermittently, with favorable results. Now the family was ready to engage in the color card game.

The family worker gave each member his or her own *Keys to Personal Success* booklet, which contained the True Color cards. They individually completed their personal color spectrum. Once they had gathered their True Color cards, each member took turns disclosing his or her personality spectrum. Joe stated that his primary color was green; Lillian said that hers was blue; Michelle reported hers as blue; and Adrian said he was an orange. The worker chose to engage the family in solving a nonthreatening problem. The question to be resolved was "where to go for the next family vacation?" Members were encouraged to self-assign tasks based on their primary personality color style. It was clear that factual information regarding length of trip and expense was best suited for Joe (his primary traits were those of a green—very detailed oriented). Adrian, an orange (creative), chose to search the Internet for fun places that all members would enjoy. He would then bring three options to the family. Lillian, a blue (values relationships and meaning), agreed to research and schedule historical and cultural sites in the surrounding area. Michelle, who was also a blue, agreed to find games and activities for the family to engage in while on vacation.

The activity proved to be a fun experience for the family. This was evidenced by laughter and joking, which took place among the members. The activity assisted Michelle by giving her an opportunity to be seen and heard by members of the family. She had been isolating herself and playing the role of lost child as the conflict between Joe and Adrian increased. Lillian expressed feelings of relief and hope that Joe and Adrian could build a successful relationship.

During the fourth session, the same procedure was used to tackle the presenting problem of doing household chores. The family worker initiated a review of communication skills and introduced techniques for resolving conflict around the daily tasks. Some examples were: to express and acknowledge feelings, to negotiate, to call time-outs, and to set boundaries. The ground rules were established and posted on newsprint. The outcome of this session resulted in a work plan for the family that included assigned tasks and rewards, as well as consequences for not completing the tasks agreed upon. The family was given the assignment of posting the family work plan in a visible place in the home. At the conclusion of the session, the worker engaged the family in a round-robin discussion using "I" statements that addressed their feelings and fears regarding the use of the suggested communication skills and the accomplishment of the work plan.

Following sessions focused on deeper issues regarding Adrian's loss of his mother's "undivided" attention and his resentment of Joe's role as the family patriarch. Joe was able to discuss his need to "be in control and do a good job." Lillian addressed her feelings regarding being triangulated by Joe and Adrian in a family sculpting session. The card game assisted the family in developing new alliances and in negotiating new rules and roles as they established a family unit with a healthier level of functioning.

Suggestions for Follow-Up

Homework can be assigned following the intervention. The worker could instruct the family to place the work plan in a visible common area of the home and to paint a portrait of the family using the color palette. The work plan and family portrait are also to be placed in a prominent location. During the next family session, the worker can explore the family members' experiences and then review the work plan. Blocks to completing the tasks are identified and successes acknowledged. The family members should be urged to use the color palette to solve day-to-day family issues, such as the assignment of family chores.

Indications and Contraindications

This activity is indicated for families who need assistance with communication, problem-solving skills, and conflict because of individual differences or with inability to function effectively as a unit. They should be experiencing mild-to-moderate levels of distress and the lack of homeostasis. It is not appropriate to address issues of family violence, addictions, infidelities, or serious psychiatric problems using this activity.

Resources for Professionals/Clients

Kalil, C. (1998). *Follow your true colors to the work you love.* Riverside, CA: True Colors.
Kalil, C. & Lowry, D. (1989). *How to express your natural skills and talents in a career.* Laguna Beach, CA: Communication Companies International.
Lowry, D. (2001). *Keys to personal success.* Riverside, CA: True Colors.

References

Carter, E. & McGoldrick, M. (1980). *The family life cycle: A framework for family therapy.* New York: Gardner Press.
Kalil, C. (1998). *Follow your true colors to the work you love.* Riverside, CA: True Colors.
Lowry, D. (2001). *Keys to personal success.* Riverside, CA: True Colors.
Myers, I. B. & Myers, P. B. (1980). *Gifts differing.* Palo Alto, CA: Consulting Psychologists.
Queralt, M. (1996). *The social environment and human behavior: A diversity perspective.* Needham Heights, MA: Allyn & Bacon.
Satir, V. (1988). *The new peoplemaking.* Palo Alto, CA: Science and Behavior Books.

– 15 –

Royal Flush

Katherine M. Hertlein

Type of Contribution: Activity

Objective

Many family members differ on how they view their family structure. The purpose of this activity is to have family members present how they see their family structure. By using picture cards, each family member selects a card that represents each member of the family and he or she arranges the cards spatially to reflect how he or she sees the family structure. This activity can be important to help parents and children in goal setting within structural family therapy.

Rationale for Use

Some families who come to therapy feel divided. Due to household arguments between parents, siblings, and between parents and children, families who come to therapy may be searching for strategies that engender better communication and increase emotional intimacy between family members. This activity promotes communication between family members and allows the family to see how each family member views distance, closeness, and process between members of the family.

Several theoretical frameworks influence this activity. It is partially influenced by structural family therapy (Minuchin, 1974), which focuses on solving a problem in a family by altering or adjusting the family structure. In this framework, problems occur within a family system when there is not appropriate closeness or distance between family members. Some examples include when the children subsystem is too close or distant to the parental subsystem, when the parents are too distant from each other, when children are parentified, or a variety of other family structures. Minuchin (1974) describes the family form that is more ideal as that in which the parents have a higher hierarchical position than the children. From this position, parents are able to provide directives to their children, and children will be able to respond more appropriately to the directives. Parents will come across as a unit as opposed to individuals who can easily be divided and conquered. Finally, appropriate boundaries between family members will also be in place, resulting in more effective management of the family.

This activity is also influenced by symbolic-experiential therapy. In symbolic-experiential therapy, clients integrate symbols and experiences (Connell, Mitten, & Whitaker, 1993). When clients use symbols to represent and describe their experiences, the therapist can help clients link experiences and events with something tangible and encourage another way for clients to express themselves. In addition, the symbols selected can be used throughout the course of therapy. The therapist and family can revisit the characters ascribed to each person or the dynamics between family members throughout therapy. For example, the therapist and family members can make comments such as "It seems like you feel like the dragon today" or ask questions such as "How did you get rid of the dragon in you?"

Within symbolic-experiential therapy, clients can also draw how close they are to one another as a way to depict emotional space (Piercy, Sprenkle, & Wetchler, 1996). In the present activity, family members assign the cards to represent each member of the family. In this way, the family members select symbols they see as being represented in each family member. Once individual family members are identified with particular cards, the members each take turns depicting what they see as the emotional space between members. Because this is occurring through the symbols and cards, it is accomplished in a nonthreatening manner. The arrangement of members to depict emotional space is also influenced by family sculpting. In family sculpting, persons in the family arrange themselves in terms of distance and closeness with one another. In this activity, family members are able to arrange the representations of themselves in relation to one another.

Finally, this activity is also influenced by the techniques of directive play therapy. In directive play therapy (as opposed to nondirective) the therapist selects the activity rather than following the child's lead. In this way, the therapist instructs each family member to complete the activity but does not put limits on what the children can choose for each family member.

Instructions

At the end of this chapter are pictures of medieval persona. The therapist photocopies the pages and cuts out each card. As a way to create cards that are sturdier, the therapist can affix the paper cards to 3½-inch by 5-inch note cards. The therapist then states that each member of the family will each have a turn to select cards that he or she believes represent members of the family. For example, the therapist might begin with the youngest child in the family and asks him or her to pick out characters that represent each person in the family. Once the individual has selected cards for each family member, the therapist instructs the individual to arrange the cards in terms of closeness or distance to one another. One manner this might be framed is for the therapist to tell the client to put the family members (represented as cards) in appropriate closeness and distance to one another. For example, who is closer to whom in the family? Which two people are farthest away from each other? The therapist tells the client that there are no right or wrong answers, just that he or she should place the cards where he or she feels is appropriate. This is important because closeness and distance as depicted by someone in the family can be used as assessment or as an intervention. For example, a child might depict his parents as emotionally distant from each other. This is an assessment in that the therapist and family come to understand the world of the child; it is an intervention in that the parents might come to an understanding of how their behavior and relationship affects their child, and may be willing to make some changes.

Colors can be very important in this activity. Family members might find value in assigning different colors to different cards. For example, a red dragon may signify anger while a green dragon may signify silliness. Likewise, a black knight may signify an element of darkness while a white knight may signify a helper or rescuer. It is important for the therapist to determine the meaning behind selected colors that are ascribed to each family member.

If the therapist chooses to pursue color within this activity, there are a few ways to accomplish it. One option is for the therapist to assign the family to color in the cards for homework and bring them to the next session. This option is limiting because family members may not agree on what colors each person should be. To avoid this problem, the therapist can make one set of photocopied cards for each member of the family. Then the therapist can assign each family member to color his or her own set of cards and bring them to the next session.

Variation with a Deck of Cards

One variation, in case the therapist does not want to use the cut-out cards within this chapter, is to do this activity with a deck of regular playing cards. The therapist will need a full deck of cards, including the jokers. This way, family members can select different cards to represent each family member. Another variation is for the clinician to use only the face cards and jokers. The benefit is that there is a more obvious hierarchy.

Variation with Puppets

Another variation is to use finger or other puppets. The store IKEA, for example, sells a set of royal family finger puppets in the children's department. These can also be used as a way to arrange the family and ascribe family members certain characteristics.

Brief Vignette

Scott Jr. was a ten-year-old client being seen for family therapy. Scott's mother, Linda, was bringing him to therapy as a result of his increasingly negative attitude toward her. She stated that her husband of fifteen years (Scott Sr.) had recently left her and had taken physical custody of Scott Jr. on the day he left. Scott Sr. left their other two children with Linda: Gregory and Steve, fourteen and five years old, respectively. After Scott Jr. left with his father, he spent every other week with his mother. Linda reported that his visits with her showed that he had a great deal of anger. Her goals for therapy were for Scott Jr. to be able to talk to her. She stated that Scott sulked about the house, often snapped when she requested something of him or tried to talk to him, and fought with his brothers.

Scott Jr. was quiet during the first session. When the therapist spoke with Scott alone, he stated that he got more annoyed at his mother's house because his brothers and his mother "treat me and my dad badly." He stated that the reason he left with his father was that he did not like the way that his older brother Gregory treated his father. When the therapist asked for some examples, Scott Jr. reported that he believed that Gregory was stealing money from his father and was also purposely losing his father's phone messages so that his father would be unable to return calls.

The therapist asked Scott Jr. how it came to be that he left the day his father left. Scott stated that he had known for some time that his father would be leaving, at least for several weeks. This was news to Linda, and she was visibly upset. The therapist asked Scott why he did not tell anyone else in the family. Scott stated that his father told him not to tell and that his brothers and mother "did not need to know." It was clear that Scott Jr. was parentified within the family system. His father had confided in him many things, and Scott Jr. placed himself above others in the family, including his mother. As a result, Scott Jr. was very loyal to his father; when his father left his mother, he sided with dad and continued his angry expressions at Linda and his brothers. In structural family therapy terms, Scott was not only parentified but also enmeshed with his father. There was a diffuse boundary between father and son, but a solid boundary between them and the other three members of the family.

Because of the problems within the organization in the family and how it affected Scott Jr.'s behavior when he was at his mother's house, the therapist decided to work to restructure the family. The therapist made a photocopy of the cards (located at the end of this chapter). The cards were then cut away from the paper and secured to note cards for stability. The therapist then presented the cards to Scott Jr. and his family in the next session (persons present were Linda, Scott Jr., and Steve). The therapist told the family that the activity would help them understand how the family structure was organized.

Steve stated that he wanted to go first. The therapist provided Steve with the cards. Steve immediately stated that he wanted his mother to be the owl. He selected the owl and placed the owl in the middle of the floor. Steve then selected himself as a jester. He placed himself to the left of the owl. Steve picked out a dragon for his brother Scott Jr., the black knight for his older brother Gregory, and king for his father. Steve put Scott Jr. and his father together at one end, and he, his brother, and his mother at the other end.

Scott Jr. went next. He selected himself as a dragon. He selected his father next, who was represented as the king. He placed himself next to his father. Then Scott Jr. selected the owl for his mother, and the jester for Steve. Finally, he selected the black knight to represent his brother Gregory. Scott Jr. placed Gregory on the opposite side of his mother, away from Steve. Finally, Linda selected herself as the queen and Scott Sr. as the king. She put the king and queen apart from each other. She then selected the dragon for Scott Jr., the bard for Gregory, and the frog prince for Steve. She placed Scott Jr. next to his father, then Steve next to him, and Gregory next to her.

The therapist complimented the family on being able to complete the activity and being respectful of everyone's opinion. The therapist then reported some observations back to the family. For example, everyone showed Scott Jr. right next to his father, and had put Linda and Scott Sr. far away from each other. The therapist rearranged Linda's depiction so that Linda and Scott Sr. were above the children, an appropriate distance apart, and the children were beneath them, an appropriate distance apart. The therapist stated that, although everybone did a great job sharing their views on how they saw the family, things might be better for the family if they looked like the structure she depicted. All three members agreed that this would be okay with them. The next week, Scott Sr. attended session. The family informed him what the structure of the family would look like. Scott Sr. stated that he would like to see the family structure set up differently as well, because he did not feel that he was able to parent effectively without being overridden by Linda. Not feeling like he had any say in the parenting, he admitted, was one of the reasons that he left the family.

Linda recently reported that Scott Jr.'s behavior has been better toward her. She stated that Scott Sr. has been taking both Steve and Scott Jr. for weekend trips as opposed to just Scott Jr. and that Steve is enjoying time with his father and brother. She stated that Scott. Jr. responded to her when she explained things from her perspective, and that he no longer has an angry reaction, but instead appears to sympathize with her.

Suggestions for Follow-Up

This activity can be supplemented by a variety of follow-up questions. For persons who select the joker, the therapist can ask, "What does a joker do? How is X like the joker in the family? How are you like a joker in the family?" A joker, for example, is typically known for juggling. Is the person in the family who was identified as the joker someone who is doing juggling in the family between two divided sides of the family, as in the vignette? Is the function of the joker in the family to be the entertainer as a way to reduce the tension within the family system? For each person in the family and each card selected, the therapist should follow up by asking the general questions and then applying them to the family. These questions include (but are not limited to) the following:

What does a king do?
How is X like the king in the family? How are you like the king in the family?
What does a queen do?
How is X like the queen in the family? How are you like the queen in the family?
What does the joker do in the family? Who would you consider to be the joker in your family?

How do a king and queen act toward each other? How do they act in your home?
Which of the characters on the cards get along? Which are at odds?
What does an owl do?

Another suggestion for follow-up is to continue the metaphors developed throughout the course of the therapy for the family. Some questions that a therapist might ask include the following:

In what ways today are you like the character you depicted? In what ways are you different? What did you do to make things different?

Contraindications

This activity is most useful when there is a relationship between the family and the therapist. In situations where children have been punished for sharing their thoughts or feelings about a given topic, it may be difficult for them to fully participate in this activity. Children in the family may feel caught between wanting to please the therapist and avoiding punishment. In this situation, the clinician should work with the parents regarding the importance of appropriate expression of emotion. Some of the negatives against emotion may be that the parents feel responsible for their children and feel that they are responsible for their child's unhappiness. As a result, when the child expresses a negative emotion, parents may personally feel attacked. In these instances, the therapist should first work with the parents to determine how much of the work they are able to handle themselves. Parents then may emphasize its importance to their child, thus increasing the likelihood of effectiveness for this activity.

Readings and Resources for the Professional

Freeman, J., Epston, D., & Lobovits, D. (1997). *Playful approaches to serious problems.* New York: W. W. Norton & Co.
Kaduson, H. G. & Schaefer, C. E. (2001). *101 more favorite play therapy techniques.* Northvale, NJ: Jason Aronson, Inc.
Landreth, G. L. (1991). *Play therapy: The art of the relationship.* Muncie, IN: Accelerated Development, Inc.
Shapiro, L. E. (1997). *Tricks of the trade.* King of Prussia, PA: The Center for Applied Psychology, Inc.

Bibliotherapy Sources for the Client

Dinkmeyer, D., McKay, G. D., & Dinkmeyer, D. (1997). *The parent's handbook: Systematic training for effective parenting.* Circle Pines, MN: American Guidance Services.
Faber, A. & Mazlish, E. (1980). *How to talk so kids will listen and listen so kids will talk.* New York: Avon.

References

Connell, G. M., Mitten, T. J., & Whitaker, C. A. (1993). Reshaping family symbols: A symbolic experiential perspective. *Journal of Marital & Family Therapy, 19*(3), 243-251.
Minuchin, S. (1974). *Families and family therapy.* Cambridge, MA: Harvard University Press.
Piercy, F. P., Sprenkle, D. H., & Wetchler, J. L. (1996). *Family therapy sourcebook.* New York: Guilford Press.

Medieval Persona Cards

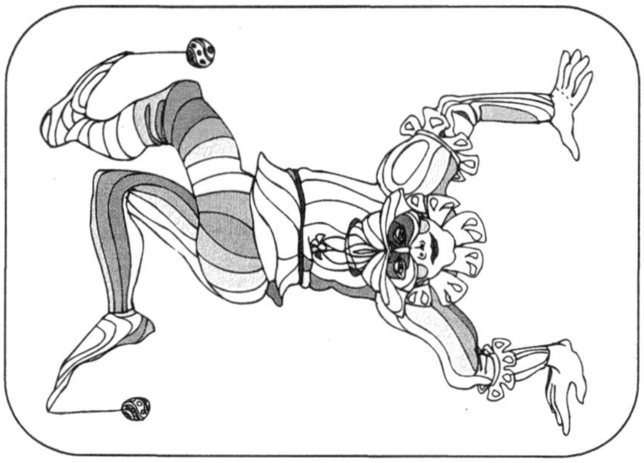

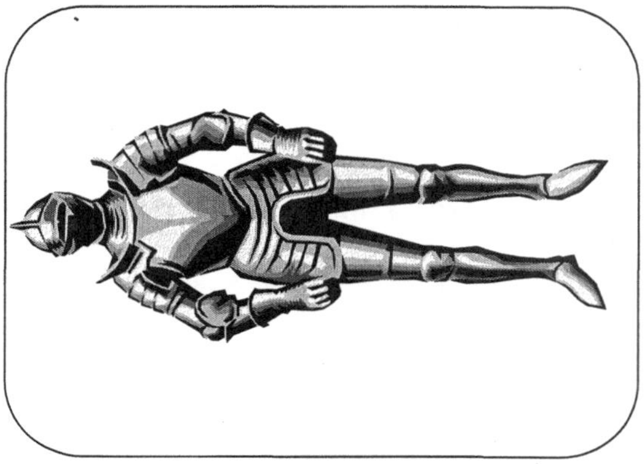

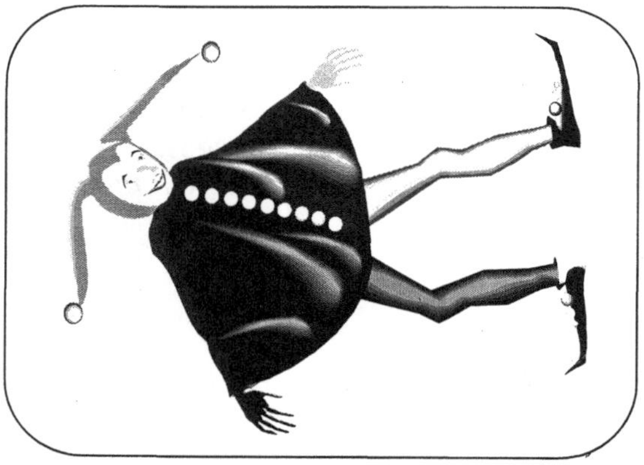

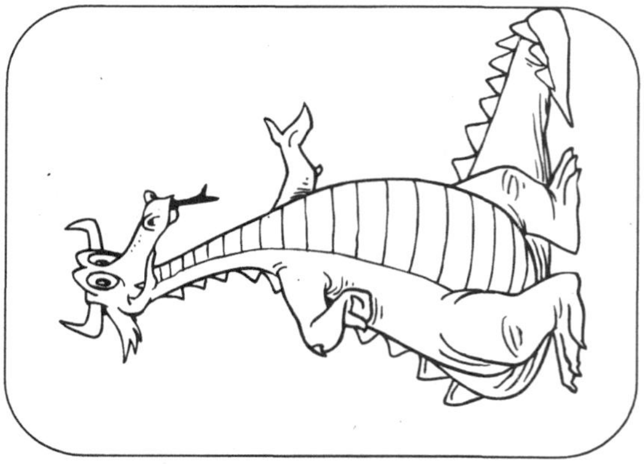

Medieval Persona Cards

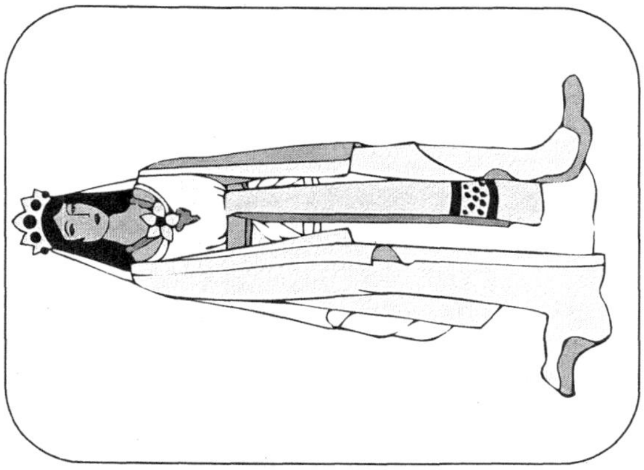

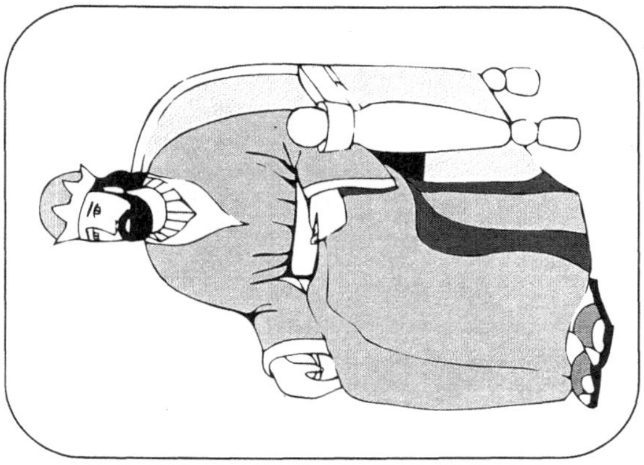

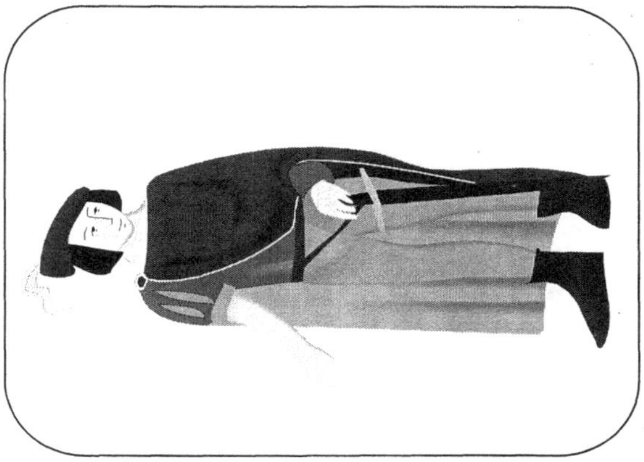

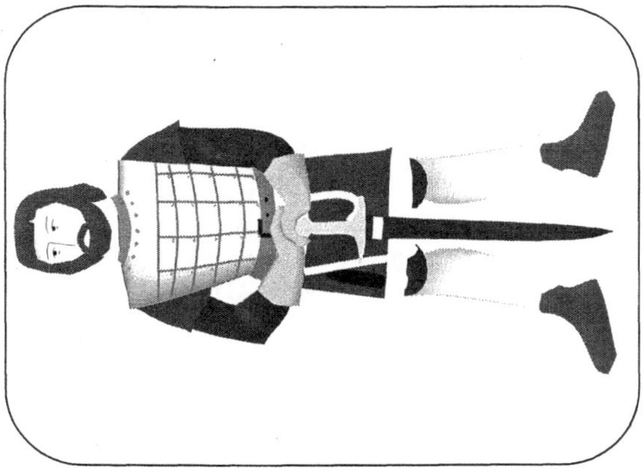

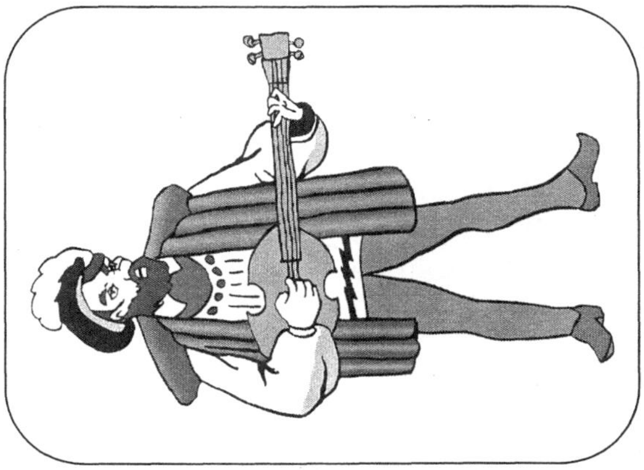

Medieval Persona Cards

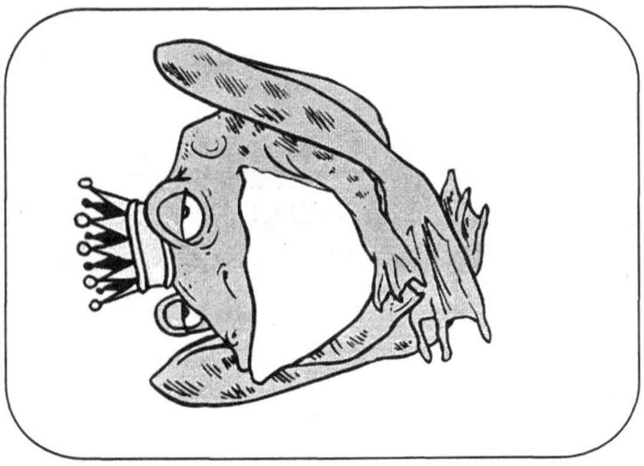

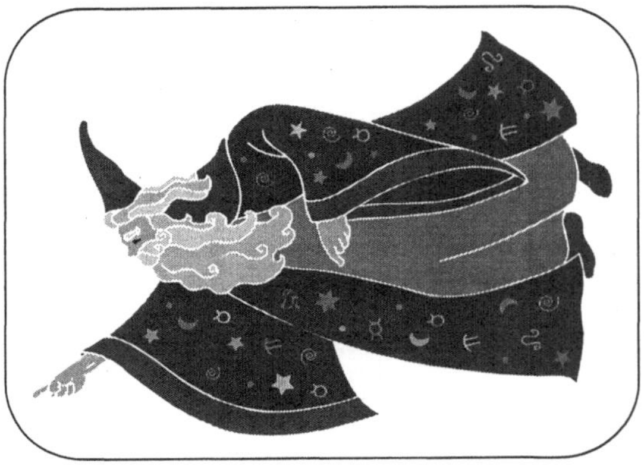

– 16 –

Put on a Happy Face

Dawn Viers

Type of Contribution: Activity

Objective

The goal of this activity is for families to recognize and express emotions that they keep buried from one another and, often, even from themselves. Helping family members to create a symbolic mask allows for the expression of covert and overt feelings and actions. This can help family members more readily identify and communicate about a broad range of feelings and emotions.

Rationale for Use

The majority of people go through life repressing certain emotions, actions, or traits. For most, this repression is a normal part of regulating thoughts and actions. For example, most children learn at a young age that they cannot scream obscenities on the playground or ask why someone does not have any hair. Sometimes, however, children (and even adults) learn to repress everyday emotions and actions. This may be the result of trying to live up to an image or playing out a role in a family. This postulation has been well documented among alcoholic families, as children often take on dysfunctional family roles, such as hero, scapegoat, lost child, or mascot (Hetherington, 1988; Mapes, Johnson, & Sandler, 1984; Veronie & Fruehstorfer, 2001). The repression of feelings can create a metaphorical mask—one portrays an image to the outside world while hiding certain traits that he or she feels would be viewed as deviant or weak. Although it can be adaptive and protective for a person to hide certain emotions, this repression can be problematic if taken to an extreme and should be addressed.

Two theoretical frameworks influence the rationale for this activity. First, the activity is based on experiential family therapy. In experiential therapy, focus is placed on present experience and may employ dreams, sensations, fantasies, and feelings (Wetchler & Piercy, 1996). Experiential therapy requires participants to experience the moment and generally involves the sharing of fantasies and fears, spontaneity, and social exchange (Neill & Kniskern, 1982). Central to experiential therapy is the concept of symbolic interaction, referred to as symbolic-experiential family therapy (Neill & Kniskern, 1982; Whitaker & Keith, 1981). Whitaker and Bumberry (1988) described symbolic-experiential therapy as "the effort to move directly into the area of living" (p. 78). Using this framework, family therapists help to decipher the messages and symbols hidden in actual conversations.

The second theoretical influence is emotionally focused therapy, a combination of experiential and more traditional systemic theories (Greenberg & Johnson, 1988; Johnson & Greenberg, 1987). Within emotionally focused therapy, emotion and the client's present experience are the primary organizing principles (Greenberg & Johnson, 1988; Johnson, 1998). Within this framework, emotional expression is a central, unifying part of healthy relationships. Greenberg and

Johnson state, "emotions are not simply inside us, but rather they are actions that connect us to the world" (1988, p. 5). Dysfunction occurs when primary biological feelings, such as fear and vulnerability, are displaced or repressed by secondary emotional reactions, including anger and stoicism. Within this frame, the secondary emotional expressions become the metaphorical mask which clients use to avoid revealing their more vulnerable emotions.

Symbolizing feelings and thoughts through an activity such as mask making is a way to identify, highlight, and access hidden emotions. Creating a mask allows the therapist and family to find the hidden meanings in common emotional expressions and conversations. As this activity is creative, rather than cognitive, it allows for the emergence of alternative modes of thought and intelligence. It also allows children and adolescents to communicate through play, which is often the natural and preferred language of children (Freeman, Epston, & Lobovits, 1997). Finally, this activity can help a client and his or her family tap into new resources and different methods of communication.

Instructions

For this activity, the therapist will need to first gather the materials for making the mask. These include newspaper strips, balloons, and a papier-mâché medium. If desired, purchased papier-mâché mix can be used; however, a homemade mixture of flour and water, mixed to a thin, sticky consistency, also works well. Stockpile other materials to decorate masks, including markers, feathers, fake jewels, ribbon or yarn, and paint. If the therapist or client is unable or uninterested in creating a three-dimensional mask using papier-mâché and balloons, a paper plate glued to a stick can be decorated and used as a mask.

Prepare the work area with newspaper or a plastic tablecloth to protect carpets and other hard-to-clean areas. The therapist should prepare the papier-mâché mixture and lay out the newspaper strips. The client or therapist will then need to blow up a balloon to a shape approximating a face. The client should be encouraged to create his or her own mask. To do this, dip the newspaper strips in the papier-mâché mixture and cover one-half of the balloon. To make a nose or ears, crumple newspaper into the appropriate shape and cover with several strips of newspaper covered in the papier-mâché mixture to adhere the appendage to the mask. Place the completed mask on a bowl, face side up, to dry (the balloon will roll over onto the mask if laid on a flat surface). Put the mask in a well-ventilated place to dry; it will initially smell like wet cement.

Let the mask dry between therapy sessions, or until all of the newspaper is dry to the touch. Once dry, pop the balloon to reveal the mask. It is now ready to be decorated. Since the mask is meant to identify covert as well as overt emotions, encourage the client to decorate both sides of the mask. The therapist should direct the client to decorate the outside of the mask to reflect expressed feelings, traits, and emotions, while the inside of the mask should reflect hidden emotions. Encourage the client to use different media to decorate the mask, as suggested previously. Making and decorating the mask will usually take two therapy sessions.

After the mask is complete, set aside time for the client and his or her family to discuss the process and meaning of the mask. Questions can include the following:

What was the process of making the mask like for you? How did you decide what traits and emotions to highlight on each side of the mask?

To whom do you show your outside face? To whom do you show your inside face?

(To family) Do you agree with the representation of the mask? Why or why not? In what circumstances have you seen the traits and emotions shown on both sides of the mask? In what ways?

What would help you show your hidden emotions and traits? When would it be appropriate to show your inside face? What stops you from showing your inside face?

Do you believe others in your family have some of the same hidden emotions as you do?

Variation: Family Mask Making

The vignette describes a case in which an individual created a mask and then brought it to a family session for a presentation and discussion of the feelings and traits depicted in the mask. However, it would be appropriate and even desirable for all family members to create a mask. In one variation, family members can create their own mask to share with one another during therapy. In another variation, family members can collaborate on a family mask that portrays the image that the family collectively shows the outside world and the image they keep hidden. Creating a collaborative family mask can be especially helpful for family members who tend to be noncommunicative with the therapist or who tend to close off from the outsiders.

Brief Vignette

A mother brought her teenage daughter, Jodie, to therapy due to a car accident involving Jodie. The mother, Linda, explained that Jodie was driving and lost control of her vehicle, causing a crash. Although Jodie and her brother, a passenger in the car, were unhurt, another family member died in the accident. Linda thought Jodie was becoming depressed over the incident, as evidenced by Jodie changing her activities, gaining weight, and letting her school grades drop. For her part, Jodie was not interested in therapy and did not think she was depressed. She attributed her change in activities and weight gain to the winter weather and hormones and the drop in grades to the challenges of being a senior. The therapist requested that the family, consisting of Jodie's brother and stepfather, attend therapy. Jodie's stepfather, Dan, was concerned about Jodie's lack of affect and was in fact angry at Jodie for not expressing the "appropriate" emotions and actions regarding the death, which he defined as remorse, sadness, and anger.

Assessment of Jodie's family history revealed her biological father (whom her mother had divorced one year earlier) was an alcoholic. He and Linda had often verbally and physically fought. Since the divorce, he had moved to another state and Jodie and her brother saw him only sporadically. Jodie stated she was the "good girl" in her family. She always received good grades, was active in student activities and sports, and had numerous friends.

In an individual session with Jodie, she talked about her role in the family. The therapist explained the roles that children in alcoholic families often take. Jodie agreed that she took on the hero role and stated that she liked this role because she felt everyone in the family looked up to her. The therapist agreed that this role had benefits, but asked if she ever felt limited in this role. Upon reflection, Jodie conceded that she thought if she broke the mold and "messed up," members of her family would come down harder on her than her brother.

The therapist introduced the mask-making activity to Jodie as a way to identify her multiple roles in her family. Jodie agreed to participate, and after some grumbling about getting her hands messy, she earnestly pieced together her mask. She formed a nose and small ears and attached them to the mask. The mask was then laid aside to dry.

During the next session, Jodie decorated her mask. With markers, she drew big blue eyes, long eyelashes, and a red mouth set in a smile on the outside of her mask. She also attached long yellow yarn to the top of the mask. On the inside of the mask, she drew large ears, very small dark eyes and eyebrows set in a scowl, and pock marks all over the face, which she stated represented her acne. Jodie talked about the differences between the two faces and the therapist suggested she bring the mask to a session with her mother and stepfather, which was scheduled for the following week. Jodie agreed and she and the therapist planned how she would reveal the mask to her family.

In the family session, Jodie presented her mask and talked about the various features and their representation. The therapist asked why she chose to highlight bright features on the outside and small, dark features on the inside. Jodie stated she felt that everyone viewed and accepted her bright side, while she felt the behaviors reflected in her dark side were acceptable only during her menstrual cycle. The therapist asked her family if they agreed with the representation. Linda agreed that Jodie saw herself as the shining star of the family, although she stated she did not understand why Jodie felt she had to save the family. The therapist explained the typical roles of children who grow up in a family where one parent is an alcoholic. Linda also stated she had seen Jodie's dark side on several occasions and proceeded to list them. Jodie seemed surprised about these events. Linda reminded Jodie that although she had shown her other face, she still loved and supported her through the good times and the bad. Dan, Jodie's stepfather, said he also wanted to support and would accept Jodie when she was angry or sad. Jodie began to cry and to talk about her sorrow over the accident and her fears that her family blamed her for the accident. Linda and Dan supported Jodie and thanked her for sharing her feelings with them. The therapist educated the family on the stages of grief to normalize the differing feelings of denial, anger, and sadness that each of the family members were feeling over the accident. Dan, Linda, and Jodie agreed that they were each in a different stage regarding the grief process.

Soon after this session, therapy started to revolve around helping the entire family go through the grieving process regarding the accident. In addition, Jodie's brother started seeing another therapist for his own anxiety issues regarding the accident. Jodie continued to remain closed about some feelings but opened up about other feelings and emotions. The family continued in therapy for another three months.

Suggestions for Follow-Up

The therapist can bring the mask into future sessions to identify overt and covert feelings and messages. For example, the therapist can ask, "Which face are you showing your family regarding this issue?" or "Is this a safe time to let your hidden feelings show?" As the client or family gets more comfortable sharing hidden feelings, they can create a new mask indicating the feelings they show the outside world.

Contraindications

As with any single activity, this activity should be accompanied by other interventions from the model that the therapist uses. This activity should not be used with a client who has severe personality or dissociative disorders, as the client could view the therapist as downplaying the seriousness of these disorders. Because this activity asks a client or family to divulge hidden parts of oneself or one's family, the therapist should be aware that abuse histories could surface during the mask making or storytelling. The therapist should let clients know that the therapist is a mandated reporter of abuse and will need to report the abuse to proper authorities.

Readings and Resources for the Professional

Freeman, J., Epston, D., & Lobovits, D. (1997). *Playful approaches to serious problems.* New York: W. W. Norton & Co.

Gil, E. (1994). *Play in family therapy.* New York: Guilford Press.

Wetchler, J. L. & Piercy, F. P. (1996). Experiential family therapies. In F. P. Piercy, D. H. Sprenkle, J. L. Wetchler, & Associates (Eds.), *Family therapy sourcebook* (2nd ed., pp. 79-105). New York: Guilford Press.

Whitaker, C. A., & Bumberry, W. M. (1988). *Dancing with the family. A symbolic-experiential approach.* New York: Brunner/Mazel.

Whitaker, C. A., & Keith, D. V. (1981). Symbolic-experiential family therapy. In A. S. Gurman & D. P. Kniskern (Eds.), *Handbook of family therapy* (pp. 187-225). New York: Brunner/Mazel.

Resources for the Client

Faber, A. & Mazlish, E. (1980). *How to talk so kids will listen and listen so kids will talk.* New York: Avon.

Nemiroff, M. A. & Annunziata, J. (1990). *A child's first book about play therapy.* Washington, DC: American Psychological Association.

References

Freeman, J., Epston, D., & Lobovits, D. (1997). *Playful approaches to serious problems.* New York: W. W. Norton & Co.

Greenberg, L. S. & Johnson, S. M. (1988). *Emotionally focused therapy for couples.* New York: Guilford Press.

Hetherington, S. E. (1988). Children of alcoholics: An emerging mental health issue. *Archives of Psychiatric Nursing, 2,* 251-255.

Johnson, S. M. (1998). Listening to the music: Emotion as a natural part of systems theory. *Journal of Systemic Therapies, 17*(2), 1-17.

Johnson, S. M. & Greenberg, L. S. (1987). Emotionally focused marital therapy: An overview. *Psychotherapy, 24,* 552-560.

Mapes, B. E., Johnson, R. A., & Sandler, K. R. (1984). The alcoholic family: Diagnosis and treatment. *Alcoholism Treatment Quarterly, 1*(4), 67-83.

Neill, J. R. & Kniskern, D. P. (Eds.) (1982). *From psyche to system: The evolving therapy of Carl Whitaker.* New York: Guilford Press.

Veronie, L. & Fruehstorfer, D. B. (2001). Gender, birth order and family role identification among adult children of alcoholics. *Current Psychology: Developmental, Learning, Personality, Social, 20,* 53-67.

Wetchler, J. L. & Piercy, F. P. (1996). Experiential family therapies. In F. P. Piercy, D. H. Sprenkle, J. L. Wetchler, & Associates (Eds.), *Family therapy sourcebook* (2nd ed., pp. 79-105). New York: Guilford Press.

Whitaker, C. A. & Bumberry, W. M. (1988). *Dancing with the family. A symbolic-experiential approach.* New York: Brunner/Mazel.

Whitaker, C. A. & Keith, D. V. (1981). Symbolic-experiential family therapy. In A. S. Gurman & D. P. Kniskern (Eds.), *Handbook of family therapy* (pp. 187-225). New York: Brunner/Mazel.

– 17 –

Speak Softly and Carry a Big Stick

Katherine M. Hertlein

Type of Activity: Homework

Objective

Referring to military preparation and the Monroe Doctrine, Teddy Roosevelt was credited as saying, "Speak softly and carry a big stick." Who thought it could apply to family therapy? The purpose of this activity is to have a family collaborate on a project to provide structure to sessions and provide safety so the family members can feel comfortable sharing with one another. As homework, the family will create an object to moderate conversation such as a "Talking Stick," and then use the Talking Stick in session as a way to regulate conversation. In this way, each family member has the opportunity to express himself or herself appropriately without monopolizing conversations. Family members have the opportunity to hear everyone's perspectives, and therapy can effectively include input from all family members.

Rationale for Use

Families come to therapy for a variety of reasons. As a result, therapy can take several shifts and the session format is sometimes dependent upon who is in the therapy room. At times the conversation in the therapy room can be chaotic. Family members may interrupt one another. Children may talk over their parents, or parents may not provide their children an opportunity to speak during the session. Another example of chaos in family communication patterns might be family members switching from topic to topic. When a topic becomes too difficult for families members to continue discussing, a chaotic environment might allow family members to switch from topic to topic, wrestling with their discomfort. At other times, therapists may feel as if they have to pull teeth to get family members to talk in front of one another; yet family members may not feel safe talking to one another. They may expect to be attacked after sharing feelings or perspectives on family events. In any of these scenarios the therapist may have a difficult time facilitating conversation.

Family members may not be able to appropriately regulate conversation with one another for a variety of reasons. One factor could be family structure (Minuchin, 1974). Children may not feel comfortable airing concerns in front of their parents due to a hierarchical nature in the family. Similarly, spouses may defer to each other as a result of a hierarchy. Creating a Talking Stick may be a helpful way to have family members communicate while respecting the hierarchy. In the activity phase, parents can dictate the materials to be used for creating the stick, but the whole family can contribute in its creation. In this way, parents retain their relative positions of hierarchy in the family, yet all can participate in the activity. During the therapy session, therapists can demonstrate respect for the hierarchy by their first participant selection. For example, the therapist can give parents the opportunity to discuss the results of the activity before the therapist asks the children, thus maintaining the hierarchy and boundaries between the subsystems.

Feminist considerations are also applicable within this activity. Werner-Wilson, Price, Zimmerman, & Murphy (1997) found that women are interrupted more frequently than men. The authors call for further investigation of this process. This activity can provide a way for therapists to be attuned to the process. The therapist can better structure therapy so the same amount of time is provided for each person to speak. As a result, women may be interrupted less in session.

This activity is also influenced by social constructionist theory. Social constructionist theories encourage a multiplicity of realities about the world. According to social constructionists, the way in which people view the world is influenced by personal beliefs and interactions with others. There is no one accurate observation about the world, as all views of the world differ from person to person. Therapists construct a reality *with* their clients rather than impose a reality *upon* their clients (Wetchler, 1996).

Social constructionism is relevant to the Talking Stick activity. In this activity, each family member can express his or her different view of the family and its problems on the stick or object. If each family member has different ideas about the problems in the family, the Talking Stick activity provides a good example of how the family resolves some of their discrepancy issues. The family can construct an object that integrates and collaborates all of their ideas. The therapist can use the process of this activity as a way to understand the process behind the decisions the family made, as well as an expressive activity.

Finally, this intervention/activity is influenced by principles of symbolic-experiential therapy. In creating an object that represents the family, the members create a symbol that the family can use to represent themselves. The therapist can use the stick or object to talk about the family, and also use it as representation to talk about the process of coming together to complete the activity. The "Speak Softly and Carry a Big Stick" intervention can be a visual reminder of conversation and expression during a session. A family member who inadvertently monopolizes the session may be more aware of the time he or she is using while others remain silent. It is a way of using symbols in therapy and is also influenced by the principles of play therapy (Landreth, 1991).

This intervention can be tailored to the various styles of individual therapists. A less-directive therapist, for example, may choose not to interrupt clients who talk a great deal during session. This intervention provides a way for less-directive therapists to structure therapy when it is therapeutically indicated to gain multiple perspectives. It can also provide a way for nondirective therapists to call attention to other family members' roles in the family conversation. Therapists can comment on who has had the Talking Stick in the session and who has not yet had an opportunity to respond. For directive therapists, this activity provides a way they can direct the family to participate in the activity, make direct comments about the use of the stick, and encourage the family to use the stick as a way to observe their conversation style.

Instructions

The purpose of this homework assignment is for the family to construct an object that represents their family. This object should be mobile enough to bring to sessions and to be used as a moderator of communication. The homework assignment can involve as many people as the therapist deems.

The therapist assigns the family members a joint project for homework—the creation of a Talking Stick, something that can be transported back to session. Family members are told the purpose of the Talking Stick. They can create the Talking Stick through a variety of ways—from organic materials, craft materials, or things around the house. The family can put as much or as little decoration onto the stick, until they are satisfied that it is a meaningful and adequate representation and expression of themselves.

The Talking Stick should be brought to the next therapy session to moderate conversation: the one who holds the stick is the person allowed to talk. Other members of the family are not allowed to interrupt the person with the stick but can respond once the stick is passed to them. The Talking Stick can be kept by the therapist in the office or transported by the family for each session.

In addition to using the stick, the therapist can also discuss the process of the homework assignment with the family, as this can provide the therapist and family with some insight about process in the family. Some of the questions a therapist might ask include the following:

What was this process like for you?
Was it easy for you to agree on what to make? How did you come to an agreement?
What was difficult about this process for you? What was rewarding about this process?
Which of you participated? Who decided who would participate?
Did anyone decline participation? Why?
Where was the Talking Stick kept before you came to therapy today? How did you decide where it was kept?
Did you learn anything you did not know before about your mother? Father? Daughter? Son? Sister? Brother? If so, what?
Where would you like to keep the stick—in the office, at your home, etc.?

Variations

There are several potential variations on this activity. Most important, it may be adjusted to fit each family. First, the family does not have to use a "Talking Stick" as the object. They can choose to create an object that means something to them, such as a ball, picture frame, card, etc. Essentially, the therapist may suggest that the family create an object on which they agree. The only parameters for the creation of the object are that (1) it be mobile enough to pass to one another during sessions, and (2) if desired, be transportable to and from therapy sessions.

Another variation is to structure who holds the stick or object at different times in the therapy session. The therapist can decide who has the Talking Stick first by dividing the family into a variety of groups. For example, families can be divided among family roles, generations, gender, hair color, etc. The parental subsystem can have the Talking Stick and choose to pass it between each other for the first five minutes. Next, the children may have the Talking Stick and pass it between themselves for the next five minutes, or another group within the family might have the stick first (such as the children), then pass it to the other groups. Depending on the topic in therapy, the therapist may want to divide the family into gender groups and have the women (daughters, mothers, aunts, etc.) speak as one collective voice about their experiences and shared views. The therapist may also divide the family into groups of extended family and nuclear family (again, depending on the presenting problem) and have the extended family start the stick, share their feelings about some issue, then pass the stick to the nuclear family. As yet another intervention, the therapist can instruct the family to divide themselves into groups. This could serve as an assessment (identifying alliances and coalitions within the family) and as an intervention by forcibly intermixing the groups at a later date and observing responses.

Finally, another variation would be to assign the Talking Stick as homework near the end of therapy. The therapist can use this as a way to capitalize on the family's successes during therapy and to make a stick for them to use during any meetings at home. In addition, the therapist can assign the activity as a postmeasure once changes in family dynamics have occurred. The therapist can compare both objects (pre- and postchanges) and discuss differences in the design, colors, shape, and meaning behind it, with the family.

Brief Vignette

The Miller family (composed of Mary and James, Mary's twelve-year-old daughter from a previous marriage, Claudia, and a three-year-old son, Dylan) had been coming to therapy for a year to address couple issues and the daughter's misbehavior. Mary and James, married for eight years, had been experiencing marital discord. After a brief period of separation during which they both dated other people, Mary and James decided to reconnect with each other and give their marriage another chance. As a result of the difficulties the couple experienced, however, Claudia did not trust James. She assumed a caretaking role for her mother and was openly defiant toward her stepfather. Claudia constantly interrupted James at home and during family therapy sessions, and James interpreted these actions as a lack of respect.

James felt that, although he had been part of the family for eight years, Claudia did not demonstrate respect for him once he and Mary reunited, with her attitude worsening over time. This was particularly upsetting to him because he had spent so much time in the family caring for Claudia as if she were his biological child. Mary felt that she was in the middle of the relationship between James and Claudia. When Claudia "mouthed off" to James, Mary wanted to discipline Claudia but was fearful of having Claudia think she was taking sides against her. As a result, James felt unsupported and like the bad parent.

The therapist inquired as to the types of family conversation that happened at home. Did the mouthing off observed in the office occur at home as well? When was the family able to have pleasant conversations? The Millers said that they were usually able to have fun when they were collaborating on projects and activities together. The family stated that they enjoyed outdoor activities, but also that Claudia had a gift for creative projects.

The therapist assigned the family to collaborate on a project as a way to structure therapy. The therapist asked the family to create a Talking Stick, an object that would be used to structure conversation in the therapy room. The therapist told the family to set aside time during the week when they could sit down as a family and work on the stick. The therapist instructed them to use any materials they wanted and to create something that represented their family. The family agreed and found time in the week to create the Talking Stick. The following week the family brought their Talking Stick to session. It was created by Claudia, Mary, and James, and had all three names around the stick.

Claudia was very proud to bring the family stick to session, showing it off to the therapist. She stated that she had fun creating the stick with her parents and reported they decorated it with colors reflecting the way she saw her family. She said that she used blue because the color "just fit"; she used green because she was angry at times, and used pink because she was calm at other times. In terms of the arrangement, Claudia reported that she mixed up all the colors on the stick because her family was mixed up together. Because Claudia was so proud of the family's Talking Stick, she took charge of enforcing the rules of the stick with the family members and therapist in session. The therapist asked Mary to discuss what the activity was like for her. Claudia handed the Talking Stick to her mother and Mary responded that she also had a good time with the assignment. She said that she felt close to Claudia during the assignment and hoped that she and Claudia would be able to maintain the closeness during other activities. Mary also commented that since the activity, she noticed James and Claudia were "getting along" better.

The therapist directed Mary to pass the Talking Stick to James and asked him to follow up on what Mary had said. James stated that he had experienced a different relationship with Claudia, and that she had begun talking with him more often and had been greeting him in the evening before she went to bed. This meant a great deal to James, and he became tearful as he described the new routine. Claudia asked for the Talking Stick and mentioned how she and James even went on a small outing over the weekend, and that this was very different than the way they used to interact. Although they were not using the stick at home, Claudia said that she felt comfortable spending time with James. Claudia also stated that she liked the Talking Stick in session because she was able to tell James how much fun she had on the outing.

The family continued to use the Talking Stick in session as a way to interact with one another. As the conversation moved from talking about the homework to talking about the way the activity changed interactions between the Miller family members, the family began to use the Talking Stick more fluently, passing it to one another, each speaking in turn. The Talking Stick was kept in the therapist's office, and the family requested the stick and used it for the duration of their sessions.

Suggestions for Follow-Up

One follow-up activity might be to include circular questioning (Boscolo, Hoffman, Cecchin, & Penn, 1987). The therapist might ask one person holding the Talking Stick to reflect on what others in the group think or might say about a given topic. For example, the therapist could ask a child holding the stick, "What do you think mom would say about the rules in the house?" After the child responds to the questions, the stick goes to mom to affirm or correct the attributions that the child prescribed, or to ask mom how the child might respond.

Another follow-up activity is to have the family use the Talking Stick at home in family meetings. Family meetings can be a helpful way for the family to reconnect during a busy week. Using the Talking Stick as a moderator for these conversations can help the family generalize the intervention to their home environment, thereby ensuring greater success. Eventually, the family will hopefully move toward moderating their conversations without using the Talking Stick.

Contraindications

In cases where a child does not feel safe to express his or her feelings in the presence of parents, the child may feel caught between therapist and parents. In this situation, the clinician should work with the parents about the importance of safety of expression. Once the parents are able to achieve this, they may be able to emphasize its importance to their child, thus increasing the likelihood of effectiveness for this activity.

This specific intervention may not initially be effective with nonverbal families, or families in which communicating safely is a concern. The therapist should determine the family's ability to actively participate in both the homework and follow-up phase of this activity. If the family is still not comfortable with the therapist, the clinician may have to spend more time joining with the family and more time with other collaborative homework assignments prior to the inception of this activity.

Readings and Resources for the Professional

Freeman, J., Epston, D., & Lobovits, D. (1997). *Playful approaches to serious problems.* New York: W. W. Norton & Co.

Landreth, G. L. (1991). *Play therapy: The art of the relationship.* Muncie, IN: Accelerated Development, Inc.

Shapiro, L. E. (1997). *Tricks of the trade.* King of Prussia, PA: The Center for Applied Psychology, Inc.

Bibliotherapy Source for Clients

Dinkmeyer, D., McKay, G. D., & Dinkmeyer, D. (1997). *The parent's handbook: Systematic training for effective parenting.* Circle Pines, MN: American Guidance Services.

References

Boscolo, L., Hoffman, L., Cecchin, C., & Penn, P. (1987). *Milan systemic family therapy: Conversations in theory and practice.* New York: Basic Books.

Landreth, G. L. (1991). *Play therapy: The art of the relationship.* Muncie, IN: Accelerated Development, Inc.

Minuchin, S. (1974). *Families and family therapy.* Cambridge, MA: Harvard University Press.

Werner-Wilson, R. J., Price, S. J., Zimmerman, T. S., & Murphy, M. J. (1997). Client gender as a process variable in marriage and family therapy: Are women clients interrupted more than men clients? *Journal of Family Psychology, 11*(3), 373-377.

Wetchler, J. L. (1996). Social constructionist family therapies. In F. Piercy, D. Sprenkle, & J. Wetchler (Eds.), *Family therapy sourcebook* (pp. 129-152). New York: Guilford Press.

– 18 –

Family Stress Balls

Dawn Viers

Type of Contribution: Activity

Objective

This activity presents a fun, hands-on way to talk about and start managing issues with which most families can relate—stress and frustration. Individually, the stress balls help to relieve stress and frustration using physical means. Collectively, the activity promotes family togetherness, problem solving, and stress management techniques. Any individual, couple, or family may find this activity useful, but stress balls seem particularly suited for families who tend to internalize problems and parents who see anger and frustration as a character flaw in their child.

Rationale for Use

In relation to people, stress is generally defined as "physical, mental, or emotional strain or tension" (*Webster's College Dictionary,* 1991, p. 1322). Stress-related illnesses at least partially account for a majority of doctor visits in the United States and are thought to cost billions of dollars per year in health care costs (Benson, 2000). Clearly, stress is a nationwide epidemic. Most families can relate to feeling stressed out and can name the problems stress has caused in their lives.

Components of relaxation to reduce stress should include (1) the repetition of muscular movements or a mental device, such as a phrase or word, and (2) ignoring distracting, everyday thoughts (Benson, 2000). Stress balls meet this criteria as they provide a physical and tactile way to address stress and frustration. Kneading the stress balls provides a physical outlet and release, similar to exercising, ripping paper, or hitting a pillow. It also provides a distraction from frustration. Williams and Williams (1993, p. 83) state, "when you start thinking about something new, you stop thinking about what is making you angry." While making and using the stress balls, everyday thoughts can be pushed aside as the client focuses on the activity.

Furthermore, naming stress helps to define the problem as an external construct rather than a personality characteristic or flaw. Among other things, this externalization decreases conflict between family members and fosters cooperation in escaping the influence of the problem (White & Epston, 1990). Externalization also helps to take the blame for the problem off the identified patient, as stress and frustration are emotions everyone in the family has experienced. Therefore, it is important to normalize stress and frustration as common, everyday occurrences and to teach skills to tackle the stress through techniques such as stress balls.

Although stress balls can be purchased, there are several reasons to encourage family members to make their own stress balls. First, the act of making the stress balls can help to reduce stress. Second, this activity encourages both children and adults to be playful. Many of my clients would run their fingers through the sand or start to build sand castles or other objects while engaging in this activity. Third, family members can create a stress ball that is representative of them as a family. This can be helpful for naming the problem and externalizing the stress. Finally, as stress balls are small, inexpensive, and easy to make, family members can make multiples. The balls can then be kept at work, at school, in a car, in a purse, or anywhere else to provide a quick release. I even had one client who kept them in her golf bag for missed putts!

Instructions

As a precursor to the project, begin to normalize stress and frustration as a process that often overcomes everybody in many given situations. This normalization process is important, as many parents tend to view outbursts as a core part of their child (or even themselves) rather than an ordinary emotion. The therapist should help the family note and process times and events that "stress them out."

Stress balls are comprised of helium-quality balloons and sand. The therapist will need to purchase and set up the activity prior to the family's arriving for the session. Newspaper or a tablecloth should be spread on the floor prior to starting the project, as the sand tends to stick in carpets. This project also works well in a sand table.

Assemble the ingredients and let the family fill the balloons with the sand. Encourage them to work together to complete the balls and to use alternative means to fill the balloons with sand. Have straws, funnels, and construction paper handy. Construction paper can also be rolled into a makeshift funnel. The family can also be encouraged to name their stress balls or decorate the balls to resemble "stress monsters." This can help families externalize the problem and place the stress outside of an individual family member.

Once the balls are complete and tied off, discuss how and when the balls can be used. I usually discuss with clients where the balls could be kept and certain situations when the balls may be helpful. I often incorporate and demonstrate other frustration and stress management techniques, such as time-outs, deep breathing, and progressive relaxation. Encourage the family to use the stress balls and other stress management techniques in session and at home.

Brief Vignette 1

A single mother, Wanda, and her eight-year-old son, Steven, came to therapy because Steven was acting out at school and home. He would talk back, not comply with rules, and throw temper tantrums. The mother worked over fifty hours a week to support her family and had little support or encouragement from friends or family. She wished to have more fun time with her son and felt that he used his anger and frustration as punishment for her working. She also felt his acting-out behavior was part of his personality, and therefore, he could not change.

I began by normalizing Steven's behavior regarding his growing independence, and commiserated with his mother over juggling parenthood with a demanding job and limited resources. I also noted that Steven's temper tantrums tended to occur during times of transition, such as when his mother returned home from work and before dinner. I reflected that Steven seemed pretty attuned to his mother's emotions and they were taking the frustration from each other. Wanda agreed that Steven and she were tied to each other's moods and that the frustration seemed to come out when the other person was also experiencing stress.

I framed making the stress balls as a way to create a positive family interaction while starting to tackle the frustration. We spent the entire session making stress balls and talking about anger management techniques. While making the stress balls, Steven and his mother were more playful with each other as they filled the balloons and played in the sand. They both seemed more relaxed at the end of the session.

At follow-up, Steven reported using the ball sporadically. However, Wanda reported that she took the ball to work and used the ball during the week, as well as other stress management techniques such as time-outs and deep breathing. She reported that Steven had fewer outbursts that week and she enjoyed spending the week with him. She felt these changes were due to the fact that she had allowed the stress to take over less often and was therefore able to handle him better.

Brief Vignette 2

I started working with an individual, Claire, who had been seen in therapy for several years for anxiety and depression. Her anxiety generally stemmed from her job and from her and her parents' health problems. During one session she was especially worried about her father's health and upcoming surgery. Claire stated that her mother was also anxious about the surgery. She did not know if her mother could handle this surgery and did not feel that she could be a support due to her own anxiety. Due to a negative experience at another clinic, Claire refused to bring her mother into therapy.

We made stress balls several weeks before the surgery. Claire made several balls during the session. At follow-up, Claire stated that she bought a bag of helium balloons and a fifty-pound bag of sand and made several stress balls to stash in her car and desk. She then took the materials to her parents' house and made stress balls with her mother. She said that the activity of making the balls helped to distract her and her mother from the upcoming surgery. As they both had health problems and were unable to engage in physical activity, she stated that kneading the balls provided a needed physical release. Claire continued to use the stress balls during times of stress and anxiety.

Suggestions for Follow-Up

After making the stress balls, the therapist should follow-up with this activity at later sessions. Ask if the family members used the stress balls and what effect they had on the frustration. If they used the balls and found them helpful, encourage them to continue using the stress balls. If they did not use the stress balls, discuss different ways of integrating the stress balls in their routines, such as putting stress balls in different locations, including the family car or a desk at work. This makes the stress balls more readily accessible and more likely to be used. If time is a factor, this activity can also be assigned as homework, as shown in the second vignette. If family members try this route, they should then be encouraged to talk about the process of making and using the stress balls.

As previously suggested, in order to extend the activity, it is helpful to teach the client other relaxation devices. These can include time-outs, deep breathing, progressive relaxation, imagery, exercise, or other relaxation techniques. *The Relaxation and Stress Reduction Workbook* (Davis, Eshelman, & McKay, 1995) is a good resource for clients and therapists to learn and integrate relaxation techniques.

Contraindications

This activity should not be used for individuals and families suffering from severe anxiety or depression, nor should it be used for families or couples who have experienced abuse, as these clients would need more intensive treatment than this activity would allow. Stress, anxiety, and frustration can cause health problems, work difficulties, and other social ills. Encourage clients dealing with these issues to stay in contact with their family doctor and seek medical attention if their stress becomes overwhelming.

This activity is not meant to be a panacea for stress, frustration, and anxiety. Rather, it is intended to begin a dialogue and is a way to take action for dealing with these issues. It is also intended to distract families from frustration and focus on fighting stress instead of fighting one another. As the materials for making stress balls are inexpensive, readily available, and easy to store, therapists can stash these materials anywhere and add the activity to their arsenal of ideas in helping manage stress.

Readings and Resources for the Professional

Bright, D. (1979). *Creative relaxation: Turning stress into positive energy.* New York: Harcourt Brace.

Davis, M., Eshelman, E. R., & McKay, M. (1995). *The relaxation and stress reduction workbook.* Oakland, CA: New Harbinger Publications.

Elliot, R. S. (1994). *From stress to strength: How to lighten your load and save your life.* New York: Bantam Books.

Forman, S. G. (1993). *Coping skills interventions for children and adolescents.* San Francisco: Jossey-Bass Publishers.

Morse, D. R. & Furst, M. L. (1979). *Stress for success: A holistic guide to stress and its management.* New York: Van Norstrand Reinhold.

Resources for the Client

Davis, M., Eshelman, E. R., & McKay, M. (1995). *The relaxation and stress reduction workbook.* Oakland, CA: New Harbinger Publications.

Elliot, R. S. (1994). *From stress to strength: How to lighten your load and save your life.* New York: Bantam Books.

Morse, D. R. & Furst, M. L. (1979). *Stress for success: A holistic guide to stress and its management.* New York: Van Norstrand Reinhold.

Williams, R. & Williams, V. (1993). *Anger kills: Seventeen strategies for controlling the hostility that can harm your health.* New York: Harper Perennial.

References

Benson, H. (2000). *The relaxation response* (2nd ed.). New York: Harper Collins.

Davis, M., Eshelman, E. R., & McKay, M. (1995). *The relaxation and stress reduction workbook.* Oakland, CA: New Harbinger Publications.

Webster's College Dictionary (1991). New York: Random House.

White, M. & Espton, D. (1990). *Narrative means to therapeutic ends.* New York: W. W. Norton & Co.

Williams, R. & Williams, V. (1993). *Anger kills: Seventeen strategies for controlling the hostility that can harm your health.* New York: Harper Perennial.

– 19 –

Up, Up, and Away in My Beautiful Balloon

Katherine M. Hertlein

Type of Contribution: Activity

Objective

The objective of this activity is twofold. First, this activity provides a way to externalize concerns and problems that families and children bring to therapy. Second, it provides a ritual to assist children and families in saying good-bye to problematic behaviors. It allows children and families to have tangible evidence of their successes during therapy and is a useful closure activity to the therapeutic process. It is based on narrative therapy and the letting go portion of a ritual as described by Whiting (1988).

Rationale for Use

This activity is influenced by narrative therapy. Narrative therapy is based on the assumption that there are two stories which one uses to interpret events and experiences: a dominant story and a subjugated story (White & Epston, 1990). A dominant story refers to a set of assumptions an individual believes about the world. It is the way that someone views the world and its events, and makes attributions about those events. Using the dominant lens, a person can make meaning out of events and experiences. Interpreting events through the dominant lens, however, can be problematic when using that lens is no longer effective. People then need another way to interpret and make meaning of the world around them. This is what brings the family to therapy.

Using a narrative therapy approach, therapists externalize problematic behaviors for families (White & Epston, 1990). Externalization refers to the process by which an individual's problems are attributed to external factors rather than internal characteristics or attributes about the person. The behavior is seen as separate from the individual or family members. In this way, family members can team up to defeat the problem or issue at hand.

This activity is also influenced by the use of rituals in therapy (Imber-Black, Roberts, & Whiting, 1988). Rituals are actions and activities characterized by the use of symbols. Typically, planning is just as important in the implementation of the ritual as is the event. Rituals are metaphorical in nature and should be broad enough so each family member can derive his or her own meaning from it (Imber-Black et al., 1988). A variety of populations can benefit from the therapeutic use of rituals, such as couples (Imber-Black et al., 1988), children (O'Connor & Hoorwitz, 1988), adolescents (Lax & Lussardi, 1988), multiple generations of families (Davis, 1988), and many other family forms with presenting problems.

According to Whiting (1988), there are several important factors in the design of a therapeutic ritual. Some important elements include symbols, the incorporation of client language, therapist directive, and client choice. Each of these is represented in this activity. First, the incorporation of symbols is when the clients draw a picture of the externalized behavior. Second, the therapist directs the activity by explaining to the clients the process of letting go of the picture with a balloon. It incorporates client choice in that the clients can choose how they want to proceed with the project—each can draw his or her own picture and set free the balloons in his or her individualized way, create his or her own picture of what the behavior looks like, etc. Other elements identified by Whiting emphasize determining what processes are open to change and which cannot be changed, and determining the setting of the ritual.

In the ritualistic activity "Up, Up, and Away," treatment revolves around externalizing the problematic behavior and promoting closure by sending a picture representing the behavior away in a balloon. This is an extrapolation of an activity briefly described by Whiting (1988) through its delineated steps and its incorporation of systemic attributes. Not only will this ritual serve to provide a bridge for saying good-bye to problematic behavior, but it can also provide a closure ritual for children and families transitioning out of therapy. By using this activity as a termination ritual, clients can better transition out of therapy, thus ensuring generalization of the technique to their home environment.

Instructions

The therapist, child, and entire family participate in this activity. Some families come to therapy having already labeled the child acting out in negative terms, such as "bad," "spoiled," or "difficult." These labels might reinforce the child's unwanted behavior as he or she gets attention for the behavior. Also, these labels might impact the child's self-esteem, resulting in further difficulty making better choices because the child does not believe he or she can. This activity may help strengthen the bonds between family members by helping the family to conquer the behavior together, rather than pitting the family and identified client against one another.

The therapist should set aside the final two therapy sessions for this activity. In the second-to-last session, the therapist asks the identified child to draw a picture of the externalized behavior, or the behavior that they tried to extinguish at the outset of therapy. Rather than the child exhibiting the behavior, the child is directed to draw that which he or she chooses to conquer. For example, if the child is hitting other children at school, the therapist can direct the child to draw a picture of this. This activity can be assigned either during the session or for homework. Unless therapeutically indicated, the therapist does not place parameters on the creation of the picture. There are no limits to size, colors, or what the child wants to do with the picture. It is also not necessary for the therapist to view the picture upon completion, unless, again, therapeutically indicated. Once the child has completed his or her picture, the therapist, family, and child attach the picture to a balloon. At this point, all involved in therapy go outdoors and set the balloon and its attached picture free.

Variations

This activity has several variations. As an alternative, the therapist can ask the family to collaborate on a picture of the externalized behavior. As mentioned previously, the activity can be assigned in-session or for homework; the therapist is not required to view the picture that the family has constructed, unless therapeutically indicated. After the picture is completed, the family and therapist attach it to the balloon. There can be one balloon for the whole family or one balloon for each member, tied together representing the unity of the family. All family members will find a place to hold the balloon(s) and release them at one time.

The therapist may also choose to have each individual family member generate his or her own picture of the externalized behavior along with the child. In this case, there can be one balloon tied to each picture for each family member. The family members then tie each of their balloons together and release them simultaneously. Another option would be to have the family members tie all of their pictures to one balloon and release the balloon together.

Brief Vignette

The Downs family came to therapy to find strategies to alleviate the children's fighting. Mark and Kara, ages eight and five, screamed, yelled, and pushed each other on a daily basis. Their mother, Laura, was a single parent. Laura reported that she had a difficult time trying to get household chores done because she felt that she had to spend a lot of energy disciplining Mark and Kara. The children had no relationship with their father, and Laura had strained relationships with her extended family. As a result of the strained familial relationships and lack of social network, Laura was experiencing a significant amount of stress and believed that she was less tolerant of Mark and Kara's problematic behavior.

Kara, five, was the identified client. Although Mark fought with her at home, he seemed able to control himself with his peers at school. Kara, however, was beginning to fight in school, arguing with both peers and teachers. Laura had been required to attend two meetings at the principal's office early in the school year regarding Kara's insubordination and "backtalk" to the faculty. Laura was becoming increasingly concerned that she was going to miss out on more time at work if Kara continued this behavior. Laura stated that she had considered putting Kara in another school but ultimately decided that these problems may continue at another school. The school referred Laura to the therapist for counseling.

Throughout the course of therapy, the therapist helped the family to externalize the fighting behavior. One of the ways this was accomplished was through the language used by the therapist. The therapist often referred to the behavior as "the fighting," making it very clear that it was different from Kara. This language change was important because it helped Laura in separating her children's behaviors from their personalities, increasing her tolerance of their fighting (it also helped the children to separate the unwanted behavior from themselves). Also important in therapy was the inclusion of a social support network for Laura, which helped her to gain some perspective and externalize her children's behavior. Once the therapist helped Laura to externalize the fighting, the therapist worked with Mark and Kara to externalize the behavior from their "goodness" or "badness" as people and empowered them against their behavior.

As therapy progressed, the family demonstrated that they were able to defeat the fighting behavior. The family believed they were ready to terminate therapy. Consistent with the course and nature of the therapy, the therapist believed that closing the sessions in a way that sent the externalized problem away might be an effective and appropriate technique for the family.

The therapist met with the family and explained that they were going to do something different from their typical sessions. The therapist instructed each family member to complete a picture of the behavior, the fighting, that they had worked to eliminate. The therapist provided no parameters about how to construct this picture and allowed each person to create the picture as he or she desired and saw to be appropriate. The family worked on their pictures in session, with Kara making three pictures and discarding them. In this way, the family was able to construct an individualized representation of the fighting behavior. This is the first important component of externalizing the behavior.

The second component, retelling the story, is emphasized in the following section. The therapist asked Laura to bring two helium-filled balloons to the next and final session. The purpose for this activity was to ritualistically release the balloons that were holding pictures of the fighting behavior. In this way, the therapist and family accounted for a second important component, retelling the story, as they added on a chapter about defeating the behavior and sending it away.

When the family arrived for the next session, Kara reported that she had completed her picture and wanted to show it to the therapist. Once she did that, she wanted the therapist to help her put it in an envelope. The therapist helped Kara with this task, and Kara attached the envelope to one of the balloon strings. Mark attached his picture to the other balloon. Laura tied both balloons together, attaching her own picture to the two balloons as she fastened them together.

The therapist led the family outdoors where the family decided that they wanted to release the balloons simultaneously. Each grabbed a section of the strings on the balloon and held the balloons. Prior to releasing the balloons, Mark suggested that the family generate a word together that, when said, they would all let go of the balloons. After some discussion, the family decided on a word. Laura counted to three, and Laura, Mark, and Kara shouted the word and released the balloons. The therapist and family returned to the therapist's office and the therapist finished the last session.

Suggestions for Follow-Up

One suggestion for follow-up is to incorporate a list of process questions for the family. For example, a therapist may be interested in what the family experienced when they were creating the symbol:

> Who was the most involved in creating the picture?
> Who was the least involved in creating the picture?
> Which family member had the easiest time developing the picture?
> Who had the most difficult time developing the picture?
> How did you make the decision of what things to include in the picture? Was this discussed as a family?
> How did you handle disagreements about how the picture should look?
> What does the balloon symbolize to you? To your family?
> Where do you think the balloon will end up?
> What is something that you learned about your family in this activity that you did not know before?

Another suggestion for follow-up can be conducted after the release of the balloons. The therapist can provide each member of the family with a balloon at the close of the session, as a way to remember the activity and the closing ritual. Yet another variation on this is to have the parent(s) each give their child a balloon at the close of session so that the children can remember the event.

Contraindications

This technique is most effective when the therapy has already externalized the problem in previous sessions. If the therapist has not already done so, he or she should consider spending the last few sessions externalizing the behavior and assisting with the process. It becomes easier for the family to ritualistically send the problem away in a balloon when they do not associate themselves with the problem, making the technique more effective. By externalizing the problem earlier in the therapy, the therapist provides a consistent treatment and metaphor throughout therapy. This activity might also not be appropriate for children who are receiving some benefit from the problem behavior, such as attention or other rewards. As a result, the therapist may desire to hold a "negative consequences of change" session, where the benefits of holding on to the behavior are discussed.

Readings and Resources for the Professional

Freeman, J., Epston, D., & Lobovits, D. (1997). *Playful approaches to serious problems.* New York: W. W. Norton & Co.

White, M. & Epston, D. (1990). *Narrative means to therapeutic ends.* New York: W. W. Norton & Co.

Bibliotherapy Source for the Client

Dinkmeyer, D., McKay, G. D., & Dinkmeyer, D. (1997). *The parent's handbook: Systematic training for effective parenting.* Circle Pines, MN: American Guidance Services.

References

Davis, J. (1988). Mazel tov: The bar mitzvah as a multigenerational ritual of change and continuity. In E. Imber-Black, J. Roberts, & R. A. Whiting (Eds.), *Rituals in families and family therapy* (pp. 177-208). New York: W. W. Norton & Co.

Imber-Black, E., Roberts, J., & Whiting, R. A. (Eds.). (1988). *Rituals in families and family therapy.* New York: W. W. Norton & Co.

Lax, W. D. & Lussardi, D. J. (1988). The use of rituals in families with an adolescent. In E. Imber-Black, J. Roberts, & R. A. Whiting (Eds.), *Rituals in families and family therapy* (pp. 158-176). New York: W. W. Norton & Co.

O'Connor, J. J. & Hoorwitz, A. N. (1988). Imitative and contagious magic in the therapeutic use of rituals with children. In E. Imber-Black, J. Roberts, & R. A. Whiting (Eds.), *Rituals in families and family therapy* (pp. 135-157). New York: W. W. Norton & Co.

White, M. & Epston, D. (1990). *Narrative means to therapeutic ends.* New York: W. W. Norton & Co.

Whiting, R. A. (1988). Guidelines to designing therapeutic rituals. In E. Imber-Black, J. Roberts, & R. A. Whiting (Eds.), *Rituals in families and family therapy* (pp. 84-109). New York: W. W. Norton & Co.

– 20 –

Drawing the Family System

Christina Dust

Type of Contribution: Activity

Objective

The purpose of this activity is to gain an understanding of a child's family system and evaluate the family relationships when parental contact is not available. Through the drawing process, children provide information for the therapist to understand their home environments and the structure of these environments from their perspectives.

Rationale for Use

At times during family treatment the parental unit is unavailable. This could be due to incarceration or a lack of desire for involvement. Working with the children to understand the presenting problem and the history of the problem can be difficult without the parents. When children are involved in a child protective services system, they are often instructed by their parents not to tell professionals about their home lives. Having the child draw the family is a creative way to investigate the family without pressuring the child to tell his or her story.

This intervention utilizes methods of art therapy. Art therapy provides an opportunity for a child to express his or her thoughts and feelings by creating drawings and illustrations (Rubin, 1984). Children are often better at nonverbal expression. Through the use of art therapy, the child can show the therapist what he or she is thinking and feeling. In this activity, art therapy is expanded to the entire family by asking the family members to work together to create a drawing of the family system.

The Kinetic Family Drawing (KFD) by Burns and Kaufman (1970) is a similar intervention. The difference between this intervention and the Kinetic Family Drawing is that this intervention is not a screening device. Instead, it is a form of joining and communicating with children, both in the assessment phase and throughout the therapy. The KFD asks the children to report how they feel about their family situations. This intervention asks children only what they know about their families, and is therefore more an intervention than a tool for assessment. Another large difference between the two interventions is that the "Drawing the Family System" intervention instructs children to work together to produce the family drawing. In the KFD each individual child draws his or her own picture. By asking the family to work together the therapist can get a better idea of the compromise skills the children have and who the leaders are in the family. This intervention can also be considered a family intervention because it engages all of the children from the same family in one activity.

Instructions

This intervention should be used in the beginning stages of therapy to assess the structure of the family system and evaluate the family relationships. During the joining process, it is critical to understand the system of which your clients are a product; in order to provide effective treatment you must know what you are treating. In a family session with children, explain how all families look and act differently. Ask them if they could draw their family and let them know they can help you understand who their family is made up of and what they look like. Provide the children with writing utensils and paper to draw on. The drawing supplies given to the children can vary. Use materials that will promote creativity in the children, possibly construction paper, colored pencils, or crayons.

Instruct the clients to draw a picture of each family member at home and an activity that person would be engaged in when at home. All of the children in the family will need to work together and collaborate on the picture. It is helpful to have the children alternate drawing the picture to ensure that each child's input is included in the end product. For example, the younger children can draw the body of the family member while the older children can draw the details of the figure. If the children disagree on how the drawing should look, they may draw the family member more than once, showing the different perspectives.

Once the drawing is complete, ask the children to explain who each person is and what he or she is doing in the drawing. Be sure to get a response from each child on each person in the picture. Using this process, the therapist can glean an idea of what life is like at home for the children, what family members are present, and what type of structure exists. Assessing the details of the drawing will also provide the therapist with important information about the children. Be sure that the children include themselves somewhere in the picture even if it is on another sheet of paper. Identifying where the children fit into the picture is important, as the role that children play in their families is often a reflection of the position that they hold in the family system. Once a child's position or role is identified, the type of family structure may become more evident. Understanding the family structure is key to helping promote change in therapy.

Brief Vignette

This intervention was developed while working with a case involved in child protective services. The children were referred for family services due to allegations of neglect. The father was incarcerated and the mother was not mandated to attend treatment. Due to the lack of court mandate, the mother refused to contribute to therapy due to her fear that more allegations would be brought against her. The children were instructed by their mother not to talk about their home life or their family because "if they did then someone could come and take them away from their mother." After several attempts to involve the mother, other methods of fact gathering and assessment were used.

After realizing that verbal expression was not an option with this case, other forms of assessment had to be done. The children enjoyed drawing, so that method was used to understand their family system. First, the children were asked to draw all of the family members that lived with them and then draw what they would be doing when they were at home. The oldest child drew his mother, her boyfriend, his maternal aunt, and his maternal uncle on one sheet of paper. The client also included his dog in the picture. The dog was drawn in the center of the paper and was the largest figure in the picture. It appeared as though the dog was a very significant figure in the child's life. The boy left himself out of the first picture. He stated that he and his sister were at school and drew the scene on another sheet of paper. Although the child did not follow the instructions given, his response provided the therapist with important information about how the child viewed his position in the family. If a child draws himself outside of the family picture, such as this child did, the therapist may want to investigate the option that the children spend more time out of the home, as opposed to in the home.

The younger child drew her mother, her mother's boyfriend, her maternal aunt, and her maternal uncle. The client placed emphasis on the maternal aunt because she was pregnant. The child even drew a baby in the center of the figure's body to signify the unborn child. The client, much like her brother, drew herself on another sheet of paper playing on a playground with her brother. Both drawings were similar in that the same characters were used in each picture and both children drew themselves in a place other than home.

Initially, each child drew his or her own picture. When they were asked to elaborate on the drawings the children came together to assist each other on explaining their pictures. Each child discussed his or her drawing and compared it to his or her sibling's drawing. In a nondirective way, the children were asked to talk about each person in their picture. By using that method of interviewing, the children did not feel the pressure of direct questioning or being put on the spot. Most times they were unaware that they were discussing their family and their home life.

After the session, the therapist had gained an understanding of the family system, the family relationships, and who made up that system. The children were relieved because they had not been verbally drilled about their parents and they had fun drawing pictures. Several times after the first session the therapist referred back to the people in the drawings to inquire about how they were doing and to utilize the information given. The mother never attended therapy and the case was dropped from the investigation process. By means of this intervention, the therapist was able to continue working with the children.

Follow-Up

Refer back to the drawing in the next few sessions to ensure that the information is consistent. Inquire as to how the family members are doing and what is happening in their lives. Discussing the drawing in future sessions will allow the children to understand the information provided is important and it will allow them to elaborate on the information given. For example, you may verify that mom is washing clothes today because it is Wednesday per the conversation with the children.

It would be helpful to have the children draw the picture again if their family structure changes later. For children in foster care it is essential to be aware of the changing family structure in the children's lives. Through the drawing process the therapist may suspect that the children are being abused. The appropriate measures should be taken if abuse is suspected. Be sure not to rely on information only from the family drawing to make that determination.

It would also be helpful in future sessions to have the children draw the family system as they would like it to look. This type of approach will provide the therapist with a solution-centered approach to begin work with. Considering that parental involvement is not an option, it would be a great alternative to work with the issue of what the children would like to have happen and who they would like as members of their family.

Contraindications

It would be best to have the parental unit involved in treatment. When that option is impossible, this intervention can be a great way to assess the family system from the child's perspective. The therapist must remember, however, that the child provides only one perspective and that this perspective is not always accurate or complete. It is merely a source of information.

This activity is most beneficial with children whose parents refuse to attend therapy or, for legal reasons, cannot attend the sessions. If the therapist has knowledge that the children have been abused, caution should be taken that the intervention does not retraumatize the child, particularly at the beginning of therapy. At this time no population is identified as not benefiting from the intervention. Therapists should select an intervention that best matches their clients' needs.

Readings and Resources for the Professional

Burns, R. C. & Kaufman, S. H. (1970). *Kinetic family drawings: An introduction to understanding children through kinetic drawings.* New York: Brunner/Mazel.

DiLeo, J. (1983). *Interpreting children's drawings.* New York: Brunner/Mazel.

Rubin, J. A. (1984). *The art of art therapy.* New York: Brunner/Mazel.

Veltman, M. W. & Browne, K. D. (2003). Trained raters' evaluation of Kinetic Family Drawings of physically abused children. *The Arts in Psychotherapy, 30,* 3-12.

Wegmann, P. & Lusebrink, V. B. (2000). Kinetic family drawing scoring method for cross-cultural studies. *The Arts of Psychotherapy, 27,* 179-190.

Bibliotherapy Source for the Client

Nemiroff, M. A. & Annunziata, J. (1990). *A child's first book about play therapy.* Washington, DC: American Psychological Association.

References

Burns, R. C. & Kaufman, S. H. (1970). *Kinetic family drawings: An introduction to understanding children through kinetic drawings.* New York: Brunner/Mazel.

Rubin, J. A. (1984). *The art of art therapy.* New York: Brunner/Mazel.

– 21 –

Family Drawings with Abused Children: Allowing Room for Expression

Lenore M. McWey

Type of Contribution: Activity

Objective

The main objective of this activity is to allow for a safe environment in which emotions can be expressed in a means comfortable and appropriate for children. Since children are often not as skilled as adults in verbalizing their thoughts and feelings, traditional talk therapy approaches may not be as effective with children (Rudolph & Thompson, 1995). Play therapy provides a means by which family members can express themselves in a safe and creative way (Webb, 1991). Family drawings are one means of allowing for such expression, and a method by which powerful assessments and interventions may be made.

Rationale for Use

Rudolph and Thompson (1995) suggest that long-term psychological and behavioral problems are potential consequences of unresolved issues regarding child abuse. Typical diagnoses of children who have been maltreated include conduct disorder, oppositional defiant disorder, depression, anxiety disorder, and attention-deficit/hyperactivity disorder (ADHD) (Harman, Childs, & Kelleher, 2000). The types of maltreatment a child experiences have been linked to the behavioral outcomes they manifest. Aggression and delinquency are the "most frequent correlates of physical abuse" along with suicide, cognitive and academic impairment, and psychobiological impairment (Kaplan, Pelcovitz, & Labruna, 1999, p. 1217). Children who have experienced emotional maltreatment tend to exhibit internalizing and externalizing behaviors, social impairments, low self-esteem, and long-term psychological impairment (Kaplan et al., 1999).

A child's age at the time of the abuse, the regularity and severity of the abuse, the relationship of the abuser to the child, and the parental response to the child after the report of victimization also contribute to how the abuse is dealt with by the child (Carmichael, 1992; Gil, 1994). For example, the situation of a child who has been victimized by a stranger would be distinctly different from that of a child whose perpetrator was the parent. In addition, how family members handle the reporting of the abuse varies from family to family and may also be a factor in the child's recovery. Each child's experience is unique, but all victims need an opportunity to express their feelings, ask questions, and replay the events if they demonstrate a readiness and desire to do so. Gil (1994) advocates for treatment as soon as possible for children who have been victims of maltreatment and asserts "every abused child deserves a one-on-one experience with a trained professional" (p. 139). In situations where abused children remain with their families, or where family reunification is the goal, family therapy becomes necessary (Gil, 1994).

Many children who have experienced maltreatment have learned not to trust others or themselves (Rudolph & Thompson, 1995). Furthermore, these children rarely enlist themselves in therapy; instead, caseworkers, parents, teachers, guidance counselors, or courts often require it. Creative measures may have to be taken to encourage participation of children and their families. According to Webb (1991), play therapy can help troubled children express their feelings, ask questions, and replay events in a safe environment through the medium most comfortable for them. Therapeutic play enables children to reenact their life experiences without fear of consequences and without having to verbally articulate occurrences if they are not comfortable doing so (Gladding, 1993). Through play, families can explore and experiment with new behaviors (McFadden, 1990). Play therapy also offers an environment where a child can develop more secure relationships with both therapists and family members. Through the process, clients may be more apt to recognize their thoughts and feelings associated with specific family dynamics.

The role of the therapist in a family play-therapy setting with an abused child is varied. Carmichael (1992) suggests that the primary function of the therapist is to be "a calm listener who can empathize and withstand the child victim's anger and anxiety reducing fear in the child" (p. 19). Other conditions the therapist should uphold are to create an atmosphere of safety for the child and family, to demonstrate patience, and to attempt to accurately reflect feelings so that family members can begin to recognize them as well (Rudolph & Thompson, 1995). Gil (1996) asserts that a primary goal of the therapist when working with abused children is to try to understand how they interpret the abuse, the meanings they make of their experiences, and how those meanings and interpretations relate to their current functioning.

Webb (1991) indicates that it is important for the therapist to tailor his or her approach around the specific needs of clients. Therapists may consider if specific objectives could be achieved more readily by therapist-directed, parent-directed, or child-directed play. This should be determined on a case-by-case basis, as each family is unique. Some children may enjoy the ability to do whatever they want to do. Other children, however, may feel comfortable taking the initiative with regard to therapeutic play.

There are a number of play-therapy modalities that a therapist can employ with families. Research suggests that although not all varieties of play therapy should be made available to children, the family should have choices (Webb, 1991). The use of art is one approach to play therapy. It is theorized that children do not conceive of their artwork as concrete representations of the self and therefore are not defensive about what they create (Rudolph & Thompson, 1995). The advantages of using art techniques are that they can be done very inexpensively, the directives can be adapted to meet the specific goals of the family, and an art activity is something that all family members can participate in, from ages two upward. Therapists may use the art to make assessments about family functioning. By watching a family play, insight may be gained into what family members are thinking and feeling. For example, a therapist can ask a family to draw their family. The therapist can then examine the details of the picture. What are the sizes of the family members? Are any people drawn closer together in proximity than others? Are any family members left out of the picture? All of these are questions a therapist can explore when observing the artwork of a client (Webb, 1991).

Instructions

Working with families in which abuse or neglect has occurred can involve a number of complications. The therapist should assess for indicators of current abuse and report any suspicions to the abuse registry immediately. It has been suggested that, if possible, the therapist should meet individually with family members until there is a sense of safety. After it has been determined that persons are not in danger, and that it is appropriate for children to be in session with other family members, therapy may proceed. Gil (1996) asserts that when working with abused children in the family context, the therapist may want to align with the child victim so that the child does not feel reabused by the therapeutic relationship but feels safe in expressing himself or herself. Although there are a number of techniques that one can use in family play therapy, this activity will be limited to the use of art in family therapy.

Specific materials needed to facilitate an art activity include washable markers, crayons, pencils, and large sheets of white paper. Having a variety of colored markers and crayons available would be desirable. Other materials, such as a dry-erase board and markers, or chalk and chalkboard are possible supplies that may be used. After the materials have been made available to the family, specific directives such as "Draw your family" or "Draw your home" can be provided. Therapists can also ask families to draw something happy, sad, and safe, or to draw the perfect world. In addition, metaphor can be used. For example, the therapist can draw the outline of a pond on a piece of paper. The therapist can then ask the family to draw themselves as creatures that live within the pond and to draw on the outside of the pond the things that they do not want in their pond.

After the therapist has given the specific directives, the therapist's primary role then becomes that of an observer. If family members ask questions, attempt to let the activity be solely their creation. For example, if asked, "Should we draw the inside of our house or the outside?" the therapist could reply, "anything you want" or "you decide." Or if asked, "What should I draw?" one response could be, "It is your activity—create anything that you want to create." If time permits, allow the family to work on the project until they indicate that they have completed the activity.

The family processes observed during a family play activity can be an excellent means of assessment. Attention to who leads, who participates, the objects drawn, who works together, or who disengages may provide meaningful insight into family dynamics. When the family indicates that they have finished the activity, begin processing the content of the project by asking questions about what has been created, remembering to stay in the realm of the family's creation. For example, if the child drew himself or herself on the picture but did not assert overtly who the person was, then do not apply his or her name to the drawing but instead ask questions such as "How is this person feeling in this picture?" Be careful not to place your own interpretations on the family's creation. Process questions such as "I see that this animal here is very small and these other animals are all large. What do you suppose this small animal thinks about that?" or "What does this animal think about this creature being way over here, away from its family?" may also be asked. Then, the therapist can also ask other family members for their perspectives on the drawing and discussions can arise from the multiple perspectives.

Brief Vignette

Jonathon was a six-year-old boy in foster care due to allegations of physical abuse and parental drug use. His biological mother was attempting to regain custody of Jonathon and was court mandated to participate in therapeutic supervised visitation with Jonathon on a biweekly basis. For our initial session, Jonathon arrived at the center first. A social services worker brought him but had another obligation to attend to, so she left rather quickly, leaving Jonathon in an unfamiliar environment full of people he had never seen before. As I approached, he was sitting very still in a chair with his hands folded on his lap. I sat in the chair next to Jonathon, introduced myself, and began to talk to him. He did not speak at all; he simply nodded "yes" and "no" in response to my questions. I asked if he wanted to go to the playroom and Jonathon shook his head no. Finally, after about ten minutes of nonverbal communication, Jonathon spoke. I asked him his favorite song, and Jonathon responded by whispering the song "Happy Birthday" in its entirety.

Available in the lobby were a few puppets and a sand tray, but when I asked Jonathon if he would like to play with them he indicated that he did not want to. Therefore, we sat together waiting for his mother to arrive. When his mother did arrive, she was very late for the session, leaving us with only about thirty minutes together. As the therapeutic goals for the family had already been decided in a previous meeting with the caseworker, the mother, and myself, the plan for our first meeting was to involve Jonathon and his mother in a family play-therapy session. Although the original plan for the family session involved another modality of family play therapy, given Jonathon's quiet disposition at the time, a family art activity became the plan instead.

A large sheet of paper and a bag of washable markers were placed in the middle of the floor. Jonathon took the bag and selected five different colored markers: green, blue, yellow, orange, and red. I then asked the family to draw something that makes them happy. Jonathon began to color immediately. His mother did not participate, but instead remained seated rather distant from where Jonathon was coloring. He colored grass and flowers. Throughout the activity, his mother would ask him "What is this?" pointing to a particular part of his picture and he would quietly respond. One time during the session, his mother asked him, "Do you want me to color?" and Jonathon shook his head "no." Jonathon colored diligently and quietly for nearly the remainder of the session.

As the end of the session neared, his mother stated, "We don't have much time left," then a change occurred in his drawing. His very elaborate, pretty, and colorful picture was becoming dark. His yellows and oranges were becoming overpowered with darker hues. He drew blue clouds and red rain, and the picture became more and more dismal as time progressed. Then, for the first time since his initial organization of the colors, he reached into the bag and pulled out a new color—black. He scribbled in black, rather aggressively, all over the once-colorful picture he had been working on for nearly the whole session. He seemed intent upon covering up almost all of his previous drawing. Then I asked, "Jonathon, what is this a picture of?" pointing to his creation, and he whispered, "Leaving." His mother began to cry.

Throughout the seven sessions I had with Jonathon and his mother, Jonathon in time did begin to participate in sessions more freely, although quietly. In each session we did an art activity, and as we progressed, Jonathon seemed actively engaged and more comfortable. His mother, however, remained distant in her participation and her attendance to sessions was sporadic. After she did not come to three consecutive sessions, the case was closed at our center. Upon last contact, the state was petitioning for the termination of the mother's parental rights and Jonathon's foster parents were attempting to formally adopt him.

Although this case did not result in the reunification of Jonathon with his mother, conducting sessions using a play-therapy modality seemed to allow Jonathon the opportunity to express his feelings in, what seemed like, much more comfortable, nonverbal means. It seemed as if Jonathon's participation in nonverbal play, such as the art activity, was a catharsis for him. In addition, through his play, both his mother and myself were able to see the depth and power of his emotions.

Suggestions for Follow-Up

When play therapy activities are used to depict real-life situations, discussing the process in the context of the activity, instead of the people involved in the real-life situation, may provide a safe, nonthreatening atmosphere in which issues may be addressed. For example, if a mother and a son had a disagreement over rules of the household and communication was thus inhibited, having each person draw a depiction of his or her version of house rules can be a means of allowing them to express themselves and discuss their perspectives. Other play-therapy modalities such as sand trays, puppet play, games, or a variety of other approaches may be used to reinforce the progress made.

The use of the family play therapy may strengthen sibling bonds, address family triangles, process family scapegoating, and illuminate family patterns and trends. Any relevant theme can be addressed through the use of family play therapy, and the nature of the modality may provide a safe opportunity for challenges to be faced and family bonds to be strengthened.

Special Considerations When Working with Abused Children

According to Knell (1993), limit setting is an important responsibility of the therapist when using a family play-therapy treatment modality. It is critical when working with children, abused children in particular, that the therapist set only those limits which encourage responsible behavior (Rudolph & Thompson, 1995). Consistency in reinforcing the established limits may help the child feel safe and accepted. If a child exhibits aggressive behavior, and therapist intervention is needed, the therapist should acknowledge the child's feelings with a reflective statement, set the limit, then describe an appropriate behavior (Rudolph & Thompson, 1995). This can then be a model for subsequent parental behavior.

Contraindications

Ensuring safety of all family members, and particularly the safety of children, is extremely important prior to engaging a family in therapy. Family therapy with abused children should be conducted only after a thorough assessment has been made regarding the appropriateness of having family members together in the same room. There should be no current abuse in the family, and if abuse is suspected, it is necessary to report the information to the abuse registry.

In addition, when working with children who have been abused, it is important to allow for flexibility during sessions so that children are free to direct, explore, and create. Gil (1994) asserts, "because physical and sexual abuse are intrusive acts, the clinician's intervention should be nonintrusive, allowing the child ample physical and emotional space" (p. 151). Therefore, entering treatment with specific activities planned for each session may be counterproductive.

Last, the field of art therapy is a distinct and well-documented form of psychotherapy. If art therapy is to be used as the primary treatment modality throughout the course of the case, extensive training on the utilization of art therapy is necessary (Gil, 1996).

Readings and Resources for the Professional

Arrington, D. B. (1991). *Home is where the art is: An art therapy approach to family therapy.* Springfield, IL: Charles Thomas Publishing.

Carey, L. (1991). Family sandplay therapy. *The Arts in Psychotherapy, 18,* 231-239.

Gil, E. (1991). *The healing power of play: Working with abused children.* New York: Guilford Press.

Gil, E. (1994). *Play in family therapy.* New York: Guilford Press.

Gil, E. (1996). *Treating abused adolescents.* New York: Guilford Press.

Thompson, C. & Rudolph, L. (1996). *Counseling children* (4th ed.). Pacific Grove, CA: Brooks/Cole Publishing.

Bibliotherapy Sources for the Client

Diamant, R. (1992). *Positioning for play: Home activities for parents of young children.* Tucson, AZ: Therapy Skills Builder.

Kraft, A. & Landreth, G. (1998). *Parents as therapeutic partners: Listening to your child's play.* Northvale, NJ: Jason Aronson.

Morin, V. & Sokoloff, D. (1999). *Fun to grow on: Engaging play activities for kids with teachers, parents, and grandparents.* Chicago: Magnolia Street Publishers.

Sawyers, J. & Rogers, C. (1988). *Helping young children develop through play: A practical guide for parents, caregivers, and teachers.* Washington, DC: National Association for Education.

References

Carmichael, K. D. (1992). *Abused and traumatized children.* Report No. CG-024-885. ERIC Document Reproduction Service No. ED 358 395.

Gil, E. (1994). *Play in family therapy.* New York: Guilford Press.

Gil, E. (1996). *Treating abused adolescents.* New York: Guilford Press.

Gladding, S. T. (1993). The therapeutic use of play counseling: An overview. *Journal of Humanistic Education and Development, 31,* 106-115.

Harman, J., Childs, G., & Kelleher, K. (2000). Mental health care utilization and expenditures by children in foster care. *Archives of Pediatrics and Adolescent Medicine, 154,* 1114-1117.

Kaplan, S., Pelcovitz, D., & Labruna, V. (1999). Child and adolescent abuse and neglect research: A review of the past 10 years. Part 1: Physical and emotional abuse and neglect. *Journal of the American Academy of Child and Adolescent Psychiatry, 38*(10), 1214-1222.

Knell, S. M. (1993). *Cognitive-behavioral play therapy.* Northvale, NJ: Jason Aronson.

McFadden, E. J. (1990). *Counseling abused children.* Report No. CG-022-287. Washington, DC: Office of Educational Research and Improvement. ERIC Document Reproduction Service No. ED 315 706.

Rudolph, L. B. & Thompson, C. L. (1995). *Counseling children.* Pacific Grove, CA: Brooks/Cole Publishing.

Webb, N. B. (1991). *Play therapy with children in crisis: A casebook for practitioners.* New York: Guilford Press.

– 22 –

Chicken Little Reconstructed: Trauma Resiliency

Wendy Danto Ellis
Muriel S. McClellan

Type of Contribution: Activity, Homework, Handout

Objective

This exercise creates the opportunity to explore the effects of deficit language and victim-themed narratives upon the ways in which they make meaning of traumatic experiences. Participants are given the opportunity to contrast alternative positive and resilient ways of talking about these events and to look at the ways in which such language invites movement into a more healthful and satisfied resolution of the trauma.

Rationale for Use

We have all heard the phrases, "I've been traumatized for life," "I am a victim," or "I'll never be the same again," from people describing the personal effects of traumatic experiences. These assertions and similar language are used every day in many cultures and represent a pervasive deficit discourse. This type of language, when persistent, invites the speaker to experience himself or herself as "stuck" and disempowered with regard to the traumatic event(s).

This activity is an interactive demonstration of the power of such deficit words and stories. It provides an opportunity for the participant to experience the juxtaposition of a deficit narrative with a more resilient view of traumatic events. This examination of language and expression is basic to the theoretical views of both social constructionism and narrative therapy. The words and language that people use and the stories they negotiate reflect their experiences, as well as shape and inform the meanings they make of those experiences. We are always in the process of constructing meanings of the words we use in conversation with others.

This exercise invites participants to become more aware of the words they choose and the stories they tell when meeting life challenges. As participants have conversations with others about a traumatic event, they experience firsthand how the ways in which we choose our words and stories influence how we think about things and, ultimately, our actions. The notion that meanings are negotiated and constructed in relationship with others becomes clear.

This exercise is presented using the story of Chicken Little and her concern that the sky is falling as our case study. Participants are first invited to apply dominant deficit ideas about post-traumatic stress disorder to Chicken Little's problem as they note her recurrent thoughts about the sky falling in. Despite her efforts to avoid feelings associated with the trauma, Chicken Little loses interest in pecking for seeds in the barnyard and gossiping with her friend, Henny Penny. It seems her sleep has been disrupted, she is irritable, and she has outbursts of anger toward Goosey Loosey. She has trouble concentrating and becomes hypervigilant. She startles easily and runs hither and yon spreading the disastrous news. If left in this state and with only this story, it is easy to see that Chicken Little would "never be the same again."

For the second part of the activity, participants are asked to apply appreciative, resourceful language and thinking as they restory the events. The questions and directions are constructed from a future-oriented, appreciative, and relational-theory base. They are designed to help shift participants' thinking and language from an individual and deficit perspective to a relational and resilient one. The differences between these two perspectives are further illustrated in the handouts at the end of the chapter. These handouts also serve to reinforce this new way of thinking and stimulate the application of this thinking in other settings, situations, and contexts.

We have successfully used this activity and the handouts in a variety of contexts including organizational consultations, critical incident debriefings, and educational settings, as well as during traditional therapy sessions, both individual and group or family.

When used in the family therapy setting with a traumatized individual, this exercise is especially helpful as it provides the opportunity for the family to experience empowerment in a traumatic situation other than the one they are personally struggling with. Alternatively, therapists may choose to forgo this and move directly to the substitution of their clients' trauma story for that of Chicken Little. In either case, all family members are actively involved in the cocreation of new meaning, new narratives, and new actions in relation to a traumatic event. The traumatized individual is able to draw upon the resources of the entire family as all members share in the creation of new possibilities.

The exercise should be introduced only after the client(s) have had an opportunity to express their experience of, and their feelings about, the traumatic incident. It is the responsibility of the therapist or facilitator to allow this expression, while at the same time not allow the client(s) to continue to repeat and revisit the tragic story. Clients must be validated for their experience of the event and acknowledged for their feelings, while at the same time, be invited into an understanding that there are multiple ways to think about any event.

Instructions

This activity is composed of three parts. In the first part, the therapist introduces the family or group to the story of Chicken Little. This is an opportunity to be playful. The therapist is encouraged to allow the participants to explore and play with deficit discourse and the trauma story. The second part of the exercise invites examples of more resilient discourses and supports the formation of more powerful and healing types of language. Each participant is encouraged to join with others as he or she resists being traumatized for life. Part three offers an opportunity to reflect upon these very different narratives and to think about which words and stories are more useful to people.

Part One—Chicken Little's Tragic Story

1. The facilator/therpist begins by asking the participants to think about the story of Chicken Little. Ask them to remember how Chicken Little is certain that the sky is falling and how she chaotically runs about spreading the word and trying to warn the other barnyard animals. Although most people remember the story, it is best to have a copy of the story, which can be read aloud at the beginning of the activity.
2. Ask the family or group members to tell a story from the perspective of Chicken Little as someone who has been traumatized for life. Encourage them to include her awful feelings, her sense of isolation, and her hopelessness in the story. (Note: If used in a large group, ask the participants to write out their stories.)

3. Invite a discussion by asking the family or group members to reflect on the story they just created. Use the following questions to stimulate discussion:
   - Were the verbs you used in your story active or passive? Did they give a sense of action or inaction?
   - What sorts of feelings do your descriptions evoke in you? Are they more discouraging or more encouraging?
   - What parts of your story included new ideas, resources, or strengths for Chicken Little to build upon for the future? (Note: The usual answer is fairly limited with this question.)

Part Two—Restorying Chicken Little

4. Ask them to retell (or rewrite) the story of Chicken Little using hopeful words and ideas. For example, ask them to try to use active words that describe movement toward the future and are hopeful about changing the situation. Encourage them to think about new possibilities by including other people in their new story, as well as their own personal resources and strengths. You can use the following questions to help them shift their thinking:
   - If Chicken Little were your sister, what would you hope she could have learned from her experience?
   - If the news covered Chicken Little's story, what optimistic message do you hope would be conveyed to the public by the reporting?
   - If Chicken Little felt supported and energized by the other members of the barnyard community, what might they be doing? What might she be doing? What might they be doing together?
5. Have the participants share their new stories.

Part Three—Reflections and Handouts

6. Point out to the family or group members that two kinds of stories have been created for Chicken Little—the first where she was severely traumatized and this second one.
7. Help the family or group members make comparisons between the two stories. Use the following questions to stimulate discussion:
   - What do you notice about your choice of words used in the two stories?
   - What do you notice about the feelings that the different words evoke in you? Did you notice a shift in tone in the stories, from dissatisfaction to more possibilities for energy and change?
8. Help shift the participants' thinking. Ask them to imagine that they are a Red Cross volunteer who has been called to the barnyard to help the occupants cope with their recent traumatic experience. Tell them that after they have spoken with the occupants they are going to leave some information to help them deal with their trauma. Ask them to look at Handout I and Handout II and invite a discussion with these questions. (Have the handouts ready to pass out.)
   - Which one of the handouts would you choose to leave with them?
   - Which one would be most helpful? Why?
   - Which one would you want given to you or to your friends and family if you or they were in a similar situation?

Brief Vignette

Joey, age twelve, and his family had been in therapy for several sessions working on their adjustment to Joey's recent diagnosis of diabetes. There were many practical as well as emotional changes that his diabetes brought to the family. All of the family members, including Joey, had strong feelings about these changes, although Joey was quite reticent about discussing his feelings.

At the beginning of the fifth session, the therapist asked the family if they would like to take a break from discussing diabetes and try something fun and different. With the family's agreement, she introduced the Chicken Little activity. Joey was an enthusiastic participant. He stated he enjoyed having all of his family members working together on something or someone other than him and his diabetes. At the next session, the family worked together on applying the second handout on signs and symptoms of resiliency to their own situation. They did so with a renewed sense of community and energy.

Suggestions for Follow-Up

This exercise is designed to help people begin to think divergently and creatively about multiple ways of responding to traumatic events. It is helpful to have participants identify some concrete ways in which they plan to implement these ideas in their daily lives. If the therapist is working with clients whom he or she sees on a regular basis, it is helpful to ask the clients to identify something they would like to do to implement some of the thinking that "bubbled up" for them as they moved through this exercise. If the client's actual trauma story was used for the experience, follow-up should flow from that. If the Chicken Little story was used, ask the clients to identify a challenge from their own lives that they would be willing to deal with in a new way. Give them copies of the two handouts and ask them to notice when they are being more resilient in their behaviors. They may even be asked to keep a brief journal of their resilient accomplishments as homework and to return with it to the next session.

Contraindications

Clinical judgment on the part of the therapist/facilitator must prevail. If working with clients in the immediate throes of a crisis or traumatic incident, it is important to help stabilize that client prior to attempting to restory the event. Client safety is at all times the number one priority.

Readings and Resources for the Professional

Durrant, M. & White, C. (1992). *Ideas for therapy with sexual abuse.* Adelaide, South Australia: Dulwich Centre Publications.
Furman, B. & Ahola, T. (1992). *Pickpockets on a nudist camp.* Adelaide, South Australia: Dulwich Centre Publications.
Gergen, K. (1994). *Realities and relationships: Soundings in social construction.* Cambridge, MA: Harvard University Press.
Higgins, G. (1994). *Resilient adults: Overcoming a cruel past.* San Francisco: Jossey-Bass Publishers.
McNamee, S. & Gergen, K. (1992). *Therapy as social construction.* London: Sage Publications.
Wolin, S. J. & Wolin, S. (1993). *The resilient self: How survivors of troubled families rise above adversity.* New York: Villard Books.

Bibliotherapy Sources for the Client

Kaminer, W. (1992). *I'm dysfunctional, you're dysfunctional.* New York: Addison-Wesley Publishing Company, Inc.
Reeve, C. (1998). *Still me.* New York: Random House.

Handout I. Common Signs and Symptoms of Stress Following Trauma

You have been through a difficult and traumatic event. It is common to experience upsetting feelings and troubling symptoms. If you notice yourself experiencing any of the following, do not be alarmed. This is normal and to be expected.

1. Difficulty in concentrating
2. Jumpiness and startling easily
3. Sadness and depression
4. Arguing and starting fights
5. Guilt and self-blame
6. Irritability and angry outbursts
7. Worrying and ruminating
8. Aches, pains, and other physical ills
9. Confusion and disorientation
10. Feeling let down by leaders and those in authority
11. Rapid, pressured speech
12. Trouble sleeping, nightmares
13. Fatigue and loss of energy
14. Anxiety and fears
15. Behaving in uncharacteristic ways
16. Eating poorly
17. Unable to perform job
18. Withdrawing or sulking

Handout II. Common Signs and Symptoms of Resiliency Following Trauma

Although you have been through a difficult and challenging time, you have done a wonderful job of dealing with it. You have been creative and resourceful in the ways in which you have uniquely coped with this difficulty. If you notice yourself feeling or doing any of the following, do not be alarmed. This is normal and natural.

1. Pride in a job well done
2. Feeling touched or moved
3. Appreciative of your resources
4. Being able to ask for support
5. Taking care of yourself
6. Doing something for others
7. Making contact with family and friends
8. Keeping a routine
9. Staying informed, but not saturated or overloaded with information
10. Looking for opportunities
11. Making positive changes
12. Eating right and exercising
13. Laughing (as humor is good medicine)
14. Setting time aside for relaxation and diversion
15. Feeling inspired to make a difference
16. Being stronger for the experience
17. Being better equipped for dealing with the future
18. Thankful for your blessings

– 23 –

Parting Is Such Sweet Sorrow: The Good-Bye Book

Katherine M. Hertlein

Type of Contribution: Activity/Homework, Assignment/Handout

Objective

Good-bye is not an easy word to say, particularly within the context of a therapist-client relationship. The purpose of this activity is to provide closure for the end of therapy with a family. The therapist and family create a book that outlines what was accomplished in therapy. This book can then be used as a summary of the therapy process and given to a transferring therapist, or the family can keep it as a reminder of the changes they have made in therapy.

Rationale for Use

The actual process of termination in therapy can be very difficult for some. Many couples, individuals, and families, upon knowing termination is evident, may cancel or not appear for the last few sessions. Not being able to consistently meet with the family toward the end of the therapy may impede the therapist's ability to have a wrap-up termination session. In this activity, the therapist and family create a book detailing the process of therapy. Each book is individualized to the therapist-client relationship and describes the interventions, the process, turning points, critical events, and other important events or processes that occurred during therapy. This assignment can provide structure to the last few therapy sessions and can enhance investment in the few remaining sessions.

Several theoretical frameworks influence this activity. First, this activity is influenced by narrative family therapy (White & Epston, 1990). Narrative therapy helps therapists work with families to experience shifts in the problem context. The therapist works with the family to move from the dominant story, which contributes to the sense of problem for the family, and move to a secondary way of understanding problematic behavior. Therapists help to externalize problematic behaviors for families (White & Epston, 1990), meaning that problems are attributed to external factors rather than some internal characteristic or attribute about the individual or family. Narrative therapy focuses on the lived experience of individuals.

It is this focus on lived experience that informs the present activity. Within narrative family therapy, White and Epston (1990) use documentation as both an intervention and a way to externalize the behavior. They provide a variety of letter types for therapeutic impact. Some of these letters include letters of invitation (letters which invite someone into therapy), letters of redundancy (those which make people redundant in roles), letters of prediction (letters which detail predictions for an individual or family, serving in part as a prophecy to be fulfilled by the cli-

The author would like to thank Dr. Carole McNamee for this suggestion for a therapy activity.

ents), counter-referral letters (of which the family may take part in writing), letters of reference, letters for special occasions, and brief letters. White and Epston contend that letters used in narrative therapy organize lived experience into a narrative (or story) that makes sense.

In narrative therapy terms, the purpose of the Good-Bye Book is to organize the story of therapy, a lived experience, into that which the family can document and recall. It literally becomes a storied therapy. This is accomplished through requesting that the family complete the Good-Bye Book toward the termination of therapy. This book can also be used in transition from one therapist to another, with the family completing the book with one therapist and presenting it to the other.

This activity is also influenced by the use of rituals in family therapy (Imber-Black, Roberts, & Whiting, 1988). In family therapy, a ritual is broadly defined as an activity or event using symbols, which represent a metaphor. Typically, rituals should allow individual members to derive their own meaning from them. Rituals are effective with a variety of therapeutic populations and presenting problems (see, for example, Imber-Black et al., 1988). Within the development of a ritual, Whiting (1988) proposes several important aspects to consider. The ritual should be written or conducted in a way that incorporates the client's language, allows for client input into the project, and has elements of both client choice and therapist direction. In addition, it is important to use symbols in developing a ritual. In this way, the client can anchor the ritual to a symbol and it can serve as a reminder of the event. The incorporation of symbols is evident in some of the tasks completed in the Good-Bye Book. For example, at times the family is asked to create a picture of a certain event or activity. The family can draw a picture that represents or is symbolic to them in relation to this activity. The Good-Bye Book activity also incorporates the aspect of client choice as it allows for the clients to freely respond to the questions and prompts in a manner of their choosing. It incorporates the therapist directive option by having the therapist provide prompts to which the family can respond.

Instructions

This activity can take place close to termination, when the therapist feels it is appropriate. In general, the therapist and family should be at a point where the termination of therapy (or transition to another therapist) is imminent. The therapist can generate the Good-Bye Book in two ways: either the therapist and family can create the book with the therapist providing prompts to the family, or the therapist can provide the family with pages from an already-made book, provided in handout form at the end of this chapter.

To begin, the therapist can copy the pages at the end of this chapter. There is also a blank book page included for the therapist to use if there are any pages the family wants to include specific to their course of treatment. With the blank page, the therapist can generate his or her own prompts for the family or leave the page blank for the family to complete as they see fit. The therapist may also instruct the family to make their own personal notes on this page.

Once the therapist makes photocopies of these pages, he or she distributes the pages to the family and instructs the family to complete the book. If the therapist and family decide that the activity will take several weeks to complete, the therapist can assign pieces of the book for homework, as opposed to assigning the entire book. When the family returns for the next session, the therapist and family will go through the book and discuss the family's responses. Another variation is for the family to complete the book as in-session activities.

If working primarily with younger children, the therapist can adjust the language of the book to reflect the reading level of the child. For example, asking a five-year-old about the turning points of therapy may not elicit a good response. Asking about what helped make things change, however, might be easier for the child to understand and therefore respond to.

Variation: Hello Book

This book could also be used as a Hello Book. The therapist can assign the book to the family as a way to get to know the individual members as well as the family as a whole. Rather than prescribing the book at the termination of therapy, the therapist should assign the book at the beginning of therapy (again, for homework or an in-session activity, depending on the appropriateness) and include such pages as follows:

What has brought you here to therapy?
What are the ways that everyone maintains the problem?
What do you expect to get out of coming here?
How do you think everyone feels about the problem?

Assigning this activity as a Hello Book also gives the therapist an opportunity to examine processes within the family at the beginning of treatment. Once the family completes the book, the therapist can ask them to comment on the processes behind putting the book together. When the family describes the processes behind the scenes, the therapist can assess whether the processes that were evident in putting the book together are those that the family sees as problematic in general, thus the reason for coming to therapy. The therapist can then implement the Good-Bye Book at the termination of therapy and use the books as assessment tools determining differences between the beginning and end of therapy.

Brief Vignette

The Markus family had been attending therapy for two years at a university clinic. As typical with the nature of a university clinic, the family had been to two different therapists and were about to be transferred to yet another therapist. As a result, they were apprehensive about beginning therapy with a new therapist. Although the present and future therapists were doing cotherapy to ease the transition, the Markus family still held some concerns about the transition. It was particularly difficult for the youngest daughter in the family. Jenny had been the identified client in the therapy, and much of the work was centered on her. For example, the therapists had worked with Jenny's parents on how to more effectively discipline Jenny and how to avoid power struggles with her. Individually, Jenny was working on completing her homework in a timely manner, respecting the rules of the house, and learning how to handle discipline and directives without throwing a tantrum. The therapist also worked with Jenny on social skills.

Because the family had made significant gains over their time in therapy, it was critical for them to maintain the changes throughout the transition to another therapist. This was particularly important because in other transitions, the family had a tendency to relapse into old patterns. Some of the strengths that the family had were the ability to collaboratively work on projects and therapy homework together, and the ability to generate their own interventions. Many times, if left to their own devices, they would identify things that they could do for homework. Finally, Jenny really enjoyed drawing.

Based on the fact that the family was transitioning, but also on the family's strengths, the therapist decided to incorporate a Good-Bye Book into the therapy. In this way, the family could ritualistically say good-bye to the present therapists, to that phase of therapy, and also build upon it with a new therapist by making a new chapter. The family could consider the most recent therapy a "closed chapter" and write a new one, rather than revisit their previous patterns of behavior.

Approximately one month before transferring the case, the therapist explained to the family that, over the next month, they would be creating a Good-Bye Book. Jenny was very interested in the idea. The therapist generated some questions and asked Jenny to respond to the questions through text and drawings. The therapist encouraged Jenny's mother to assist Jenny in the project, as well as incorporate her own ideas in the book. Jenny's stepfather, John, also agreed to be part of the book process. The therapist assigned the family to start the book, providing them with prompts.

The family returned the following week with some ideas about what they did for homework. As the family spoke, the therapist recorded the interventions they had completed. The therapist provided the family with some interventions that were not mentioned. As the therapist talked, Jenny wrote the ideas on a piece of paper and talked about what she could draw to represent those ideas.

The next week the family selected several interventions to describe and depict within their book. One of Jenny's favorite interventions was when she and her mother were assigned to spend time together. Although this was an activity that had been assigned early on in the therapy, and the therapist had encouraged the family to maintain this activity throughout the course of therapy, the family did not keep up with this activity. When the family created the book, they decided to revisit the activity and implement it on a weekly basis.

The final week, the therapist and family met together with the new therapist. The family presented Jenny with the book and all they had done during therapy. Jenny appeared eager to take the new therapist through the book that she and her family had created. With this book, the new therapist was brought up to speed on the case and the family also had a reminder of their successes in therapy.

Suggestions for Follow-Up

After completion of the book, the therapist can ask several important process questions. These questions will serve as a way to solidify the information that the family has brought to therapy within the contents of the book. The therapist can ask such questions as, "Who took initiative in starting the book?" and "What was it like to put this book together and see how far you've come?" These questions ask the family to comment on their successes, something they may not have overtly done in the past. In this way, the therapist and family frame what they have experienced as something in the past, thus externalizing the problem even further. Some additional questions include the following:

> Which interventions were easier to remember?
> Which were more difficult? Why?
> What do you think changed things for your family?

Contraindications

This activity may not be appropriate with families who blame a single family member for their problems. The last thing a therapist wants is an entire book directed at someone and his or her problems. This intervention works best when individuals in families are knowledgeable of and have each accepted their systemic role in maintaining a problem.

Resource for the Professional

Imber-Black, E., Roberts, J., & Whiting, R. A. (1988). *Rituals in families and family therapy.* New York: W. W. Norton & Co.

Bibliotherapy Source for the Client

Bruckner-Gordon, F., Gangi, B. K., & Wallman, G. U. (1988). *Making therapy work: Your guide to choosing, using, and ending therapy.* New York: Harper and Row.

References

Imber-Black, E., Roberts, J., & Whiting, R. A. (1988). *Rituals in families and family therapy.* New York: W. W. Norton & Co.

White, M. & Epston, D. (1990). *Narrative means to therapeutic ends.* New York: Guilford.

Whiting, R. A. (1988). Guidelines to designing therapeutic rituals. In E. Imber-Black, J. Roberts, & R. A. Whiting (Eds.), *Rituals in families and family therapy* (pp. 84-109). New York: W. W. Norton & Co.

Good-Bye Book

Good-Bye Book

Good-Bye Book

Good-Bye Book

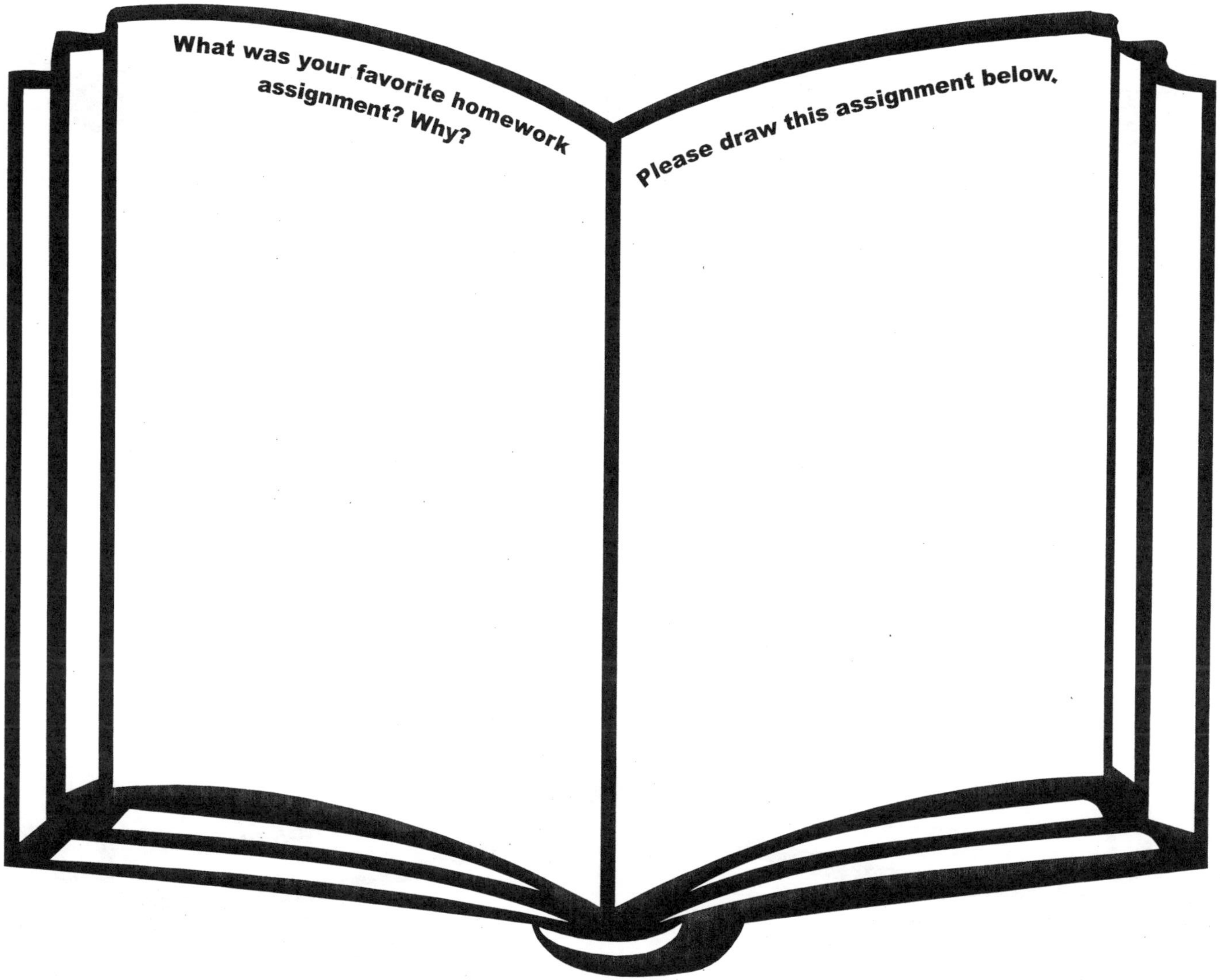

Good-Bye Book

Good-Bye Book

Good-Bye Book

The Pen Is Mightier Than the Sword: Writing to Combat Adolescent Silence in Family Therapy

Katherine M. Hertlein
Liddy B. Hope

Type of Contribution: Activity

Objective

Silence in therapy is a controversial subject. Often, clients who are silent are thought of as being resistant to therapy. Silent adolescents are typically labeled as such. Adolescent clients may be "forced" to come to family therapy and, in an attempt to exert some control over the situation, may refuse to speak in session. The purpose of this chapter is to present alternative means for the therapist working with adolescents within family therapy who choose to be silent in session.

Rationale for Use

According to DeVito (1989), "Our silence communicates just as intensely as anything we might verbalize" (p. 153). Silence allows speakers time to think and may be used as a response to feeling anxious or threatened. Some may use silence to prevent the verbal communication of certain messages, or even as a weapon to hurt others. Silence also has the potential to communicate a variety of emotional responses (DeVito, 1989) and can be used strategically. For example, silence can be used to gain interpersonal attention. In this sense, others will begin to question why the silent person is not talking, and make judgments and inferences as the attention comes to that person. This chapter addresses the benefit of silence in the therapy room as a communicative function and provides creative techniques for working with silent adolescents.

The awareness of silence differs from person to person and situation to situation. Silence is acceptable in some relationships and not in others. With close friends, silence is more acceptable than in groups of people that are not well-known to one another. Some propose that silence promotes closeness between two people (Bruneau, 1973). It is also more acceptable in some situations as opposed to others. For example, silence at a library is more acceptable than silence at a party. The use of silence might also differ culturally. For example, silence in Japan is used for disagreeing with others (Hasegawa & Gudykunst, 1998).

When clients in psychotherapy are silent, therapists might view them as resistant (e.g., Marshall, 1972). Adolescents who come into family therapy, for example, may sulk, sit with their arms crossed, and only answer questions with the statement "I don't know." Parents become frustrated with the behavior of the nonresponsive adolescent in session and a power struggle may emerge within the session itself. Although silence is a common way in which clients avoid parts of the interview process, silence should not be overlooked as an important form of communication. The adolescent may simply be communicating autonomy in some way, or communicating difficulty handling the conversation. It is a juggling act to keep the adolescent connected with the family and engaged in therapy, while also demonstrating respect for the adolescent's autonomy and independence.

Developmentally, adolescents who are silent may be attempting to develop autonomy. Attending therapy, especially at the urging of one's parents, limits a youth's autonomy and authority. This creates resistance, particularly when the family members are there, hanging on the adolescent's every word. Developing intimacy is another issue for adolescents. All clients, adolescents included, should feel comfortable with their therapist and with the process of expressing emotion. However, therapists should also consider the context in which the silence resides. For example, if the family system is not one in which the adolescent feels comfortable sharing emotion, he or she may be viewed as resistant when it is really unsafe for him or her. Resistance should therefore be considered in the terms of the system of which it is a part (McHolland, 1985).

Therapists might not be comfortable with silence, be it the clients' or their own. Being silent may seem against our nature or training as therapists. The therapist's job often is to facilitate communication; psychotherapy, after all, means "talk" therapy. Reik (1968) describes a detriment to the emphasis on talk in therapy is that the emotional effect of silence is ignored in the therapy room. The reality is, in therapy, silence induces a high degree of internal activity. It promotes emotional readiness to receive information. It shares and gives resonance to clients' emotional experience and inner condition. Martryes (1995) contends that silence promotes emotional experiences and moves clients to attain a significant emotional level. The drawback to avoiding silence in the therapy room influences client-perceived rapport. Sharpley (1997) discovered that it was during these periods of silence that clients reported a stronger rapport with the therapist. In addition, avoiding silence robs the client of the opportunity to think about what is being discussed in therapy and to internalize the changes made. Clients most value silence when they are working or are at decisional stages of the session (Sharpley, 1997).

How can we use silence to the benefit of the adolescent in family therapy? McHolland (1985) presents some techniques for use with adolescents who manifest resistance through silence. Typically, these clients are coerced into therapy or give the impression that they do not need to come and thus remain apathetic. Some of the strategies include relabeling the silence, prescribing it, reflecting on the practitioner's feelings, recognizing the feelings of being hassled, and scheduling a silent session. When working with the apathetic adolescent, the therapist can engage in a nonverbal session in which the therapist asks the adolescent to respond to questions by nodding or shrugging. Other techniques include engaging in a family sculpting activity and instructing the adolescent that others will be allowed to speak for him or her. Rather than simply presenting strategies in which the therapist does not speak and waits for the client to speak, this chapter provides a nonwritten strategy to use with adolescents that will still achieve therapeutic goals via a new route of communication.

Instructions

The therapist should assess the degree of anxiety experienced by the adolescent client at each session. Although it is important not to be too intrusive, it is also important to not allow the silence to become overwhelming to the client. To avoid the potential intolerance of silence for the client, certain questions or statements can be used. Some examples of these questions are "What was happening in the silence?" and "What were you feeling just then?" The therapist can also use process statements such as "You are uncomfortable with the silence" (Martryes, 1995).

Once the therapist determines the level of anxiety within the session, the therapist should attempt to determine the reason for the silence (Leira, 1995). Is it a silence through which the adolescent means to communicate something? Or is it part of the personality of the teen? Clinicians who treat adolescents who are silent as "resistant clients" might be missing the message being sent by the teen, leading to unproductive behavior and responses by the therapist (McHolland, 1985).

The therapist should then consider the context of the silence and the clients. How has the adolescent client learned to define and use silence within communication in this family system? Equally important is the clinician's own understanding and use of silence. The goal is to use silence in a way that is effective for all participants. Then the therapist should prescribe the intervention. One technique, rather than being verbal, is to have a written conversation with the adolescent. The materials needed are markers (at least one) and a large sheet of paper. This activity is also useful with a wipe board and wipeable markers.

The therapist should start this activity by introducing benign questions. Using benign questions, or questions that are general and do not carry a great deal of meaning, allows the therapist and adolescent to join. This activity might scare the adolescent or other family members off if the therapist starts with a heavy question such as "Why have you come here today?" "Hi" and "How are you?" are good ways to start. Once the therapist has engaged the teen in the activity, he or she can then introduce more challenging questions.

Brief Vignette

Jimmy, a fifteen-year-old, was brought to family counseling by his mother as a result of his falling grades and emotional withdrawal. His parents were in the midst of filing for divorce, yet both still lived in the family home. Jimmy's mother often came to session, but Jimmy's father did not attend sessions on a regular basis, attending only two sessions over the course of therapy. His mother June believed the impending divorce was causing the falling grades and the isolation. Jimmy considered himself a loner at school. He stated that he did not have many friends, and that he liked a girl at school but was concerned that she would reject him.

After several sessions, it became clear that Jimmy was remaining "stuck" because of his dependence on "surface" communication—small talk. Any time the family therapist asked a question requiring Jimmy to move beyond small talk, Jimmy did not speak. This happened with Jimmy's mother June in the room as well as when Jimmy and the therapist were meeting alone. June had a tendency to rescue him when he was silent in the room. She would answer questions for him, would rephrase things when he did not respond as an attempt to get him to respond, or would make excuses as to why he would not respond. The goal of therapy was to move the therapeutic relationship to a point where Jimmy was able to communicate his feelings about the impending divorce.

The first goal was for the therapist to work with June toward her not rescuing Jimmy when he was silent. The therapist and June discussed how she felt when Jimmy was silent. She stated that she was scared when Jimmy was silent because she was not sure what was going on in his mind. She said she was concerned that he was thinking about the impending divorce and any anger he had toward her. June was worried about his social withdrawal at home, and became even more concerned when he refused to speak in session. The therapist and June worked on her anxiety related to Jimmy's silence in session. The therapist encouraged June to refrain from saving Jimmy in session and to allow Jimmy the autonomy to be silent.

The therapist drew the family's structure on a piece of paper during a session. The therapist asked if this was how the family looked. Jimmy did not agree. The therapist asked Jimmy to correct the picture. Jimmy sat silent. Any other question the therapist asked, Jimmy remained silent. After a period of silence, the therapist reached for the marker and flipped the big piece of paper onto the other side. The therapist wrote, "hi" on the paper. Noticing that Jimmy was watching, the therapist handed Jimmy a marker. Jimmy wrote back, "hi." The therapist wrote,

"What's up?" Jimmy wrote, "Nothing." This taking of turns writing questions and answers continued. As it did, the therapist was able to get answers to questions that had previously been answered with silence.

It was through this exercise that Jimmy disclosed to the therapist his fears, the concern he had that if his mother's miscarriage had not occurred, he would not be here, etc. It proved a very productive session in terms of expression of feeling and assessment. It was the beginning of a working relationship between Jimmy and the clinician. In addition, it provided a place to which the clinician could later refer in order to connect situations to Jimmy's feelings.

Suggestions for Follow-Up

One suggestion for follow-up is that the therapist can assign some of these activities for homework. For example, the therapist can assign the family to set a time to have a nonverbal, written conversation. The therapist can assign the family to select a thirty-minute time frame to have a written conversation. Members can select what style and color they choose to write and represent themselves with, and the family can determine the rules regarding the activity. They can decide who will start writing first and in what order the other members will follow.

Contraindications

Although this activity may work for some adolescents, it certainly will not be completely effective for each adolescent. For example, it may not be effective for an adolescent who is in a system in which silence is the predominant and ineffective pattern of communication. This intervention is not recommended for situations in which abuse is occurring or where intervention needs to occur immediately.

Resource for the Professional

Landreth, G. L. (1991). *Play therapy: The art of the relationship.* Muncie, IN: Accelerated Development, Inc.

References

Bruneau, T. J. (1973). Communicative silences: Forms and functions. *The Journal of Communication, 23,* 17-46.

DeVito, J. A. (1989, Summer). Silence and paralanguage and communication. *Et cetera,* pp. 153-162.

Hasegawa, T. & Gudykunst, W. B. (1998). Silence in Japan and the United States. *Journal of Cross-Cultural Psychology, 29*(5), 668-684.

Leira, T. (1995). Silence and communication: Non-verbal dialogue and therapeutic action. *Scandanavian Psychoanalytic Review, 18,* 41-65.

Marshall, R. J. (1972). The treatment of resistances in psychotherapy of children and adolescents. *Psychotherapy: Theory, Research, and Practice, 9*(2), 143-148.

Martyres, G. (1995). On silence: A language for emotional experience. *Australian and New Zealand Journal of Psychiatry, 29,* 118-123.

McHolland, J. D. (1985). Strategies for dealing with resistant adolescents. *Adolescence, 20*(78), 349-368.

Reik, T. (1968). The psychological meaning of silence. *Psychoanalytic Review, 55,* 172-186.

Sharpley, C. F. (1997). The influence of silence on client-perceived rapport. *Counseling Psychology Quarterly, 10*(3), 237-246.

– 25 –

Communicating with Teens: Movie Exchange

Glenn W. Lambie
Shari Sias

Type of Contribution: Activity/Homework

Objective

Communicating with adolescents is often a challenge for both parents and therapists. The objective of this activity is to support family communication with teens, while facilitating transference of therapeutic learning to the daily family interactions through the use of a transitional object, in this case a movie videotape or DVD.

Rationale for Use

Family factors such as a low degree of parental nurturance and poor parent-child communications have repeatedly been found to be positively related to adolescents' dysfunctionality (Lambie & Rokutani, 2002). Therefore, supporting healthy family communication and interaction is likely to foster greater family functionality. In today's high-speed and often chaotic society, it can be difficult for family members to gather and simply interact with one another. In many families, parents and children are involved in work-related activities (i.e., job and school responsibilities), as well as a wide range of extracurricular obligations, all of which decrease the time family members are able to spend together. This reduction in family interaction can reduce a family's potential to fully develop their communication skills.

Some studies maintain that adolescents are the most challenging group of clients to work with in counseling (Hanna, Hanna, & Keys, 1999). For example, adolescents may be reluctant to communicate with adults and often are poorly motivated to improve their communication style (Lambie & Rokutani, 2002; Sommers-Flanagan & Sommers-Flanagan, 1995). For adults, working with adolescents is a form of multicultural counseling because of the unique cognitive, emotional, and social developmental transitions occurring during adolescence (Sommers-Flanagan & Sommers-Flanagan, 1995). Further complicating working with adolescents in family therapy is that they are generally the identified client (IC) and often come to counseling with negative expectations and with their defenses up.

Family therapists need to use different strategies, methods, and approaches to engage the different subsystems within a family (Liddle, 1995). Clinical awareness is necessary for therapists to appropriately match their therapeutic style to the different development levels of the family members (Guldner, 1990). When teens are present in a family configuration, the family therapist needs a clear conceptual understanding of adolescence and developmental psychology in order to establish and maintain a therapeutic relationship. Therapists also need to be more flexible and creative in an effort to join with the adolescent using the young person's style of communication, which is primarily activity and play (Stith, Rosen, McCollum, Coleman, & Herman, 1996). Not surprisingly, research has found that adolescents are more comfortable with counseling activities than with verbal communication (Guldner, 1990).

Among the various approaches to working with adolescents, the use of music has previously been recommended as an effective counseling approach (Erickson, 1998; Guldner, 1990). Similar to music, movies are of interest to most teens and adults, and viewing movies is a "normal" activity. Therefore, families are more likely to complete a therapeutic homework assignment involving viewing a movie together than other traditional counseling homework assignments such as bibliotherapy, the use of books as a therapeutic strategy. Movies can have a more powerful effect on an individual than any other form of art, engendering an array of emotions (Wedding & Boyd, 1997). Viewing movies can help reduce defense mechanisms (Sharp, Smith, & Cole, 2002), and increase the potential for more genuine communication between viewers (i.e., family members). Last, having the therapist and family members view the same movie offers a common shared experience that may strengthen the therapeutic relationship (Sharp et al., 2002).

Cinematherapy is an established therapeutic strategy that involves selecting movies for the counselee(s) to view individually or with a group, followed with therapeutic processing within the subsequent therapy session as a method of supporting therapeutic growth (Berg-Cross, Jennings, & Baruth, 1990; Sharp et al., 2002). Movie Exchange differs from traditional cinematherapy in that the focus is on family interactional processes and interactions (i.e., having family members gather and interact while viewing a video/movie), not the message or theme communicated in the movie.

Significant to the effectiveness of family therapy is a family's ability to transfer therapeutic insight acquired during counseling to everyday interactions. A strategy to promote such application of learning is the use of therapeutic transitional objects. The concept of the transitional object, as originated with Winnicott (1971), referred to children's objects such as teddy bears and blankets that substituted for parental nurturance during a young child's attempt to separate from his or her parents, providing the child with a sense of security (Sadock, Sadock, & Kaplan, 2002). Within this family therapy model, a transitional object is an object such as a videotape or DVD that is acquired within counseling and is used outside of the therapy session by the family in its "normal" interactions to stimulate and reinforce the family's therapeutic learning. In Movie Exchange, this involves viewing a movie. The family comes together to watch the video or DVD, which promotes the family member's recall of the insight gained in counseling, as well as relates the learning to their current context (i.e., everyday life).

Instructions

Effective use of Movie Exchange requires preparation. First, the therapist needs to gather a series of movies he or she feels are appropriate, avoiding movies generally considered inappropriate for adolescents' viewing, such as films containing excessive violence. It is important that the therapist view the potential movies to become familiar with the content and, therefore, be able to discuss a given film with the family. The next step is to construct a list of appropriate movies and periodically update it.

Once the therapist determines that Movie Exchange would be an effective therapeutic strategy for a family, the activity should be presented to the entire family. The therapist first explains the requirements of the activity. These requirements are prescribed, not suggested: (a) the entire family views the movie together during a collectively set, predetermined time between the present and the following counseling session; (b) the family collaboratively selects a movie from the inventory (all family members have a voice in the selection process, but the parents/guardians have the final input); and (c) the family discusses the movie and processes the experience in the subsequent therapy session. It is important that the therapist explains these requirements in the family's "own language" and confirms that all family members agree with and understand their responsibilities related to the activity. A useful strategy to assess the family members' understanding is to have each family member report to the therapist in his or her own words what the expectations are for the activity.

Once the family has agreed to the Movie Exchange homework assignment, the next step is for the family to select a movie. In Movie Exchange, the family is given the list of videotapes/DVDs and selects the movie; the therapist does not select the movie for the family. However, the therapist may provide a recommendation to the family. Once the selection has been made, it is essential that the therapist process the experience with the family in the subsequent therapy session. As mentioned, the focus of the experiential processing is not on the content of the movie, but on the family process. It is important to provide all family members an opportunity to respond to the activity process questions (i.e., circular questioning). Circular questions stimulate family members to think about systemic processing and reciprocal interactions. They promote an attitude of curiosity among the family members, increasing the family's awareness about itself and its interactions. Circular questions examine human differences and are categorized into five types of questions:

1. relationship differences,
2. degree differences,
3. behavior consequences,
4. hypothetical future, and
5. now and then differences (Benson, Schindler-Zimmerman, & Martin, 1991; Fleuridas, Nelson, & Rosenthal, 1986).

Typical process and circular questions include the following:

1. What were the challenges faced in getting everyone (i.e., all the family members) together to watch the movie?
2. What did you like/dislike about the movie?
3. Watching the movie as a family is one activity that all family members can do together. What are some other activities that you do (or could do) as a family?
4. How did you feel about your family's movie selection process? How did you go about choosing which movie to watch?
5. What do you think your parent(s) liked best about this activity? What do you think your child(ren) liked best about this activity?
6. Do you think that having your family gather for an activity such as viewing a movie is something you would like to have occur more often? How often should your family engage in an activity such as this one?
7. On a scale of 1 to 10, how enjoyable was gathering together to watch the movie?
8. What happened prior to your family gathering together to watch the movie? What happened immediately after watching the movie?
9. How do you think it will be the next time your family gathers together to watch a movie?
10. Did your family communicate more before or after gathering together to watch the movie?

It is important for the therapist to process these questions in an open-ended fashion, allowing all members to express their feelings.

Brief Vignette

Movie Exchange has been effective with numerous families with diverse configurations. The following is an example of a multistressed family with a multigenerational history of sexual abuse. The family configuration included the father (Andy) and his thirteen-year-old son (John). Andy had been divorced for approximately five years, and his ex-wife lived across the country with their four children. The previous year, John, Andy's second-oldest child, came to live with him after having severe school behavioral problems (threatened with expulsion) and psychological/emotional difficulties (history of depression, suicide ideation, attention-deficit/hyperactivity disorder [ADHD], and specific learning disabilities [LD]). In addition, John had been sexually molested by his older brother, Willie, who was incarcerated in a juvenile facility for the molestation of his brother and other children in the community. Andy, himself, was sexually molested as a child by his father, who was never prosecuted, and has since discontinued communication with his parents. Andy and John were referred by the school system to family therapy to support John's multiple needs.

Similar to many adolescents, John was not interested in attending family counseling to such an extent that on one occasion Andy was the only person present in the family therapy session because John "refused to come." The therapist worked to engage John in counseling through the use of activities such as drawing on a dry-erase board. It seemed that John felt more comfortable and engaged in therapy when he was involved in an activity rather than just talking, where it often appeared he was in the hot seat. Andy appeared to have a difficult time relating to his son and easily became frustrated and angry; Andy seemed to have a lower frustration tolerance than John. Both John and Andy expressed wanting to spend more time together. However, they seemed to have a difficult time achieving this because of Andy's work (self-employed) and because "something always seemed to come up."

Based on the family's assessed needs, the following counseling goals were established and agreed upon: (a) improve family communication/relationship, (b) increase parental involvement, and (c) clarify and strengthen Andy's role in meeting John's emotional needs. A first step to achieving these goals was simply to get Andy and John to communicate more appropriately. Their current pattern of communication was emotionally laden and critical. Similar to many families, movies seemed to be a common ground for Andy and John. Therefore, Movie Exchange seemed to be a well-suited therapeutic strategy for this family.

The therapist introduced Movie Exchange to the family. Both Andy and John appeared excited about the activity, especially because the family struggled financially and was unable to rent or go to the movies often. The therapist explained the requirements of the activity, and both Andy and John repeated their responsibilities to the therapist in their own words. Next, the therapist provided them with a copy of the movie directory. Andy allowed John to go through the list and select a movie. John selected *Godzilla* (1998), which Andy agreed would be a good choice and enjoyable to watch. Following the selection, Andy and John determined a day and time when they would sit down and watch the movie together (Friday evening at 8:00 p.m.).

At the next counseling session, John seemed more energetic. Upon entering the room, he sat down, leaned over and handed the videotape to the therapist, saying "thank you." The therapist asked both Andy and John if they had any difficulties staying with their predetermined time for viewing the movie. They both said "yes," and explained that Andy got home from work later than he planned and by the time they had eaten dinner and cleaned the dishes, it was 9:00 p.m. However, that was the only challenge and they watched the movie together at 9:00 instead of 8:00. Next, the therapist inquired how they felt about the experience. Andy was pleased about the experience, and John was particularly happy because Andy had followed through with the plan, allowing him time with his father without arguing. The therapist next asked if the family would like to continue this activity and how often they should gather together to watch a movie.

Andy and John said they would like to continue with the activity and possibly increase the activity to twice a week. Both Andy and John expressed that they enjoyed the movie and acknowledged that it provided them with something to talk about without getting frustrated with each other. They said that they would like to continue with Movie Exchange.

The family's in-session interactions appeared to improve, with John becoming more invested in the therapeutic process. In addition, the movie seemed to provide Andy with a subject that allowed him to engage with his son without being "negative" or "critical." Andy reported that it was no longer a challenge to get John to attend family therapy sessions. Once Andy and John's communication and relationship improved, John was better able to express his needs to his father and Andy was better able to hear them.

Movie Exchange was an effective therapeutic intervention with this family. The videotape seemed to serve as a reminder and reinforced the work the family had been doing in therapy. At the conclusion of the therapist's work with this family, he gave them the videotape *Shrek* (2001), a family favorite. Using the videotape as a transitional object, the therapist explained that his hope was that they would be reminded of all the work they had done together in therapy whenever they viewed the movie or just simply saw the videocassette.

Suggestions for Follow-Up

Follow-up in Movie Exchange involves the therapist processing the experience with all the family members (circular questioning). Each time a family is prescribed to view a movie, it is essential that time be allotted during the therapy session to process the activity. The therapist must also remember to collect his or her videotapes/DVDs from the family before another movie is assigned.

Contraindications

This activity can be helpful for almost any family with any problem. It is an especially helpful activity to employ with families who are not spending much time together.

Readings and Resources for the Professional

Dermer, S. B. & Hutchings, J. B. (2000). Utilizing movies in family therapy: Application for individuals, couples, families. *The American Journal of Family Therapy, 28,* 163-180.

Hesley, J. W. & Hesley, J. G. (1998). *Rent two films and let's talk in the morning: Using popular movies in psychotherapy.* New York: John Wiley & Sons.

Mangin, D. (1999, May 27). Cinema therapy: How some shrinks are using movies to help their clients cope with life and just feel better. *Health and Body.* Retrieved on July 10, 2003, from http://www.salon.com/health/feature/1999/05/27/film_therapy/print/html.

Bibliotherapy Sources for the Client

Steinberg, L. A. & Levine, A. (1997). *You and your adolescent, Revised edition: A parent's guide for ages 10 to 20.* New York: Harper Resource.

Vernon, A. & Al-Mabuk, R. (1995). *What growing up is all about: A parents' guide to child and adolescent development.* Champaign, IL: Research Press.

References

Benson, M. J., Schindler-Zimmerman, T., & Martin, D. (1991). Accessing children's perceptions of their family: Circular questioning revisited. *Journal of Marital and Family Therapy, 17,* 363-372.

Berg-Cross, L., Jennings, P., & Baruth, P. (1990). Cinematherapy: Theory and application. *Psychotherapy in Private Practice, 8,* 135-156.

Erickson, M . J. (1998) Teenage clients' favorite music as an aid in therapy. In L. L. Hecker, S. A. Deacon, & Associates (Eds.), *The therapist's notebook: Homework, handouts, and activities for use in psychotherapy* (pp. 375-376). Binghamton, NY: The Haworth Press.

Fleuridas, C., Nelson, T. A., & Rosenthal, D. M. (1986). The evolution of circular questioning: Training family therapists. *Journal of Marital and Family Therapy, 12,* 113-127.

Godzilla. (1998). Produced by D. Devlin. Directed by R. Emmerich. Columbia Tristar Home Video. [Videocassette.]

Guldner, C. A. (1990). Family therapy with adolescents. *Journal of Group Psychotherapy, Psychodrama, and Sociometry, 43,* 142-150.

Hanna, F. J., Hanna, C. A., & Keys, S. G. (1999). Fifty strategies for counseling defiant, aggressive adolescents: Reaching, accepting, and relating. *Journal of Counseling & Development, 77,* 395-404.

Lambie, G. W. & Rokutani, L. J. (2002). A systems approach to substance abuse identification and intervention for school counselors. *Professional School Counseling, 5,* 353-359.

Liddle, H. A. (1995). Conceptual and clinical dimensions of multidimensional, multisystems engagement strategy in family-based adolescent treatment. *Psychotherapy: Theory, Research, Practice, and Training, 32,* 39-58.

Sadock, B. J., Sadock, V. A., & Kaplan, H. I. (2002). *Kaplan and Sadock's synopsis of psychiatry: Behavioral science/clinical psychiatry* (9th ed.). Baltimore, MD: Williams and Wilkins.

Sharp, C., Smith, J. V., & Cole, A. (2002). Cinematherapy: Metaphorically promoting therapeutic change. *Counseling Psychology Quarterly, 15,* 269-276.

Shrek. (2001). Produced by A. Warner, J. H. Williams, & J. Katzenberg. Directed by A. Adamson & V. Jenson. DreamWorks Home Entertainment. [Videocassette.]

Sommers-Flanagan, J. & Sommers-Flanagan, R. (1995). Psychotherapeutic techniques with treatment-resistant adolescents. *Psychotherapy, 32,* 131-140.

Stith, S. M., Rosen, K. H., McCollum, E. E., Coleman, J. U., & Herman, S. A. (1996). The voices of children: Preadolescent children's experiences in family therapy. *Journal of Marital and Family Therapy, 22*, 69-86.

Wedding, D. & Boyd, M. A. (1997). *Movies and mental illness: Using films to understand psychopathology.* Boston: McGraw-Hill College.

Winnicott, D. W. (1971). *Playing and reality.* New York: Basic Books.

Movie List

Batman (1989)
Batman Forever (1995)
Batman Returns (1992)
Beauty and the Beast (Disney, 1991)
Bebe's Kids (1992)
Daredevil (2003)
Dead Poets Society (1989)
Forrest Gump (1994)
Free Willy (1993)
Godzilla (1998)
A Goofy Movie (1995)
Harry Potter and the Chamber of Secrets (2002)
Harry Potter and the Prisoner of Azkaban (2004)
Harry Potter and the Sorcerer's Stone (2001)
Hercules (Disney, 1997)
Hook (1991)
How the Grinch Stole Christmas (2000)
Hunchback of Notre Dame (Disney, 1996)
Ice Age (2002)
Jungle 2 Jungle (1997)
The Jungle Book (1967)
The Land Before Time (1988)
The Last of the Mohicans (1992)
The Lion King (1994)
Lord of the Rings: The Fellowship of the Ring (2001)
Lord of the Rings: The Return of the King (2003)
Lord of the Rings: The Two Towers (2002)
The Matrix (1999)
The Matrix Reloaded (2003)
The Matrix Revolutions (2003)
Mrs. Doubtfire (1993)
The Mummy (1999)
The Mummy Returns (2001)
Parenthood (1989)
Planes, Trains and Automobiles (1987)
The Princess Bride (1987)
Robin Hood (Disney, 1973)
The Rock (1996)
The Santa Clause (1994)
The Santa Clause 2 (2002)
Saving Private Ryan (1998)
Shrek (2001)
Shrek 2 (2004)
Spider-Man (2002)
Spider-Man 2 (2004)
Tarzan (Disney, 1999)
What About Bob? (1991)
X-Men (2000)
X2 (X-Men United) (2003)

– 26 –

The "Puppet Reflecting Team" Technique

Darryl R. Haslam

Type of Contribution: Therapeutic Activity

Objective

The intervention described in this chapter is designed to achieve the effect of a "reflecting team approach" in working with families or individuals through only one therapist (or a pair of therapists). The reflecting team approach is a postmodern model of therapy developed primarily by Tom Andersen (1991) of Norway. The central intervention in this approach involves creating a situation or an environment where the client system can observe itself from a different perspective by listening to reflections offered by a neutral set of observing therapists. At a predetermined segment of a therapeutic session, the team of reflecting therapists would enter the therapy room and offer unrehearsed impressions about the clients while the clients observed them. The reflections are typically offered from a nonknowing, social constructionist stance. After the team has reflected their observations, the clients and the attending therapist discuss the clients' counterimpressions of the team's observations, and incorporate them into the therapeutic process. In this way, clients hear observations about themselves and their problems from an uninvolved group of outside observers. The clients have a chance to see themselves and their problems in a different way.

Rationale for Use

Although the intervention described in this chapter does not claim to replicate a true "reflecting team" approach, it does attempt to offer a more feasible way of achieving a similar effect in session. In order to employ a reflecting team approach per Andersen (1991) and colleagues, a therapist would normally need to have a group of professionals who are trained in theory and method of reflecting teams and are available during a session to perform a reflecting team. While the therapeutic potential of such an intervention should be recognized, the logistics of having such therapist resources in actual clinical settings can be difficult or somewhat impractical to achieve. Because most therapists work in settings where they either practice alone or with other therapists who typically have their own time constraints and sizeable caseloads, the logistics of availability become a problem. At best, a pair of therapists may be able to team up to do cotherapy but even this would still be insufficient to employ a true reflecting team approach. Indeed, training and academic settings may be the only environments where sufficient numbers of therapists can be trained and available to do a traditional reflecting team approach.

Therefore, the following intervention is an adaptation of this approach that can be employed quite easily with one or two therapists. Although it cannot truly replicate the reflecting team approach, it is designed to serve as a more practical version for the average clinician and can at least replicate many of the key components of a "reflecting position" that would be sufficient for clinical impact.

Puppets are used in this intervention because they become excellent mediums that can replicate multiple therapeutic perspectives and have these perspectives attributed to them directly, since puppets are designed to represent or invoke some form of unique character by nature. Indeed, puppets have been used in art and drama for centuries as important elements of human expression (Bratton & Ray, 1999). In recent times, the use of puppets has been documented extensively in therapeutic practice, such as in play therapy with children (Landreth, 1991), group play therapy (Bratton & Ray, 1999), and family play therapy (Gil, 1994).

Instructions

The "Puppet Reflecting Team" intervention involves creating a reflecting experience for a client system by attempting to achieve, in essence, the effect of multiple observers. The intervention uses hand puppets to create the effect of different characters and perspectives in the therapy room as if they were neutral observers to the therapy process.

Therefore, through the medium of puppets, the therapist can offer reflective insights that he or she may feel are more appropriate to be shared by another perspective than directly as the "therapist." In fact, the evocative power of puppets is so luring that many of us can scarcely resist the temptation of animating a hand puppet once we have put it on. Indeed, the shroud of the puppet can often give people permission to let different, freer sides of themselves come out. Thus, the power of puppets in therapy should not be ignored.

An acceptance of the evocative power of puppets is a basic foundation for therapists to have when using this approach. One must also understand the premise that puppets can simulate the presence of multiple perspectives by helping the therapist access different parts of himself or herself in a way that can simulate the interactions of other team members. In this way, the therapist can allow the natural properties of the puppets to open up their own therapeutic creativity.

Introducing the Puppet Team

To employ the intervention in therapy, the therapist must introduce the puppets and convince the clients that they have a life of their own. He or she would bring out a set of puppets, preferably selected in advance, at a certain point in the session when the reflecting team effect is desired. Typically, around midsession would be an ideal time to employ the technique. The therapist would then introduce the "reflecting team" members to the client, as if they were real. This may be done perhaps by calling them a "team of neutral colleagues" or a "standard part of my therapeutic team." The therapist could then introduce their intentions by saying something such as, "They have been observing your case for a while now and want to have a conversation to share their impressions about what *they* think is going on." The therapist would then instruct the clients to sit back and listen to what the puppet team has to say, after which they will be given a chance to discuss their counterimpressions.*

The effect of introducing the puppet team can be further enhanced by having each puppet introduce itself directly to the client, demonstrating its unique character and describing its role on the team. This sort of interaction between the puppets and the clients may initiate some level of relationship-forming quality (as if "real colleagues") and may make it easier for the clients to accept them as distinct entities. Another potential enhancement is to have the set of prechosen puppets already set aside in the room in view, either on a bookcase, desk, or cabinet. In this way, they can metaphorically be watching the session and become a more natural part of the session.

*The exact dialogue and manner of introducing the team can be done in various ways and should be phrased in a manner that is comfortable for the therapist. Ad libs and spontaneity are encouraged and will only add to the realness of the puppet play.

Although these enhancements require some additional imagination and may cause some awkwardness, they can enrich the intervention greatly for those comfortable in using them.

A critical aspect of this intervention is that the therapist must act as if he or she believes the puppets are really part of the therapy process and have their own life to a degree. A halfhearted or unconvincing stance by the therapist will create doubt in the clients' minds about whether the approach will be a productive part of the therapy process.

Conducting the Reflecting Team's Dialogue

After the introduction of the team, the next step would be conducting the actual reflecting team dialogue, the therapist speaking and acting directly through the puppets. Here is where the highest amount of creativity and "dramatic flair" is required of the therapist. The exact interplay of characters and the nature of the clinically relevant reflections offered by them are completely up to the discretion of therapist. Humor could easily be used here, as appropriate, to dramatize or even exaggerate thoughts and attitudes in the family; this can become an amusing way to help them reflect on these attitudes. Strengths and weaknesses, doubts and hopes, and optimistic and pessimistic forecasts can all be displayed by various team members. Again, the intent of a reflecting approach is to allow the client system to see themselves from an observing perspective, rather than a perspective of being directly saturated in their problems. Hopefully, the reflections offered can trigger thoughts or feelings that will become important catalysts for change in future therapy sessions.

The style of the statements used by the team members is also up to the discretion of the therapist. A purely social-constructionst stance would include reflective statements with a more tentative quality, such as "I wonder if . . ." phrases. This attitude would portray a more "nonknowing" perspective by the team. If a more positivistic stance is used, statements would be more direct and may involve phrases such as "I bet . . ." or "I think . . ." Again, the comfort level of the therapist and congruence to his or her theoretical orientation are important factors to be conscious of throughout the approach.

Selection of the Puppets

The selection of the puppets is also a very important factor in using this technique. Depending on the effect the therapist wants to create with the reflecting team, the cadre of puppets chosen should be conducive to that effect. A variety of puppets should be selected in a similar fashion as members of a real reflecting team would be: recruiting a sufficiently diverse set of individuals with unique perspectives and thoughts to create an enriching interplay.

Some puppets are naturally aggressive or ill-tempered, such as "predator puppets" (e.g., alligators, carnivorous dinosaurs, wolves, tigers, sharks, etc.). These puppets can be used for an effect of offering a pessimistic or confrontational perspective on the team. Due to their inherent personalities, reflections they offer could be done in direct and unfettered ways, as appropriate. Such puppets may make paradoxical statements such as "I wonder if the family has too many troubles to deal with and if they are really as messed up as people say." This manner of dialogue may mimic the client's dominant story and allow them to hear it in a direct but insightful way.

This type of puppet can be easily balanced with a more nurturing and optimistic perspective using a docile or tame puppet (e.g., a cat, dog, teddy bear, tropical bird, etc.). Such puppets could offer comforting or reassuring messages such as "I have a different view. I wonder if this family really has a lot more strength than they realize in order to have come this far. They seem to be really interested in working together to find a solution and I believe that good things happen when people work together."

Other types of puppets may produce other effects on the team. Puppets can be used as analytical members (e.g., an owl, a wizard, a doctor, etc.), shy or fearful members (e.g., a mouse, turtle, or other "weak" puppets), or strong and powerful members (e.g., an eagle, lion, etc.). A docile puppet, such as a turtle for instance, can reflect the doubts and fears of the clients as in "people are out to step on them" or "they should just hide in their shells and stay closed in." The effect of a turtle retreating into its shell can reflect fears and avoidant tendencies in clients' real lives, especially if withdrawal or denial is used as a coping mechanism. Strong puppets can express confident or conquering attitudes about problems. Likewise, real-life professional mental health roles can be dramatized. For instance, the therapist can use a "doctor puppet" to state that "she just needs to get on drugs and be done with it," while another puppet (perhaps a "family therapist" puppet) could say, "No, I really think she has the capacity to get out of this on her own."

A couple of methods can be used in selecting the exact cadre of puppets in the preparatory stage of using this technique, whether it be with the same or different clients. One method is to have the same cadre of preselected puppets comprise the team each and every time the intervention is used; the other method is to have the members of the puppet team chosen anew prior to each session in which the intervention is to be used. An advantage of the fomer approach is that consistency could make the role acting easier for the therapist since he or she can become better acquainted with the character that each puppet represents and be more familiar with how they interact together for more realistic dramatizations. An advantage of the latter approach is that it would allow the therapist more flexibility in creating a particular blend of puppets that may match the needs of a particular case or session, thus causing the team makeup to be a more dynamic process. This, however, may also be more difficult since the therapist would need to have sufficient insight and experience in using puppets to accurately discern the best combination of puppets and types of animations desired or needed for each clinical situation.

Other Considerations

The number of puppets a therapist chooses can vary depending on the effect desired and the therapist's comfort level and experience with puppets. Starting off with even two puppets is perfectly acceptable and can be effective. Alternately, a therapist can have more than two puppets but animate only a pair at a time. Although the transitions between puppets may seem awkward, if done confidently and smoothly, there is a high chance they will not detract from the overall interplay. Stuffed animals could also be used and would not require a hand placed inside of them. If a cotherapist were available, then a larger team of puppets (four or more) could be used. As an additional and more divergent adaptation to the approach, one puppet could be used as an effective tool for therapy as a simulated cotherapist. One puppet could not act as a "reflecting team," but it could interplay with the real therapist in a way that could achieve a similar purpose by offering an alternate perspective in therapy.

Puppets both new and used can be purchased from a variety of sources. However, it is strongly recommended that generic puppets be used whenever possible and that popular or trendy puppets be avoided. The rationale behind this distinction is that popular puppets tend to have formalized, preattached personalities in the minds of the therapist and/or clients and may restrict the range of creativity and utility for the therapist, possibly diminishing the potential to be clinically effective. Therapists must decide whether exceptions to this rule are acceptable, but generic puppets tend to be more effective for reflective activities.

Applications to Individuals and Couples

The main variable in applying this approach to different constellations and types of clients would be in the type, manner, and content of the reflective comments devised for the exercise.

Again, this is an area where the therapist's discretion is the most important determining factor and where less specific guidance is given, due to the wide variance and complexity of presenting problems clients bring into therapy.

In use with a single adult client, the reflections would be directed more toward the individual and how he or she functions in the familial and other external systems related to the problem at hand. Likely, the therapist would devise reflections aimed at causing the client to view his or her world and his or her role in it in a significantly different way; this new insight would in turn lead to new reactions and behaviors in the client's relationships with these systems, thus having a systemic impact. The client may need to hear a message of validation that will give him or her confidence in dealing with the problem. Other times, the client may respond well to a paradoxical message where he or she is challenged to not get better in an effort to prove the therapist wrong. Whatever the style or therapeutic stance taken, the goal would be on insight and behavior.

With a couple in therapy, the reflections would still be aimed at the individuals (the partners) but be in the context of helping the couple system see each other and/or their relationship in a significantly different way. Similar to working with an individual, whether a validating or paradoxical approach is taken, the goal is to make an impact in the form of perceptual and behavioral changes in the couple system. For example, the therapist may have the puppets reflect a central problem in the couple's interactions in an effort to allow them to hear it in a different light, given in a third-party format (the reflecting team).

For more assistance and guidance in developing effective reflections in this approach, the reader is encouraged to review sources that discuss the traditional reflecting team model in detail, especially Andersen's (1991) book. This will give the therapist a firmer theoretical and practice base to use this approach in an even more effective way.

Brief Vignette

The following is a real-life case example of how the adaptation previously described (using one puppet to create a cotherapist effect) was used with a deeply troubled girl in a family session.

The family consisted of a father, a six-year-old daughter, and a five-year-old son. The presenting problem involved the children experiencing adjustment difficulties related to the recent divorce of their parents; this was complicated by frequent periods of no or unpredictable contact with the mother and often distressing encounters with her when they did have them. At one point in a family session, the girl became overcome with emotion, suddenly shut down, and refused to engage in the therapy session. Her major coping style was avoidant in nature, so we had seen similar behavior before. However, on this occasion, she became particularly shut down, burying her face in her lap and crying to the point that it stopped the flow of the therapy process. The therapist sensed that her sadness was related to issues of grief and abandonment related to her mother and felt that it would be beneficial for her to acknowledge them. However, the girl had become so unresponsive that any efforts by the therapist or her father to elicit responsiveness from her completely failed.

The therapist decided to use a box of puppets that were already in the room to employ a therapeutic intervention intended to help her express (or at least normalize) her grief in session. The therapist looked through the box of puppets and found a "Papa Smurf"* puppet to become the new cotherapist. This puppet was selected due to its availability at the time and its representation

*Although some readers will surely remember the Smurfs former popularity on TV and may see this puppet as "trendy" (as previously advised against), the Smurf shows are old enough that most children tend not to be extremely familiar with them and most adults would not be sufficiently attached to them to expect a particular character representation of Papa Smurf; therefore, the therapist felt this exception was acceptable.

of wisdom and reflective insight that the therapist hoped would be an appropriate ingredient to add to the situation.

The therapist animated Papa Smurf first by having him move around the family and introduce himself. After some initial amusement from the father and son, the therapist began using the reflections. The therapist asked the puppet, "What do you think is going on for [the girl] right now?" The therapist had Papa Smurf offer some empathic remarks to show that he was a compassionate observer, such as "I can see that she is very sad." The therapist and Papa Smurf then dialogued about some general theories about why the little girl was so sad. Papa Smurf said things such as "I think she's very hurt about her mother not being around anymore" and "I bet she's sad about her mom not contacting her more. She may even think that it's her fault." Other general observations came out through the dialogue as the therapist used the puppet to speculate about thoughts and feelings that may be related to the girl's own experience.

At several times the dad nodded spiritedly in agreement to the observations that Papa Smurf offered, and the girl's countenance slowly became less withdrawn. After about ten minutes of Papa Smurf in the session, she finally blurted out, "I hate my mother!" Then she paused and made another statement: "I'm mad that she doesn't come and see me more!" Then she withdrew again and cried. The therapist was very pleased with this breakthrough and did not try to bring her out again. He used Papa Smurf to make some final statements to validate her feelings and express appreciation for her courage (e.g., "I bet a lot of girls feel sad when they miss their mommy," and "I can sure understand why those mad feelings are inside of you"). The session ended soon after this.

In this example, the puppet became a vehicle of reflection for the girl and her feelings. She was able to hear a "neutral observer's" observations about her experience, which allowed her to gain the courage to overcome her avoidance and engage her pain in the session. Although she had been completely unresponsive to the father and therapist only a moment earlier, she saw herself or the therapeutic environment differently when Papa Smurf was there. Even if the therapist, rather than Papa Smurf, had directly offered similar reflections to the girl, it is doubtful that it would have been as successful (or successful at all) since she had typically resisted his efforts in the past. Instead, the intervention allowed the girl to make a significant step in acknowledging and working through her issues with her mother. Thus the puppet created a neutral context to offer a more unbiased perspective in the room, an effect that attempted to emulate the spirit behind Andersen's "reflecting team."

Although certain dynamic differences will exist in this example, as opposed to the multiple-puppet approach described earlier in this chapter, the basic way of applying the puppets in session, as well as the potential impact, would be quite similar.

Suggestions for Follow-Up

Typically this intervention is not intended to be the sole intervention in one's therapeutic work with clients but used as a complement to an insight-oriented style of therapy. As time permits at the end of the session in which this technique is used, the therapist should process with the client system about their initial reactions to the "puppet reflecting team." Future sessions could then continue the work of processing the experience by discussing any insights received from the reflecting team along with insights gained through other therapeutic methods. The "puppet reflecting team" could then be used as many times as needed to create the reflecting position with the clients.

Contraindications

This intervention is ideally designed for insight-oriented approaches to therapy and with clients who are able—mentally, emotionally, and psychologically—to engage in insight-oriented work. Because the act of being able to recognize and assimilate insights from the "puppet reflecting team" requires cognitive processing, some clients may be less apt to respond to this approach, especially those with cognitive or mental deficits.

Moreover, the attitude of the therapist in approaching this intervention is critical. The therapist needs to act comfortable in the medium of puppets and in using his or her own spontaneity and creativity in the approach. In order to make the puppets believable, a therapist would need to get into the act of making the puppets come to life. In this way, he or she would need to treat them as if they were really separate members of the treatment system and act out their parts as realistically as possible, giving the illusion that the reflections indeed are coming from them. Having said this, professional acting ability is not required, only an attitude in the therapist that is flexible, creative, and willing to do play acting with his or her clients. While adult clients will never be fooled into believing the puppets truly have their own personalities separate from the therapist's thoughts and motives, they can accept the illusion if done in a sufficiently convincing way. If the therapist did not act as if the puppets were real or acted awkwardly toward them, then the family will probably have difficulty accepting the puppets as legitimate. Therefore, characteristics of the therapist can enhance or hinder this approach.

Naturally, this intervention would work ideally with children or families with young children (many parents being open to using play in therapy due to the presence of their children); however, this would not necessarily be the only case. In working with dyads or families consisting of adults or adolescents, this approach could still be quite appropriate and effective. Play-oriented approaches have been used successfully with adults in many clinical situations and problems; moreover, adults are not incapable of accessing the parts of their selves that allow them to play and use imagination. Certainly, some adults have distanced those parts of their selves more than others and may be less readily able to "go there." However, a skilled clinical assessment should be able to ascertain which types of adult clients this intervention could be used with and/or how much preparatory work would be needed first. For those adults who are willing to use this medium as a therapeutic intervention, it can become a powerful approach and have profound therapeutic effects, since it is capable of accessing deep feelings and thoughts not always as available in verbally based approaches.

In the author's experience in using play-oriented approaches with adults, even if they show some initial reluctance to engage in play, they often eventually become willing to do so with appropriate therapist prompting. Once they actually engage, they tend to do very effective projective work.

Conclusion

In summary, the "Puppet Reflecting Team" activity is an innovative and effective way of creating a "reflecting team" effect by incorporating the illusion of multiple perspectives in therapy with only one therapist and the use of puppets. It utilizes elements of play in a clinically effective way that is versatile, both in being adaptable to various clinical situations and environments and in being successful with both children and adult clients. It draws from the natural creativity of the therapist and allows him or her to use parts of himself or herself not as readily able to be expressed—thus enhancing the therapy process. Clients in the reflecting position, in turn, can see their behaviors or situations in a different light and be able to use that insight for future therapeutic progress.

Readings and Resources for the Professional

Kaudson, H. & Schaefer, C. (1997). *101 favorite play therapy techniques*. Northvale, NJ: Jason Aronson.

Webb, N. B. (Ed.). (1999). *Play therapy with children in crisis, Second edition: Individual, group and family treatment*. New York: Guilford Press.

Bibliotherapy Sources For the Client

General books or articles about puppetry (of which there are many) seem to be written for a more general audience, addressing the use of puppets in entertainment or storytelling. None known to this author are written specifically for consumers of the therapeutic use of puppets. Any resources that did fit in the latter category would most likely be addressed to a professional therapeutic audience, not to clients.

References

Andersen, T. (Ed.). (1991). *The reflecting team: Dialogues and dialogues about dialogues*. New York: W. W. Norton & Co.

Bratton, S. C. & Ray, D. (1999). Group puppetry. In D. S. Sweeney & L. E. Homeyer (Eds.), *The handbook of group play therapy: How to do it, how it works, whom it's best for* (pp. 267-277). San Francisco: Jossey-Bass, Inc.

Gil, E. (1994). *Play in family therapy*. New York: Guilford Press.

Landreth, G. (1991). *Play therapy: The art of the relationship*. Muncie, IN: Accelerated Development, Inc.

– 27 –

"Eyes on the Prize": Incorporating Cultural Knowledge into Goal Development for the African-American Family with a Child with Serious Emotional Disturbance

Nicole Lynn Lee

Type of Contribution: Activity/Handout

Objective

African-American families have a rich and diverse history in America. During their enslavement, they developed coping mechanisms that enabled them to survive the hardships of confinement while flourishing into a family-centered community with rich traditions. Many of these coping mechanisms were predicated on the belief that eventually good would prevail and things "would be all right." Thus the motto "keep your eyes on the prize" became a rallying cry for the importance of having a goal and remaining cognizant of that goal.* Today, African-American families are not physically enslaved, yet many still suffer from the legacies of physical confinement and subsequent Jim Crow laws. However, regardless of their situation, many African-American families still face hardships with the belief that things "will be all right." Keep your eyes on the prize still resonates and serves as a rallying cry for the community.

The purpose of this activity is to demonstrate a new approach for goal development for African-American families with children with serious emotional disturbance (SED), one that incorporates the historical experiences of African Americans into the process. This chapter explains how mental health practitioners may work in partnership with family members to create tangible goals using a "Prize Sheet."

It is important to preface this chapter with a statement concerning the variability of the African-American community. This chapter summarizes beliefs that have existed within the African-American community; however, the author does not imply that all members share these beliefs. African Americans represent a diverse segment of society. This chapter should serve as a guide for work with African-American families, not as a mutually exclusive body of knowledge.

---

*The phrase "eyes on the prize" is an expression that has meaning in the African-American community. It is also the name of a documentary produced by Blackside, Inc. (1987) that chronicled the civil rights movement. This is found in the reference list under Hampton, 1987.

Rationale for Use

Children labeled as emotionally disordered have increased risk for behavioral, academic, and social difficulties. These difficulties can significantly reduce a child's ability to function effectively in family, school, social, and community roles. For instance, some children with emotional disorders have poor self-management, trouble following time limits, less proficiency in peer group activities, and difficulty managing anger and following rules (e.g., Riley, Ensminger, Green, & Kang, 1998). Children with SED experience academic difficulties including lower grade point averages and higher school absenteeism than children within the general population (Riley et al., 1998; Wagner, 1995). In addition, there is evidence to demonstrate that behaviorally disordered children may have lower levels of self-esteem (Dumont & Provost, 1999; Nielsen & Metha, 1994) and may feel stigmatized by continuously being labeled "emotionally disturbed," "troubled," or "bad."

In addition to these characteristics, African-American families who have children with SED may experience additional difficulties related to the stresses of discrimination, poverty, or insensitive organizational practices (e.g., Stern, Smith, & Jang, 1999; Wright & Anderson, 1998). Often, African-American families with children with SED are hesitant to participate in the therapeutic process. Families may have concerns that clinicians will identify their family dynamics, family communication patterns, and lifestyle as deviant or problematic. For instance, African-American families may be concerned that a white or even a middle-class African-American clinician will identify a single-parent or grandmother-headed family as abnormal and the cause of SED instead of being "alternative forms of family organization" (Sudarkasa, 1996, p. 29). African-American families may feel that a clinician will not see or understand the benefits of alternate forms of family organization. In addition, African-American families may be fearful that clinicians unfamiliar with them may not understand their traditional communication patterns or type of discipline. For instance, the African-American community has traditionally valued an expressive communication style. Stories are sometimes told by white bystanders of the "angry black parent" hitting his or her child at the grocery store or the "uppity black woman" confronting authority figures while her children watch. However, these persons may just be using the communication skills deemed necessary to survive in a predominately white world.

Other reasons can also explain why African-American families may be hesitant to come to therapy. Many of these reasons center on families' fears of intrusiveness by the clinician as well as the fear of exposing private matters in a way that emphasizes what is negative about family functioning, instead of what is positive about family functioning. Furthermore, African-American families may feel hesitant about the therapeutic process because of past misunderstandings with clinicians or perceived discrimination from service providers (Hill-Collins, 2000). These experiences may have been exacerbated by an inability of clinicians to develop rapport with African-American families. For instance, developing a partnership with African-American families instead of a "practitioner as expert" model improves the communication between clinician and family and helps to build trust.

The Prize Sheet is important and valuable for use with African-American families with a child with SED because the Prize Sheet

begins with an acknowledgement of strengths instead of deficits,
uses an already understood metaphor,
makes African-American families partners in the therapeutic process,
emphasizes the use of traditional coping skills that have garnered past success for the family, and
acknowledges the importance of visualization.

The Prize Sheet is grounded in the Africentric, strengths, and empowerment perspectives, perspectives that have proven successful with African-American families (e.g., Gutierrez, 1990; Gutierrez, GlenMaye, & DeLois, 1995; Gutierrez, Oh, & Gillmore, 2000).

The Africentric perspective is an emerging paradigm that brings the beliefs, values, and customs of African-American people into the scholarly literature (Schiele, 1997). The Africentric perspective posits that all things are connected; the individual is important, but the family and community are paramount and shape the individual (Schiele, 2000). The empowerment and strength perspectives encourage marginalized individuals and groups to acknowledge and cultivate their strengths and talents and use these to improve themselves as well as their communities (Gutierrez, 1990; Saleebey, 1996, 1997). This mandate underscores the responsibility that the individual has to the larger society. It also posits that in order to understand the individual, the practitioner must understand the individual's environment (Lee, 1996). Instead of "blaming the victim" for his or her deficiencies, the empowerment perspective seeks to understand how the individual's environment contributes to his or her specific circumstances (Lee, 1996). In summary, the Africentric, strengths, and empowerment perspectives are congruent with work with African-American families.

The Prize Sheet is similar to other goal development activities. However, this goal development activity is rooted in an important and relevant metaphor. In addition, the Prize Sheet uses language that articulates the child and family's ability to impact their community.

Instructions

An important part of completing the Prize Sheet is to make sure that the clinician has established a rapport with the family. Establishing rapport is an important process and increases the probability that the clinician and the family will establish an environment of trust. Unfortunately, due to space limitations, establishing rapport is not covered in this chapter; however, a list of books and articles that discuss this topic are listed at the end of the chapter.

Step 1: We've Gotten This Far

The purpose of this step is to make an assessment or inventory of the family and child's strengths. The goal is to evaluate these strengths independent of the child's SED. Family members must think of one nice quality about the family and the child. The clinician is not ignoring the SED; rather, the clinician begins by acknowledging that the child and family have "gotten this far together."* If families have difficulty thinking about strengths, the clinician may ask the family to think about the hardships they have experienced and how they "got through them." It is important to consider nontraditional resources such as a strong female-headed household. Further, it is important to consider personal as well as community resources available to the family.

Step 2: Prize Identification

The clinician asks the child and family to visualize a prize, something that would bring honor to the family and community. If the child could accomplish ___ the child and family could contribute ___ to the community. As the Africentric perspective articulates, it is important to acknowledge the child and family's connection to the community. In essence, the child and family work toward a prize that can benefit the family as well as the community.

*"We've come this far by faith" is an expression commonly heard in African-American churches.

The clinician must help family members choose a prize that is realistic. To facilitate the process, the clinician may ask clarifying questions to help the family fine-tune their selection of a prize.

Step 3: Resource Gap Identification

Child and family strengths were identified in the first step. This step provides an opportunity for the child and family to think about barriers that exist that may prevent them from achieving their prize. Barriers could be physical, environmental, or even mental. It is important to include structural barriers such as racism or other forms of discrimination experienced by the family. After the family identifies barriers, the child, family, and clinician think about what they could substitute to overcome or ameliorate the barriers. The emphasis is on nontraditional resources, such as grandparents, the church, and women's groups.

Step 4: Prize Steps or Action Steps

Action steps are the actual steps that the entire family will take to help the child and, ultimately, the community. These steps are specific and should include a notation identifying the person responsible for certain actions. However, it is important to remember that although individual family members may be listed to perform certain duties, it is the entire family unit that works together. As articulated in the Africentric perspective, helping one involves collective action.

Step 5: Evaluating the Prize

The child and family think about the prize and action steps that were identified. Then they decide how they will keep themselves motivated and what success will look like. In essence, this step involves the child and family making decisions about how they will monitor and evaluate their work. For instance, the family may decide to share a small cake or even have their success announced in a church bulletin or newsletter.

At the end of each step, the clinician should paraphrase what members agreed to do and write it on the Prize Sheet. Then, the clinician should ask each member whether the paraphrased account is accurate. This allows the family to clarify comments as well as receive feedback from the clinician. After the Prize Sheet is completed, the clinician should make copies and distribute them to all participants.

It is important to remember that the process is just as important as the prize. The process provides opportunities for the child and family to communicate with each other. Family members may learn things about one another as well as identify previously unarticulated strengths. This also provides opportunities for the family to work on a structured task together while receiving feedback from a trained third party (the clinician).

Variations

There are several variations. The practitioner may work with the family over a series of sessions to develop the prize. The "family" may consist of biological parents or nonbiological members depending on who has custody and is invested in the child's life. Also, if the clinician works with a family that includes small children, the children may be too young to verbalize certain feelings. In this case, the clinician may ask the child to draw or act out a potential prize. This way, the child remains involved in the process. Finally, the clinician may decide to change the existing Prize Sheet or develop a different one. However, it is important to retain the heart of the activity, the prize metaphor.

Brief Vignette

The Clarke family, consisting of Leroy, the father, Teisha, the stepmother, Ted, the son, and Tyis, a newborn, came to therapy because Ted, age twelve, who had been labeled as severely emotionally disturbed (SED), was verbally abusive to his stepmother. Ted was impulsive, had frequent crying spells, and had attempted suicide. After an initial referral to a psychiatrist, the entire family decided that they were ready to begin family therapy.

After the first session, it was clear to the clinician that the family had difficulty communicating with one another. Whenever Ted attempted to speak, his father interrupted with negative comments about Ted's behavior. At the end of the first session, the clinician asked the participants if they would mind filling out a Prize Sheet. Ted seemed very interested in the Prize Sheet and wanted more information. Leroy said, "See, Ted only is interested when it benefits him." The clinician replied, "This is a Prize Sheet for everyone, an opportunity for us to think about the positive things about your family and then think about one goal we will work toward."

During the next session, the family and clinician completed the Prize Sheet. At first, it seemed that Leroy would again monopolize the conversation. However, Leroy did not; rather, he seemed very interested in what Ted had to say about him. When asked about family member strengths, Ted commented that his father was a good athlete. His father seemed surprised by Ted's comments and responded that one of Ted's strengths was that he took care of his baby sister. Teisha began to discuss how Ted had rocked the baby to sleep several nights ago. Ted seemed surprised that Teisha noticed and said, "You saw me do that?"

The family continued discussing strengths. Leroy said that Ted was strong willed and could be a leader if he got himself together. Ted rolled his eyes and the clinician noticed that Leroy was about to make a derogatory remark. The clinician quickly said, "Ted, why that look? I don't understand what that means. Can you explain?" Ted said, "I can't be no leader." The clinician asked Leroy to explain why he thought Ted could be a leader. Leroy stammered at first but then began to discuss Ted's strengths.

After Leroy finished, the atmosphere seemed more relaxed. Ted did not make eye contact with his family or the clinician, but his face was less tense and he occasionally had a slight smile.

Next, the clinician and family began to discuss potential "prizes." Leroy suggested that a good prize would be for Ted to decrease his angry outbursts. Ted seemed distracted and when asked how he was feeling he said, "It's always my fault. I'm the problem." The clinician listened to Ted. He had interpreted his father's statements as an indictment against him. He believed, once again, that he was the source of all of the difficulties instead of a symptom of the family's communication and functioning difficulties.

The clinician saw this as an opportunity to reiterate the philosophy behind the Prize Sheet. Specifically, the clinician reiterated to the family that the prize is something that the entire family will work to achieve. After a brief discussion, the family decided that the prize would be a reduction in angry outbursts for the entire family unit. To achieve this, the family said that one action step would be to have weekly family meetings during which family members had the opportunity to discuss weekly events with one another.

The primary purpose of the Prize Sheet is to develop and obtain goals; however, the process is as important as the product. The Prize Sheet becomes a communication tool, a way for participants to acknowledge one another while working toward a common prize. This example demonstrates how the Prize Sheet was used to help family members discuss family strengths and past and current family practices. Sometimes family members, particularly family members living with a child labeled SED, may have difficulty identifying and articulating strengths to one another. After completing the Prize Sheet, family members had a greater understanding of their strengths and their value to the family unit. This case also demonstrates how important it is to reiterate that each family member has a responsibility to the family. Ted believed that he was responsible for family difficulties; however, the Prize Sheet activity helped Ted to begin the process of believing that he was not the sole cause of family difficulties.

Future sessions included the family reporting information from their weekly meetings. Ted took the responsibility of copying and distributing revised copies of the Prize Sheet. In summary, the Prize Sheet provided a plan that the family used to "chart" their strengths, desired goals, and accomplishments.

Suggestions for Follow-Up

Follow-up consists of tracking the family's progress. An important part of follow-up is for the clinician to provide motivation. For example, if the family is having difficulty obtaining a prize, they may need to reevaluate and modify their prize. The clinician should use a strengths perspective and help the family feel proud of the work that they have done while encouraging the family to continue the process.

Contraindications

The "Eyes on the Prize" metaphor is well understood within the African-American community. However, non-African-American clinicians need to make sure that they do not use this activity in a way that is insensitive to African-American families. The prize metaphor may seem condescending if a person unfamiliar with the African-American community uses it. The clinician must conduct a self-analysis and determine if he or she is comfortable using a metaphor that is part of the African-American experience.

Readings and Resources for the Professional

Beckett, J. (1994). *Cross-cultural communication: A video/workbook self-instructional training package.* Richmond: Virginia Geriatric Education Center, Virginia Commonwealth University, Medical College of Virginia.

Blundo, R. (2001). Learning strengths-based practice: Challenging our personal and professional frames. *Families in Society: The Journal of Contemporary Human Services, 82,* 296-304.

Costello, J., Angold, A., & Keeler, G. (1999). Adolescent outcomes of childhood disorders: The consequences of severity and impairment. *Journal of the American Academy of Child and Adolescent Psychiatry, 38,* 121-129.

Goldstein, H. (1997). Victors or victims? In D. Saleebey (Ed.), *The strengths perspective in social work practice* (2nd ed., pp. 21-35). New York: Longman Publishers.

Lane, K., Gresham, F., & O'Shaughnessy, T. (2002). Identifying, assessing, and intervening with children with or at risk for behavioral disorders: A look to the future. In K. Lane, F. Gresham, & T. O'Shaughnessy (Eds.), *Interventions for children with or at risk for emotional and behavioral disorders* (pp. 317-324). Boston: Allyn & Bacon.

Livingston, R. (1999). Cultural issues in diagnosis and treatment of ADHD. *Journal of the American Academy of Child Psychiatry, 38,* 1591-1594.

Reid, R., DuPaul, G. J., Power, T. J., Anastopoulos, A. D., Rogers-Adkinson, D., Noll, M. B., & Riccio, C. (1998). Assessing culturally different students for attention deficit hyperactivity disorder using behavior rating scales. *Journal of Abnormal Child Psychology, 26,* 187-198.

Walrath, C., Sharp, M., Zuber, M., & Leaf, P. J. (2001). Serving children with SED in urban systems of care: Referral agency differences in child characteristics in Baltimore and the Bronx. *Journal of Emotional and Behavioral Disorders, 9,* 94-105.

References

Dumont, M. & Provost, M. (1999). Resilience in adolescents: Protective role of social support, coping strategies, self-esteem, and social activities on experience of stress and depression. *Journal of Youth and Adolescence, 28,* 343-364.

Gutierrez, L. (1990). Working with women of color: An empowerment perspective. *Social Work, 35,* 149-154.

Gutierrez, L., GlenMaye, L., & DeLois, K. (1995). The organizational context of empowerment practice: Implications for social work administration. *Social Work, 40,* 249-258.

Gutierrez, L., Oh, H., & Gillmore, R. (2000). Toward an understanding of empowerment for HIV/AIDS prevention with adolescent women. *Sex Roles: A Journal of Research, 2,* 581-612.

Hampton, H. (Producer). (1987). *Eyes on the prize: America's civil right's years (1954-1965)* [Motion picture]. United States: Blackside Publishing.

Hill-Collins, P. (2000). Core themes in black feminist thought. In P. Hill-Collins (Ed.), *Black feminist thought: Knowledge consciousness, and the politics of empowerment* (2nd ed., pp. 45-201). New York: Routledge.

Lee, J. (1996). The empowerment approach to social work practice. In F. Turner (Ed.), *Social work treatment: Interlocking theoretical approaches* (4th ed., pp. 218-249). New York: The Free Press.

Nielsen, D. & Metha, A. (1994). Parental behavior and adolescent self-esteem in clinical and nonclinical samples. *Adolescence, 29,* 525-543.

Riley, A., Ensminger, M., Green, B., & Kang, M. (1998). Social role functioning by adolescents with psychiatric disorders. *Journal of the American Academy of Child and Adolescent Psychiatry, 37,* 620-629.

Saleebey, D. (1996). The strengths perspective in social work practice: Extensions and cautions. *Social Work, 41,* 296-304.

Saleebey, D. (1997). Introduction: Power in the people. In D. Saleebey (Ed.), *The strengths perspective in social work practice* (2nd ed., pp. 3-18). New York: Longman Publishers.

Schiele, J. (1997). The contour and meaning of Afrocentric social work. *Journal of Black Studies, 27*(6), 800-820.

Schiele, J. (2000). *Human services and the Afrocentric paradigm.* Binghamton, NY: The Haworth Press.

Stern, S., Smith, C., & Jang, S. (1999). Urban families and adolescent mental health. *Social Work Research, 23*(1), 15-27.

Sudarkasa (1996). *The strength of our mothers: African and African American women and families essays and speeches.* Trenton, NJ: Africa World Press.

Wagner, M. (1995). Outcomes for youths with serious emotional disturbance in secondary school and early adulthood. *The Future of Children, 5,* 90-112.

Wright, O. & Anderson, J. (1998). Clinical social work practice with urban African American families. *Families in Society, 79,* 197-205.

"Eyes on the Prize" Goal Formation Steps

Step 1: We've Gotten This Far

What skills have helped us to get here? What current skills does each family member possess? It is important to consider nontraditional resources such as a strong female-headed household. Furthermore, it is important to consider personal resources as well as community resources available to the family.

If families have difficulty thinking about strengths, the clinician may ask the family to think about the hardships they have experienced and how they got through them.

Step 2: Prize Identification

The clinician may want to ask the family to remain silent for a few minutes and think about a prize. He or she may also want to use miracle statements/questions to determine the prize: "If I could do [this prize] I could help my family and my community do ___."

Using information gathered from miracle questions/statements, negotiate with the family to find out the most realistic change that is possible. This helps to develop a tangible "prize." Prize should be measurable (e.g., behavioral) and feasible. If the family develops a goal that is not feasible, the clinician should ask questions such as "Specifically, what are the steps to accomplishing this prize?" and "If I had to accomplish this prize, what would I do?"

Also, the clinician wants to connect how this prize could help the family and community. This helps the client to put the proposed prize into perspective and examine its feasibility and practicality. It also makes the family responsible for considering the potential long-term implications of the prize. Critical yet supportive questioning can be empowering. The "identified" problem might be present in the child labeled as SED; however, the entire family must take responsibility for the prize. Specifically, everyone has to contribute to attaining the prize.

Step 3: Resource Gap Identification—"What Keeps Us from the Prize?"

Permanent changes are possible but require time and resources in place to sustain them. If the family is going to make the identified change and get the prize, do they have the resources available to do so? If not, are there substitutes that can fulfill the need(s)? This is important and is a second test to determine if the identified change is realistic based on existing resources. This is also an opportunity to understand the family's beliefs about their community and if they believe their resources are limited due to exposure to racism, sexism, or classism.

Step 4: Prize Steps or Action Steps—Developing Action Steps or Task-Setting

What are the actual steps that the family will take to fulfill the goals? These should be small, specific, and measurable. They should logically lead to the larger goal. For example, if the goal is to improve grades, all of the steps should get the child closer to his or her goal. As with step three, the practitioner should make sure that the action steps are feasible and culturally appropriate. Step four should also include a discussion about how the client is feeling. Often, practitioners working with children develop goals based on behavioral indicators because behaviors are easier to witness than cognitions. Internal functioning is important, and the practitioner should ask questions to determine if action steps will help the client develop higher self-esteem and self-concept. Specifically, do goals and their subsequent action steps contain activities that help the client develop mastery of skills, improve feelings about himself or herself and what he or she is capable of, and motivate him or her to continue the process?

Step 5: Evaluating the Prize

This step involves a discussion that specifies what success looks like. How will the family know that they have attained the prize, and what happens if they do not attain it? It is important to think about the indicators and assess their cultural relevancy. This helps to evaluate their progress. In addition to monitoring and evaluation, the family must also think about how they will celebrate their successes. This celebration may involve other family or community members.

EYES ON THE PRIZE

As a family we have sacrificed . . .
but we realize
that our eyes
will never leave our prize.

Step 1: We've Come This Far
Step 2: What's the Prize?
Step 3: What Keeps Us from the Prize?
Step 4: Miles to Go: Family Action Steps
Step 5: Realizing the Dream: How Will We Monitor and Evaluate? How Will We Celebrate?

Toward a Culturally and Spiritually Consonant Treatment of Native Hawaiians: An Integration of Family Therapy and *Ho'oponopono*

Bill Forisha
Carol Wright
Margaret Tucker

Type of Contribution: Activity

Objective

The objective of this activity is to explore therapeutic interventions that are relatively more consonant with indigenous or traditional healing and religious practices than interventions derived solely from mainstream approaches to family therapy. In so doing, this activity seeks to answer the call of the Association for Multicultural Counseling and Development for developing culturally appropriate intervention strategies and techniques (Hurdle, 2002). Similarly, McGoldrick and Giordano (1996) call for "a radically new conceptual model of clinical intervention," one that facilitates the resolution of conflicts within the family as well as cultural conflicts between the family and the professional community (p. 20). Such a model, according to these authors, requires the conscious selection and utilization of particular values, beliefs, and ways of being and acting that have broad appeal. It is the intention of this activity to realize these requirements in a cross-cultural integration of selected spiritual and therapeutic concepts and processes.

Rationale For Use

In Hawaii, the challenge of providing culturally consonant therapy must be met within a historical context that entails the triumph of one culture and the collapse or disintegration of another. Such social upheavals are painful and people suffer the effects of the physical, economic, social, and psychological challenges inherent therein for many generations (Mokuau & Matsuoka, 1995). According to the United States *Census of the Population* (2000), 6.6 percent of the population of Hawaii identify themselves as being solely of Hawaiian descent; however, this figure rises to 23.3 percent as people identify themselves as being of Hawaiian descent in combination with one or two other peoples of Pacific Islander descent. These persons have a higher rate of suicide, depression, substance abuse, imprisonment, and death than any other ethnically identifiable portion of Hawaii's diverse population (Marsella, Mokihana, Oliveira, Plümmer, &

The authors wish to thank Kamuela Ka'Ahanui, PhD, of the Department of Education, Antioch University Seattle, for his willingness to lend both his personal and professional assistance to the production of this paper.

Crabbe, 1998; McCubbin, Thompson, Thompson, Elver, & McCubbin, 1994). In other words, the loss of their lives, land, language, and traditions continue to impact on the current psychological and physical health of Native Hawaiians. Counseling that ignores these collective losses may only serve to increase rather than decrease the ability of families to cope with the present circumstances within which they conduct their lives.

Psychosocial Outlook

The Native Hawaiian worldview entails an intersection of four elements: person, family, nature, and the spirit world. These elements are not wholly separate entities but are, in fact, interconnected and exist as a psychic unity (Marsella et al., 1998). In addition to this unity, the attempt to achieve a state of balance and purity in one's life is known as *pono* and is a culturally supported goal (Ito, 1985a). In this state of balance, one feels a sense of *lokahi* or harmony with the world as well as a kind of physical and psychological contentment (Marsella et al., 1998). This harmony is nurtured in the family by placing the group's needs over the individual's needs and by being of service to others. It is nurtured in nature by conserving and caring for the land and it is nurtured in the spirit world by respecting the gods through ritual and *pule* or prayer (Ito, 1985a).

According to Ito (1985a), Native Hawaiians see themselves as connected to one another by "emotional bonds that support and protect each member" (p. 302). These bonds are the essence of Hawaiian interpersonal relationships and would seem to resemble a web in which all members are connected. These bonds are sustained and nourished by a generosity of self that ensures they thrive with *aloha* or love, *na'au* or sincerity, and *pumehana* or warmth. Living with a generosity of spirit also ensures that the same quality of affect and good fortune will be reciprocated through any number of these ties. *Hala* or selfishness or jealousy or any persistent negative emotion and/or an act of transgression, however, may not only impede the exchange of positive affect but also create a reciprocal negative exchange that may culminate in a *hihia* or entanglement (Ito, 1985a).

The larger one's web of connection or network, the more protected the individual (Ito, 1985a). It is for this reason that children are thought to be most vulnerable, as they have had insufficient time to create their networks and, thereby, the opportunity to cultivate protection against ill fortune. Until they can construct their networks, the parental bonds keep them safe—unless these bonds become entangled through negative exchanges (Ito, 1985a). When illness, injury, calamity, or even untimely death occur, they may be seen as public manifestations of this negative effect. More than being viewed as causative, these are, in fact, messages from God or from the ancestors, warning the individual that he or she is taking the wrong road. If the negative effect continues, an individual's connection to the familial network might be at risk (Ito, 1985a; Marsella et al., 1998).

Families and the Family Schema

The primary social unit in Native Hawaiian society is the *'ohana* or family. Its composition includes the immediate family, the extended family, those affiliated by marriage, those chosen to join the family, and the *'aumakua* or ancestors (Arsenault, 2000). The family schema is comprised of mutually shared and interconnected beliefs about family structure and function, self, community, spiritual and material nature, and time (McCubbin et al., 1994). For instance, *Kupuna* or grandparents are respected and revered for their knowledge and wisdom and for being the conduits of Hawaiian culture to the next generation (Arsenault, 2000; Shook, 1985). They often take on the role of primary caretakers. In fact, a senior person of either gender may, by informal consensus, play the role of *po'o* or head of household. Although all family members are seen as being responsible for the psychological and spiritual—and even to some extent financial—well-being of the family, the *po'o* is seen as being relatively more responsible (Arsenault, 2000). All youth and adult family members are expected to help with the children and support parents during crises. Interestingly, it is believed that one of the effects of persistent negative emotions is that a child may be singled out for retribution. If this occurs, restoring harmony or *kokahi* to the unity of self, family, nature, and spirit world—for the sake of an individual child—becomes the task of the whole family (McCubbin et al., 1994).

Ho'oponopono and Family Therapy

Ho'oponopono, or to make right through active participation, is an eloquent method of conflict resolution by which grievances may be aired and harmony restored (Ito, 1985b). Believed to have existed in the days before contact with people of European descent, it was and remains a religious ritual that seeks to block the growth of complex *hihia* or entanglements by resolving conflicts between family members (or between families) (Ito, 1985a). *Ho'oponopono* differs from most Western therapeutic practices in at least three ways—the spiritual focus, the emphasis on forgiveness, and the ritualized format (Shook, 1985). Nevertheless, this rather ancient religious practice appears to have much in common with at least two modern, scientifically oriented approaches to helping families: Bowenian family therapy and structural family therapy. This commonality may be seen in both the processes of intervention as well as in the conceptual content of these theories.

Similarities to Bowenian Family Therapy

The primary goal of Bowenian family therapy is to increase the level of *self-differentiation* within an emotional system (Kerr & Bowen, 1988). The concept of self-differentiation has two interrelated and inseparable aspects: (1) to increase a person's experience of individuation from an emotional system while still remaining an active, responsible, and viable participant and (2) to increase a person's experience of separating his or her cognitive from his or her emotional responses while still remaining aware of his or her full range of feelings. In terms of the latter, a relatively differentiated individual is informed by his or her feelings without being compelled or dominated by them. Interestingly, Bowen maintains that such a person will seek to balance the needs of the family as a whole with the needs of the individual members, including the self (Kerr & Bowen, 1988).

Furthermore, self-differentiation is an ongoing, dialectical process (Bowen, 1978). The concept describes two equal yet opposite forces that are found everywhere in nature: a force for togetherness or fusion and a force for individuality and autonomous functioning (Kerr & Bowen, 1988). When the equilibrium between these two forces becomes unbalanced in either direction, both the group and the individual members suffer. For instance, if fusion prevails, the community or family loses access to the creative ideas of its individual members. If individuality prevails, the group cohesion that is necessary for the survival of all individual members may be in jeopardy.

Although Bowenian family therapy seemingly emphasizes the *individuation process* and Hawaiian culture seemingly emphasizes *group cohesion,* these orientations may not be as mutually exclusive as they otherwise appear, when supporting concepts and beliefs are considered. For instance, maintaining an *emotional cutoff* from a significant other (or others) paradoxically deters growth toward individuation (Kerr & Bowen, 1988). This is, perhaps, not too dissimilar from maintaining negative energy toward another member of one's familial network. Another example is provided by Bowen's seminal concept of *triangulation*—a process which reduces anxiety between relatively less differentiated members of a dyadic relationship by directing the anxiety toward a third entity, most often a child (Kerr & Bowen, 1988). This process does not appear altogether different than the Native Hawaiian notion of a child being singled out for retribution by those adults persisting in negative emotions.

During the *ho'oponopono* process, the leader often engages in dyadic linear communication with each member. In fact, all communication is controlled by the leader, who may choose to inhibit spontaneous, unauthorized communication between family members (Shook, 1985). This has the effect of reducing the risk of runaway escalation of the problem and increasing the probability of mutual understandings. This appears to be quite similar to the Bowenian style of interviewing couples; one partner talks with the therapist while the other listens (Klever, 1998). This tends to decrease emotional reactivity and increase cognitive reflection—thus facilitating the experience of empathetic listening and the resolution of problems between the partners.

Additional similarities include the following. In Bowenian theory, a presenting symptom is considered to be multigenerational in origin—with all family members being actors and reactors (Bowen, 1978). Similarly, in *ho'oponopono* extended family members and the spirits of deceased family members are considered viable parts of the relational web and, hence, are invited to attend and to participate—but without calling undue attention to themselves (Ito, 1985b). The leaders of both approaches often coach or direct participants to engage in *relationship experiments,* that is, to act intentionally different in present or upcoming familial interactions (Bowen, 1978; Ito, 1985b). Finally, much like a Bowenian therapist who takes care to avoid being triangulated into the emotional system of clients, the leader of *ho'oponopono* must be able to be fully present with family members yet remain somewhat apart from them (Bowen, 1978; Ito, 1985b).

Similarities to Structural Family Therapy

The primary goal of structural family therapy is the restoration of a family system to a level of functioning that ensures the integrity of itself and its subsystems and their ability to interact in an open fashion with other systems (Minuchin, 1974). Each system (or subsystem) evolves patterns of interaction that create invisible psychosocial *boundaries*. Relatively *clear* boundaries promote the optimal development of life-enhancing skills within a system by balancing the need for new information with the need for space and time to assimilate and use the information. Relatively more *rigid* boundaries unduly restrict the flow of information between systems, thus promoting subsystemic autonomy or *detachment*—quite possibly at the cost of systemic or communal nurturance and support. Relatively more *diffuse* boundaries encourage an unrestricted flow of information between systems, thus promoting subsystemic dependence or *enmeshment*—quite possibly at the cost of autonomy and mastery and even structural integrity.

Boundary clarification is also central to the *ho'oponopono* process. In fact, restoring familial harmony and balance may require altering boundaries between various subsystems such as generations, spouses, siblings, men and women, and family and nonfamily members. Therefore, although relatively more interested in the history of a presenting problem and relatively more guarded against runaway escalation than a structural family therapist, an elder conducting *ho'oponopono* is also interested in observing and understanding the verbal and nonverbal interactions of participants—whether spontaneously engaged in or deliberately precipitated by the leader (Arsenault, 2000). According to Minuchin and Fishman (1981), such observations are necessary for a structural analysis of systemic boundaries and, hence, for subsequent interventions. However, boundary clarification actually starts for both approaches when the leader asks each participant to describe his or her relation to the issue at hand. This inquiry begins to alter the structural underpinnings of any *hihia* or entanglements. Furthermore, when connecting with one person at a time, the leader of *ho'oponopono* may subtly and temporarily support one side of a dispute (Arsenault, 2000). This appears similar to using Minuchin's technique of *unbalancing* in order to realign boundaries between subsystems.

Ho'oponopono and structural family therapy appear to share additional common ground. For instance, both approaches encourage participation in treatment by all relevant family members (Minuchin, 1974; Shook, 1985). However, in *ho'oponopono* relevancy is more broadly defined—as is the composition of most Native Hawaiian households—both nuclear and extended family members and both adults and children (and even infants) are more often included (Shook, 1985). Furthermore, the leaders of both approaches gain access to the family by joining the family, that is, by establishing rapport based upon adaptation to the family's interactional style and to the family's traditions, values, and beliefs (Arsenault, 2000; Minuchin, 1974). This allows for the formation of an alliance for change with the family as a whole and with each member of the family. In *ho'oponopono,* this is primarily accomplished by the opening ritual, *pule wehe* or prayer. However, in both approaches, joining also occurs when each family member is interviewed about his or her own relation to the problem (Arsenault, 2000).

Instructions

Ho'oponopono is a complex and often quite lengthy problem-solving process (Shook, 1985). This complexity is reduced or at least managed by following the time-honored stages and instructions that follow. A senior family member or, if necessary, a respected senior person from the Native Hawaiian community is a natural candidate for leading *ho'oponopono* (Shook, 1985). Utilizing a family member in such a role may be somewhat akin to Minuchin's (1974) practice of joining the more powerful family members in order to gain entrance to the family as a whole and/or to create leverage with other family members. The role may also be similar to Bowen's technique of *coaching* the single most differentiated family member in order to change the whole system (1978). In any case, utilizing a family member as a coleader may be a necessary compromise of mainstream therapeutic traditions in order to develop an approach to family therapy consonant with indigenous cultural traditions.

In either case, the *haku* or leader may work as a cotherapist with a Western-trained family therapist in the initial sessions and remain available as a consultant as both *ho'oponopono* and therapy progress in an integrative manner. With sufficient experience, a culturally knowledgeable and sensitive family therapist may merge the roles of leader and therapist into one integrated role (Shook, 1985). It should be pointed out that *ho'oponopono* does not always follow a rigidly structured pattern but instead allows for flexibility at the leader's discretion (Shook, 1985). For example, rather than prayers being used only during the opening segment, they may be utilized anytime the leader deems it necessary. Also, if negative feelings become too intense or forgiveness is not forthcoming in response to an apology, the leader may call a *ho'omalu* or cooling-off period (Shook, 1985; Ito, 1985b).

Stage One: Pule Wehe *or Opening Prayer*

In the first phase of this stage, the *haku* or leader begins by invoking spiritual support in an effort to create an environment characterized by honesty, openness, strength, and commitment to the process. The spirits invoked may be a combination of the Christian God and Hawaiian *'aumakua* or ancestors (Shook, 1985; Ito, 1985b). Invoking their aid simply means asking for their support, not their direct intervention. The environment that is cocreated with the spiritual support of ancestors and the openness of the family members ensures that they will be able to resolve the conflict themselves. During the second phase of *pule wehe,* called *kukulu kumuhana* or the identification of the issue at hand, the leader elicits the perspective of each participant on the issue (Shook, 1985; Ito, 1985b). The leader then identifies the general relevancy of the issue for the family as a whole and identifies the existence of a *hihia* or negative entanglement between particular members. The former action may be similar to systemizing the presenting problem—a type of reframing that is routinely done in structural family therapy (Minuchin & Fishman, 1981). Other issues may appear during this or subsequent sessions; however, traditionally any particular issue is resolved before moving on to the next issue (Ito, 1985b).

Stage Two: Mahiki *or Discussion*

Mahiki literally means to peel off, as in peeling off the layers of a problem through an in-depth discussion thereof; it also means to pry or exorcise and in this case signifies efforts by the leader to uncover and process any covert painful emotions or hostile intentions (Ito, 1985b; Shook, 1985). Each participant who has been affected by the issue at hand in some identifiable way is encouraged to expand on his or her thoughts and feelings about the issue by talking directly and only to the leader. The leader then engages in *kukulu kumuhana* or exploration on an individual level in order to explore and clarify each individual's perceptions and emotions about the issue. Participants must be fully engaged in the process. Verbal responses to questions must be forthcoming; avoidant nonverbal responses such as shrugging or head nodding are not acceptable (Ito, 1985b). Further, participants are expected to maintain self-control and respond rationally. They are also expected to become increasingly aware of both self and others in terms of behavior, intentions, and emotions. As a result, they are expected to increase their level of empathy and respect for the experiences and viewpoints of others in the family (Ito, 1985b). This manner of discussion provides the leader and the participants with a more complete understanding of the history and the meaning of the issue in the life of the family.

During the discussion with each participant, the leader may avail himself or herself of diverse interventions. Group prayer, of course, may be used at any time. If the discussion becomes heated with anger or any strong emotion then the leader may invoke *ho'omalu* or cooling-off period (Shook, 1985; Arsenault, 2000). The length of the cooling-off period is at the discretion of the leader. This technique allows participants to regain control of their emotions and ponder the problem accordingly. If an individual who is one of the critical participants in the original issue or in the resulting entanglements continually refuses to cooperate in the prescribed manner, the leader may interrupt the process and cancel *ho'oponopono* accordingly. Hopefully, this will not be necessary and the process will proceed to the next step.

Stage Three: Mihi *or to Apologize and to Forgive*

When the discussion is complete, that is, when negative emotions have sufficiently subsided and empathy between entangled participants sufficiently increased, sincere apologies may be made and sincere forgivenesses offered (Shook, 1985). The offending family member must state the transgression, apologize, and request forgiveness. The victim must not only grant forgiveness but also acknowledge any actions or thoughts about revenge and be willing to apologize for those and request forgiveness. In this way, neither holds a position of righteousness and the relationship returns to an even footing (Ito, 1985b). Sometimes, however, restitution is necessary in order to move forward; if that is the case, the terms are negotiated accordingly (Shook, 1985). Following the exchange of apologies and forgivenesses, both participants are asked to *kala* or loosen the negative entanglement that has bound them together in the first place. This is accomplished by affirming their desire for reconciliation and by *'oki* or excising the negative emotions from their own minds—so that although the incident may be remembered, the negative emotions are consigned to the past (Shook, 1985; Ito, 1985b).

The Last Stage: Pani *or the Closing Ritual*

The last stage in *ho'oponopono* has three formal components: a closing prayer or *pule, ho'opau,* an expression of gratitude to the spiritual forces, and the sharing of food (Ito, 1985b). However, these may be preceded by the leader summarizing what has taken place and reaffirming the family's strengths and enduring bonds (Shook, 1985). The particular issue that was worked on is declared closed; traditionally, it is never to be mentioned again. If other issues were raised during any of the preceding stages, the present closing continues but the final closing is postponed and another *ho'oponopono* is scheduled accordingly (Shook, 1985).

Brief Vignette

Preparing for Ho'oponopono: *Intake and Evaluation*

A former client referred Elena to Carol Wright. Carol is a Caucasian who has lived and worked as a family therapist in an agency setting on Maui for five years. Elena is a forty-eight-year-old Native Hawaiian with six living children. During the intake session, Elena's opening statement was, "I understand you are open to the Hawaiian culture and *ho'oponopono;* I need that for my family and myself." Elena complained that her adult children treated her disrespectfully and were unduly interfering with her parenting of her minor children (their half siblings). In addition, she was concerned that her adolescent son was beginning to use cannabis and alcohol. Borrowing her frame of reference from Minuchin, Carol tentatively hypothesized that generational boundaries were too diffuse in Elena's blended family and that at least one member may have developed symptoms that put him at risk.

Elena disclosed that she was presently married to her third husband, Kali. She claimed that Suporro, her second husband, had been physically abusive and that she had feared for her life during most of their marriage. In tears, she said that she felt shame for having abandoned her children to Suporro's care in order to protect herself. She stated that it was time for *pono* or to make right and restore balance with these children, now adults, some with children of their own and living with her. Carol asked if there was an elder in the family, or an elder close to the family, who was familiar with the *ho'oponopono* process and would be willing to act in the role of *haku* or leader. Elena said that Kali was familiar with *ho'oponopono* and was respected by her children and grandchildren and by many others in the native community. Carol scheduled the second session with Kali and Elena alone in order to commence a multigenerational assessment of Elena's family of origin and to determine Kali's potential for acting as coleader or cotherapist in the ensuing integrated intervention process.

Carol was able to construct a detailed history of Elena's family. As a result, she added a Bowenian perspective to her working hypotheses—namely, that severe abuse experienced in Elena's family of origin had been reenacted in her family of procreation and that this in turn reflected an unrealistic appraisal of herself (a characteristic of relatively lower levels of self-differentiation) as a victim who did not know how to change undesirable patterns of interpersonal interaction. Carol was impressed, however, with how far Elena had already grown in her struggle with such a legacy and with her continuing desire to improve her familial network. She was also impressed with Kali's overall demeanor and his desire to be helpful. Thus, it was agreed upon that *ho'oponopono* would be used in conjunction with family therapy. Elena volunteered to invite her children to participate in an all-day meeting. (*Ho'oponopono* most often continues until the issue at hand or some specific portion thereof has been resolved.) In closing, both clients shared their appreciation for Carol's cultural sensitivity and their trust in her professional competence.

Integration: Ho'oponopono *and the First Family Marathon Session*

Kali introduced Carol as a family therapist who was interested in and respectful of Hawaiian traditions. Kali explained that he would be acting as *haku* or leader and, if and when relevant, also as a participant. He pointed out that Carol's leadership would be direct, active, and imbued with *malama* or caring and that both of them would be working with the *mana* or life force to start the healing process. He then thanked family members in turn (as in structural family therapy) for their willingness to explore blending *ho'oponopono* with family therapy. Carol shared that she felt particularly honored at being included in this process and expressed her gratitude accordingly.

Kali started the proceedings with *pule* or prayer. (Elena's children who could not attend due to distance were included in *pule* by speakerphone.) In *pule,* Kali invited the ancestors to join and support the process—but without interfering in it. He also, in *pule,* admonished everyone to come with a loving, open, and honest heart and be willing to seek balance, restore harmony, and make right, that is, to apologize and to forgive. Kali ended this stage in the process by admonishing everyone to have courage and to "be warriors; let go of resentments, establish harmony and togetherness while maintaining individuality." He added, "although *lokahi* (harmony) should be sought, in the end, the *'ohana* (family) must be placed ahead of the individual, if unavoidable conflict arose between two or more persons." He was, thus, setting clear boundaries and guidelines—as determined by Native Hawaiian values and traditions—for this marathon session and all subsequent sessions.

After a break, Kali asked everyone to reassemble for the *mahiki* or discussion stage of *ho'oponopono.* Carol then invited each person to share what he or she would like changed in the family. As in Bowenian family therapy, she asked that each person speak directly to the leaders—who were intentionally sitting side by side. Elena spoke first and shared, "I want more respect from my daughters, Lisa and Lana, and I want them to stop parenting my son (their younger half brother), Kimo, so much." Carol turned to Lisa and invited her to respond to what Elena had shared. Lisa said, "I know there are a lot of issues and a lot of anger and hurt—whether it comes up in here or not." Carol responded directly to Lisa by stating her hope that she and other family members would trust the combined processes of *ho'oponopono* and family therapy and take the opportunity to open up and share their hurts and resentments. Kali reminded everyone that in doing so they would be helping the family regain harmony and balance.

Lisa seemed to relax a little and stated, "I am concerned about Kimo because he has always been pressured by everyone to grow up faster than he should have; the animosity in the family has torn him emotionally." Acting upon her earlier hypothesis regarding diffuse boundaries, Carol gently challenged Lisa's role as a *parentified child:* "Sounds like you have had to grow up faster yourself and take care of others in the family." Lisa, appearing downcast, agreed. "I dropped out of school when I was only fourteen and I have always worked to support others in the family; I just don't want Kimo to go through what I went through." Carol thanked her for being forthcoming about her parental involvement in Kimo's life.

Distracted by her facial grimaces, Carol invited Lana to share what it was that she wanted or expected from these meetings. However, just as Lana was about to speak, Elena interrupted and complained, "When both of us come home from work, Lana gets mad at me when I ask her for help with the house cleaning." At this moment, Carol, acting as both a Bowenian and a structural family therapist, challenged the enmeshment (or fusion) of mother and adult daughter by modeling the use of "I" statements and by directing the interaction. After this, Elena, rather more calmly, shared, "Lana says things to me like, 'what does the bitch want now' or 'how come Kimo doesn't do a damn thing.'" Lana concurred and said that she and her mom tended to get angry at each other easily.

After some moments of silence, Carol switched from Bowenian interviewing to precipitating an enactment between mother and adult daughter (a technique used in both *ho'oponopono* and structural family therapy). She directed both Elena and Lana to tell what they wanted of each other. They did so, but their interaction did not produce reconciliation or resolution of their differences. As if moving into the third stage *(mihi)* of *ho'oponopono* (at least for this particular subsystem on this particular issue), Kali invited both women to declare to each other their deepest and truest intentions in this matter. Elena replied, "I'm sorry. I will work on my tone and I hope you will too." Lana cried and said, "I want it to work better, but I need help. I am a single parent and I need my family to understand how hard that is, but I'm willing to start all over, to forgive, and to learn to talk more gently." Both women embraced and cried together.

After a lunch break, Kali and Carol reconvened the minimarathon and returned to Bowenian interviewing. At Carol's invitation to continue sharing, Elena declared rather forcefully that she did not feel respected by her daughters regarding her parenting of Kimo. Lana started to respond directly to Elena, but Kali interrupted her and reminded her to speak directly to the leaders. Lana did so and said, "Kimo needed us. Yes, Mom was a wonderful mother for us; she protected us. But after she left, Kimo took the brunt of Suporro's abuse. We were there for him; she wasn't." Lisa also chimed in, "When I was pregnant she asked me if it was Suporro's child—like I was having sex with my father. I felt like a whore. [To Elena] How could you think that?" Elena responded (before Kali or Carol could interrupt), "I did not mean it like that. I was concerned that maybe he had sexually abused you." Lisa said, "Then why didn't you say it that way? And why did you leave us with a father who was violent?" At this point the room became rather quiet.

Carol invited Elena to respond (directly to her and Kali) to Lisa's last question. Elena did so tearfully. She said, "I don't always say things the way I mean them; I am very sorry for that miscommunication. I regret leaving my children, but I was afraid for my life. I hope they will forgive me?" Lisa told the leaders, "I'm not ready to yet. I also want to know why she gave my brother Rico away." Again the room was quiet. Kali reminded everyone that although forgiveness was ultimately required in *ho'oponopono,* being honest and sincere was also important. Deciding that it was too late in the day to bring up another issue, Carol asked if anyone in the family or *'ohana* was ready to forgive their mother for leaving the way she did. Kimo responded tearfully. "I forgive her but for restitution she should continue to seek counseling for the family. I don't like being here but I realize that I need help." Carol asked Kimo if he would be willing to undergo an assessment for substance abuse. He nodded his head affirmatively. Kali asked Lisa if she would be willing to work on her resentments at a future meeting. She said she would try. Carol thanked her accordingly. In order to strengthen the executive subsystem (often a goal in structural family therapy), Carol invited Elena, Lisa, and Lana to act as *coparents* of Kimo until the next *ho'oponopono*. They agreed to do so and also agreed to meet twice a week as a parenting discussion group—with Elena as chair and Kali as advisor. Carol promised to provide some written resources for the group to study.

In closing, Carol acknowledged that many issues still needed attention and eventual resolution. She added that she was very impressed with how much love and courage had survived years of parental violence and abandonment. Several members thanked Carol and Kali for leading the sessions. All agreed to reconvene in three weeks to continue *ho'oponopono*. Kali ended the entire day in the traditional manner—with *pule ho'opau*—blessing the family, the therapist, and the ancestors. He then invited the family and Carol to share a meal in a symbolical expression of trust and unity.

Suggestions for Follow-Up

Hopefully, *ho'oponopono* will, in the vignette, be continued until all outstanding threats to harmony have been addressed—one at a time—and, in particular, until all necessary requests for forgiveness have been made and accepted (Ito, 1985b). Since this is the expected and normal course of events, *following up* is not, per se, part of *ho'oponopono*. However, it would be advisable to follow-up should the therapist discern that the process had been prematurely concluded. In fact, following up by continuing to work with various familial subsystems is the norm in Carol's practice. For instance, seeing Kimo individually for a few sessions may provide additional opportunities for protecting him from being singled out for retribution or, in Bowenian terms, for helping him extricate himself from overlapping triangles. In any case, to follow-up would probably be experienced as helpful by the *haku* or leader and/or by the *po'o* or head of household and as an act of caring by family members.

Indications and Contraindications

It is the assumption of this study that interventions derived from indigenous or traditional healing practices increase the probability that family therapy will be experienced by clients from corresponding cultural groups as relatively more syntonic with their basic values and worldviews. The previous case illustrates the viability of creating a culturally consonant intervention program for Native Hawaiian families by integrating indigenous spiritual traditions with imported, professionally derived treatment approaches. Similar integrative processes have been suggested for other ethnic minorities residing in the United States (Sue & Sue, 1990). For instance, Bermudez and Bermudez (2002) suggest that the effectiveness of family therapy with Latinos will be increased by sensitively utilizing selected cultural orientations, particularly those of a spiritual or religious nature. (Interestingly, Becvar [2003] makes a similar suggestion in her call for using specific spiritual practices as adjunctive interventions in the routine practice of family therapy.) In their review of various studies of both Hispanic and Native American cultures, Sue and Sue recommend modifying Western-oriented clinical goals and techniques associated with *doing* (acting on the world) by placing greater value on the spiritual quality of just *being* (living in harmony). The writers maintain that "the ability to integrate the different value systems as they relate to the problems of the client are critical" (1990, p. 238).

Using any model of intervention that integrates indigenous or traditional ways of resolving conflicts with therapeutic approaches from the dominant culture should be undertaken only with cultural understanding and sensitivity and due regard for the ethical requirements of each tradition. For instance, it would be a mistake to assume that every person of Native Hawaiian descent would automatically want to participate in *ho'oponopono* or would automatically exhibit those personality traits (such as honesty, openness, and interdependency) deemed essential for success (Shook, 1985). In reviewing work done with Hispanic and other minority families, Sue and Sue (1990) point out that the between- and within-group cultural differences must be examined before counseling can proceed. In fact, information, otherwise vital to culturally and spiritually consonant family therapy, can be "misused, if generalizations are made in a stereotypic fashion" (p. 242).

In terms of ethical considerations related to the practice of family therapy, appropriate, individualized waivers of confidentiality and statements of informed consent are, of course, prerequisites for intervention. In addition, if any of the participants present under the influence of drugs or alcohol or if there is a conflict of interest among participants or between any participant and any leader or coleader, such as landlord and tenant, treatment should be rescheduled or cancelled altogether (Shook, 1985).

Bibliotherapy Sources for the Client

Ito, K. (1985a). Affective bonds: Hawaiian interrelationships of self: Exploring Pacific ethnopsychologies. In G. M. White & J. Kirkpatrick (Eds.), *Person, self and experience* (pp. 301-327). Berkeley: University of California Press.

Ito, K. (1985b). Ho'oponopono, "To make right": Hawaiian conflict resolution and metaphor in the construction of a family therapy. *Culture, Medicine, and Psychiatry, 9,* 201-217.

Marsella, A. J., Oliveira, J. M., Plummer, C. M., & Crabbe, K. M. (1998). Native Hawaiian (Kanaka Maoli) culture, mind, and well-being. In H. McCubbin & E. Thompson (Eds.), *Resiliency in Native American and immigrant family series* (Vol. 2, pp. 93-113). Thousand Oaks, CA: Sage Publications.

Mokuau, N. & Matsuoka, J. (1995). Turbulence among a native people: Social work practice with Hawaiians. *Social Work, 40*(4), 465-475.

Shook, V. E. (1985). *Ho'oponopono.* Honolulu: University of Hawaii Press, The East-West Center.

References

Arsenault, D. (2000). The modification of Ho'oponopono as group therapy in a male adolescent residential group home setting. *Journal of Child and Adolescent Group Therapy, 10*(1), 29-45.

Becvar, D. (2003, September-October). Utilizing spiritual resources as an adjunct to family therapy. *Family Therapy Magazine, 2,* 31-33.

Bermudez, J. M. & Bermudez, S. (2002). Altar-making with Latino families: a narrative therapy perspective. *Journal of Family Psychotherapy, 13*(3/4), 329-347.

Bowen, M. (1978). *Family therapy in clinical practice.* Northvale, NJ: Jason Aronson.

Hurdle, D. E. (2002). Native Hawaiian traditional healing: Culturally based interventions for social work practice. *Social Work, 47*(2), 183-192.

Ito, K. (1985a). Affective bonds: Hawaiian interrelationships of self: Exploring Pacific ethnopsychologies. In G. M. White & J. Kirkpatrick (Eds.), *Person, self and experience* (pp. 301-327). Berkeley: University of California Press.

Ito, K. (1985b). Ho'oponopono, "To make right": Hawaiian conflict resolution and metaphor in the construction of a family therapy. *Culture, Medicine, and Psychiatry, 9,* 201-217.

Kerr, M. E. & Bowen, M. (1988). *Family evaluation.* New York: W.W. Norton & Co.

Klever, P. (1998). Marital fusion and differentiation. In P. Titelman (Ed.), *Clinical applications of Bowen Family Systems Theory* (pp. 119-145). Binghamton, NY: The Haworth Press.

Marsella, A. J., Oliveira, J. M., Plummer, C. M., & Crabbe, K. M. (1998). Native Hawaiian (Kanaka Maoli) culture, mind, and well-being. In H. McCubbin & E. Thompson (Eds.), *Resiliency in Native American and immigrant family series* (Vol. 2, pp. 93-113). Thousand Oaks, CA: Sage Publications.

McCubbin, H., Thompson, A., Thompson, E., Elver, K. M., & McCubbin, M. (1994). Ethnicity, schema and coherence: Appraisal processes for families in crisis. *Resilience in families series* (Vol. 1, pp. 41-67). Thousand Oaks, CA: Sage Publications.

McGoldrick, M. & Giordano, J. (1996). Overview: Ethnicity and family therapy. In M. McGoldrick, J. Giordano, & J. Pearce (Eds.), *Ethnicity and family therapy* (pp. 1-27). New York: Guilford Press.

Minuchin, S. (1974). *Families & family therapy.* Cambridge, MA: Harvard University Press.

Minuchin, S. & Fishman, H. C. (1981). *Family therapy techniques.* Cambridge, MA: Harvard University Press.

Mokuau, N. & Matsuoka, J. (1995). Turbulence among a native people: Social work practice with Hawaiians. *Social Work, 40*(4), 465-475.

Shook, V. E. (1985). *Ho'oponopono*. Honolulu: University of Hawaii Press, The East-West Center.

Sue, D. W. & Sue, D. (1990). *Counseling the culturally different: Theory and practice*. New York: John Wiley & Sons.

U.S. Bureau of the Census. (2000). *Census of the population: Supplemental report—Profile of general demographic characteristics: 2000* [Data file]. Available from http://www.cityofpsl.com/Plan%20apps/census.pdf.

SECTION III: INTERVENTIONS INCLUDING LARGER SYSTEMS

– 29 –

The Healing Journey: Celebrating the Past and Envisioning the Future

Chunhong Zhang
Abigail Tolhurst Christiansen

Type of Contribution: Activity

This activity* is well suited for groups of individuals, couples, or families working on recovering from a past trauma, a medical condition, or a loss (e.g., sexual abuse, physical abuse, infertility, grieving, etc.). It can also be adapted for use in a couple or family therapy setting when similar issues are presented.

Objective

1. To review and integrate clients' experience with the trauma and their healing process.
2. To integrate experience of healing into a lifelong perspective by establishing connections between present, past, and future.
3. To facilitate personal expression of this experience through artwork.
4. To identify personal strengths utilized and gained during the healing journey in a safe group setting.
5. To celebrate the progress made and help clients to take pride in themselves.
6. To envision the future of the healing and set concrete goals.
7. To build motivation for achieving identified goals.

This activity encourages individuals or families who are recovering from a trauma, a loss, or a medical condition to review and reflect upon their experience of coping and healing. This reviewing helps them to highlight, appreciate, and take ownership of the progresses they have made, as well as to identify strengths they possess or have gained through the healing process. It also helps clients to integrate their experience of healing into a lifelong perspective, which helps them gain a better understanding of who they are and where they have come from. Through the activity, clients take pride in their strengths and build motivation for the next step on their healing journey.

Rationale for Use

Reviewing and reflecting on the past helps one establish an existential sense of self and wholeness, derive personal strengths, and clarify directions for the future (Linley & Stephen,

*This activity was developed and field-tested with a women's support group for childhood incest survivors. Suggestions for adaptations for use with groups of families or couples are provided in a later section.

2003). This is especially true for individuals and families who are working through traumatic experiences or the loss of a loved one. For these individuals and families, there can be a long, uneven road toward recovery, sometimes interspersed with setbacks (Bass & Davis, 1990; Courtois, 1988). The metaphor of a "healing journey" vividly captures the essence of this long, complex, and recursive process (Bass & Davis, 1990; Kirschner, Kirschner, & Rappaport, 1993). Periodically reflecting on the roads they have traveled, the healing journey helps individuals and families to better understand where they have come from, to locate where they are on their own path to recovery, and to gain a sense of direction for the future (Davis, 1990). It is a time to celebrate and take pride in how far they have progressed and to recognize personal strengths. It is also a time to clarify what is left on the journey, to create goals, and to build motivation for the next step on the journey.

Having this celebration in a group environment allows individuals or family members to receive validation, support, and encouragement from other group members. Group therapy is believed by some to be the treatment of choice for adult trauma victims (van der Kolk, 1987). For example, Chew (1998) pointed out that group treatment in conjunction with individual therapy is one of the most effective ways of healing sexual abuse. Being in a homogeneous trauma group can be immensely validating and normalizing for group members (Chew, 1998): experiences can be shared and understood, commonalities can be recognized, etc. Groups also provide a setting for members to experience safety, break secrecy, decrease isolation and stigma, and learn new ways of relating (Courtois, 1988; Kirschner et al., 1993).

This activity also helps the group as a whole to gain a better sense of where each group member is in his or her recovery. The activity establishes a baseline reference for future group discussions. The use of art as the method of expression empowers group members and provides an additional way of creating connection in the group (Anderson, 1995; Baerg, 2003).

Instructions

The first step of the activity is to introduce the "healing journey" concept. This concept may come up during group discussions, which offers a natural transition to the activity. If it does not, facilitators are to bring it up and ask questions to start the discussion. Such statements and questions can include the following: Change or healing is a process. Do you think you are on a journey of healing? What does the journey mean for you? How long do you think the journey will last (i.e., does it have an ending point or is it a lifelong process)? During this initial conversation group members may bring up their religious or spiritual beliefs.

Next, group leaders provide rationale for the activity and pass out the activity sheet (see The Healing Journey Handout at the end of the chapter). The activity asks group members to reflect upon their healing journey, then create an artwork that captures their experience on this journey. We strongly suggest having group members work on the activity at home, as this allows them the freedom to take as much time as they need and to use whatever materials they wish to work on the project. It also allows group members to reflect and work in privacy if they desire. The process of working on the activity can be therapeutic in its own right. We find that doing this activity during a group meeting limits the creativity and depth of processing primarily due to time and other logistic constraints. A good strategy is to introduce the activity at the end of a group meeting, assign it as homework, and then use the subsequent group meeting for sharing, processing, and envisioning.

At home each group member spends a minimum amount of time (e.g., twenty minutes) working on the activity. The minimum time requirement is one way of ensuring that sufficient attention is given to the activity. Group members are asked to reflect on their healing journey with the help of a set of guiding questions and then create a piece of artwork based on their reflections. This artwork can take any form the group member wishes (e.g., writing a letter, creating a collage, drawing, painting, sculpture, etc.). The artwork can focus on two or three of the guiding questions, or it can answer all of them. Questions are adapted from Davis (1990).

How long have I been actively dealing with this problem?
What are the different aspects of healing?
What aspects of healing have I mostly resolved or achieved?
What is left for me to do?
What issues am I most concerned with right now?
Where has my journey taken me? (Where have I come along my journey of healing?)
Where am I heading on this journey of healing?

Group members are asked to bring their art projects to the next group meeting and share their experiences of working on the project. Creating safety for this sharing is important. We recommend that certain rules or guidelines be discussed up front. If confidentiality is already a rule the group maintains, this may be a good time to remind members of this rule. Guidelines should also cover whether it is okay for a group member to pass on sharing. We recommend that those group members who decide to pass share their experience and reflections of listening to other group members instead. The group will also need to decide if it is okay to ask questions while someone is sharing or if questions should be held until the person finishes. It is possible that sharing or answering questions may overwhelm a group member. The group should also set up guidelines for handling this situation (e.g., whether it is okay for the person to leave the group for a few minutes to regain composure).

Facilitators are encouraged to ask processing questions to help group members further process this experience. Processing questions are also encouraged from group members. These questions can include but are not limited to the following:

What was your experience of doing this activity (i.e., easy or hard)?
What parts did you find most easy/difficult?
What emotions did it bring up while you were working on it?
What have you learned through the journey?
What did you learn about yourself when you finished the project?
Have other group members had a similar experience?
What are you most proud of?

It is important to emphasize and validate that healing is an ongoing and often nonlinear process. At times group members feel as if they are moving backward rather than moving forward. Group members should be encouraged to raise this topic whenever they feel the need to further reflect on their experience, even after this activity. The Instruction Sheet at the end of this chapter provides a summary of these steps.

Hints for Adaptation for Multiple Family Groups and Family Therapy

Healing from a past trauma, a loss, or a difficult medical condition is rarely an individual matter. In some cases the entire family experiences the trauma or loss. Even in cases in which only one individual directly experienced the trauma, family members and partners often suffer from the "ripple effects" and are intimately involved and influenced throughout the healing journey (Davis, 1990; Harkness & Zador, 2001). It is important, therefore, that interventions treat the entire family system whenever possible instead of focusing exclusively on the traumatized individual. Marriage and family therapy (MFT) and multifamily group therapy (MFGT) are good formats for achieving this goal. When adapting this activity for multifamily groups or marriage and family therapy, changes in instruction are necessary. If the presenting trauma is one that the entire family experienced and is trying to heal from, the instructions could be framed so that each family member is encouraged to reflect and report on his or her individual experience with the trauma and healing, as well as his or her perceptions of how the family as a whole, or how other family members experienced and coped with it. If it is a trauma that one specific family member experienced and the family as a whole are trying to heal from its secondary impacts, family members could be asked to reflect on their "distal" experience of the trauma: how they perceived the trauma had changed their relationship with the person who experienced it and how the family as a whole has coped with the experience. Facilitators also have a choice between asking each family member to create his or her own artwork/representation or have the family work as a team to create one artwork and present it together to the rest of the group. Ensuring safety in family or couple groups is necessarily more complex than in individual groups due to the added layer of family dynamics. It is requisite that all members in the group, including the partners or family members, are supportive of the healing of the person recovering from the trauma.

Brief Vignette

We used this activity with a women's support group for adult survivors of childhood incest. All current members of this small group have participated in the group for a minimum of five years and have been working on recovery for a much longer period of time.* Each member is currently in individual therapy or has been in individual therapy in the past. Given the length of time these women have worked together, they are very familiar with one another and have a good sense of support and safety. The group meets biweekly and is semistructured: alternating between sharing sessions and activity sessions.

Although the group has been in existence for a long time, it had experienced several transitions over a short period of time, including the frequent turnover of facilitators and group members leaving. This transition and turnover sometimes resulted in a lack of focus or direction. This activity, as it turned out, also helped the group to maintain a sense of continuity in addition to the other functions it was designed to fulfill.

The group members greeted the activity with interest. The artwork they produced was powerful, reflecting the deep processing that had occurred. Two group members wrote poems with themes of personal empowerment and increasing openness and awareness through the journey. One group member presented a collage that vividly depicted the different stages she experienced through the journey: the little girl who lived in intense fear forever chased by a monster, the depressed, suicidal young to middle-aged adult, and the more self-assured although still struggling middle-aged adult. Another group member presented a sculpture that characterized her experience as a spiraling upward and widening movement with the theme of incest weaving in and out, gradually transformed from a dark, heavy presence to a lighter and more harmonious presence along the way. A different group member drew a picture of a tree with the branches representing paths her life had taken up to this point. One group member chose to pass—this decision was met with respect and understanding by the entire group.

Group members commented that this activity had been very helpful and growth promoting. Some group members reported that they experienced a new freedom from the family triangles following the activity. Although we were unable to devote additional group time to the follow-up questions for "envisioning the future," group members were encouraged to think about it be-

*The length of group membership is partly due to the fact that this is a community support group, not a therapy group in the strict sense. All group members are currently living functional lives. Group members mainly use this group for community, support, and continued personal growth.

tween meetings. Since implementing this intervention, group members have referred to their artwork in describing where they are in their journey. Group members have reminded other members of their goals in an effort to support one another. This intervention has also been helpful for group members when introducing a new group facilitator to their achievements, struggles, and goals. Several group members brought in their artwork a second time for the new facilitator to review.

Suggestions for Follow-Up

To follow-up this activity, group members are asked to envision the future of their healing journey. Group members considered the following questions and discussed them during a subsequent meeting:

What do you envision the future of your journey to be like?

If you were to take one more step down the journey, big or small, what would that be? (To be a little bit more assertive? To confront a co-worker? To mentor someone just starting this journey? etc.) Describe it in as specific terms as you can.

How can the group help you with these goals?

Contraindications

For the "Healing Journey" activity to be used successfully, the group must first be perceived as a safe place by group members (Harkness & Zador, 2001). If any intragroup conflict exists, it is important to resolve that conflict before venturing into this activity. Second, group facilitators need to set the tone for valuing sharing and diversified experience. Although the likelihood of this activity turning into a "competition" (i.e., whose art work is best) is low given the nature of the activity, it is still best for group facilitators to take precautions. For example, when introducing the activity, facilitators could stress, "Each individual's/family's healing is different. Each artwork created is meaningful for that person/family in its own way." If a sense of competitiveness does transpire in the group, facilitators could redirect the conversation by asking, "In what ways are each of the artworks shared uniquely meaningful to each individual/family?" Third, this activity works best with a population who have been on the healing journey for some time. Depending on the nature and intensity of the trauma, the activity may not work well with individuals or families who are just embarking on their healing and are still overwhelmed with intense emotions, flashbacks, or crises, as often is the case with incest survivors during the awareness stage (Bass & Davis, 1990). This activity takes a considerable amount of energy and may not be appropriate for beginners on the healing journey who have more urgent things to deal with. Fourth, since this activity depends on participants being comfortable working with or creating metaphors to represent their experience, some group members may find it too abstract and refuse to participate. When this is the case, it is advisable to encourage the group member to do the reflection and review part of the activity but represent his or her experience in whatever way he or she feels most at ease.

Readings and Resources for the Professional

Bass, E. & Davis, L. (1990). *The courage to heal: A guide for women survivors of sexual abuse.* New York: Perennial Library, Harper & Row.

Courtois, C. (1988). *Healing the incest wound: Adult survivors in therapy.* New York: W. W. Norton & Co.

Davis, L. (1991). *Allies in healing: When the person you love was sexually abused as a child.* New York: Harper Collins.

Rosen, E. J. (1996). The family as a healing resource. In C. A. Corr & D. M. Coor (Eds.), *Handbook of child death and bereavement* (pp. 223-243). New York: Springer.

Wilson, J., Friedman, M., & Lindy, J. (2001). *Treating psychological trauma and PTSD.* New York: Guilford Press.

Bibiotherapy Sources for the Client

Bass, E. & Davis, L. (1990). *The courage to heal: A guide for women survivors of sexual abuse.* New York: Perennial Library, Harper & Row.

Chew, J. (1998). *Women survivors of childhood sexual abuse.* Binghamton, NY: The Haworth Press.

Davis, L. (1990). *The courage to heal workbook: A guide for women survivors of childhood sexual abuse.* New York: Harper Collins.

Davis, L. (1991). *Allies in healing: When the person you love was sexually abused as a child.* New York: Harper Collins.

Herman, J. L. (1992). *Trauma and recovery.* New York: Basic Books.

Kirschner, S., Kirschner, D., & Rappaport, R. (1993). *Working with adult incest survivors.* New York: Brunner/Mazel.

Rich, P. (1999). *The healing journey through grief: Your journal for reflection and recovery.* New York: John Wiley & Sons.

Rosenbloom, D., Williams, M. B., & Watkins, B. E. (1999). *Life after trauma: A workbook for healing.* New York: Guilford Press.

References

Anderson, F. E. (1995). Catharsis and empowerment through group claywork with incest survivors. *Arts in Psychotherapy, 22,* 413-427.

Baerg, S. (2003). "Sometimes there just aren't any words": Using expressive therapy with adolescents living with cancer. *Canadian Journal of Counseling, 37,* 65-74.

Bass, E. & Davis, L. (1990). *The courage to heal: A guide for women survivors of sexual abuse.* New York: Perennial Library, Harper & Row.

Chew, J. (1998). *Women survivors of childhood sexual abuse.* Binghamton, NY: The Haworth Press.

Courtois, C. A. (1988). *Healing the incest wound: Adult survivors in therapy.* New York: W. W. Norton & Co.

Davis, L. (1990). *The courage to heal workbook: A guide for women survivors of childhood sexual abuse.* New York: Harper Collins.

Harkness, L. & Zador, N. (2001). Treatment of PTSD in families and couples. In J. Wilson, M. Friedman, & J. Lindy (Eds.), *Treating psychological trauma and PTSD* (pp. 335-353). New York: Guilford Press.

Kirschner, S., Kirschner, D., & Rappaport, R. (1993). *Working with adult incest survivors.* New York: Brunner/Mazel.

Linley, P. A. & Stephen, J. (2003). Trauma and personal growth. *Psychologist, 16,* 135-141.

van der Kolk, B. A. (1987). The drug treatment of post-traumatic stress disorder. *Journal of Affective Disorders, 13,* 203-213.

The Healing Journey Handout

Spend roughly twenty minutes creating a piece of artwork based on your reflection on the following questions. This artwork can be writing, a collage, drawing, painting, sculpture, or any other method of your choice. It can answer all of the questions or focus on the two or three that are most relevant to you.

How long have I been actively dealing with this problem?
What are the aspects of healing?
What aspects of healing have I mostly resolved or achieved?
What is left for me to do?
What issues am I most concerned with right now?
Where has my journey taken me? (Where have I come along my journey of healing?)
Where am I heading on this journey of healing?

Please bring what you have created to the next activity session. During the session we ask that you share the parts of your artwork that you are comfortable talking about. If you feel uncomfortable or unsafe in talking about certain questions, it is okay to pass, but please bring your creation with you to reflect on as you listen to others.

Instruction Sheet

1. Introduce the "healing journey" concept.
2. Provide rationale for the activity and pass out handout I "The Healing Journey" (see Healing Journey Handout).
3. Group members take the activity home and reflect on their experience of the healing journey with the help of guiding questions. They are to make an artwork (poem, collage, painting, etc.) based on their reflections.
4. Group members bring their artwork to the next group session.
5. Create group rules for sharing.
6. Group members volunteer to share their artwork with the group.
7. Process the experience of the activity with processing questions.
8. Summarize and close the activity.

– 30 –

If You Work with Families, Get to School! Family-Based School Interventions

Laurie L.Williamson

Type of Contribution: Activity

Objective

The objective of this activity is to encourage communication and collaboration among therapist, parents, and school personnel.

Rationale for Use

Difficulties at school influence family relationships at home. However, these challenges also provide an opportunity to promote therapeutic growth. Collaboration among the therapist, home, and school is essential to successfully support the whole child. It does, indeed, take a village to raise a child.

Parents and school officials often fall victim to children's attempts to divide and conquer; therapists can also become ensnared. Testing the limits is part of a child's developmental growth. Our jobs, as child and student advocates, are to maintain appropriate limits and provide a consistent and safe environment that facilitates growth. Just like an effective parenting team, therapists, schools, and homes need to communicate regularly to provide the child with unified support (Fuller & Olsen, 1998).

One common response to the many and varied academic, social, and personal problems that students bring to school is the development of a student support team (SST). There are many versions of the student support team. Each SST's charge is to identify the individual needs of at-risk students, frequently making referrals for counseling or treatment. The SST coordinator is an invaluable resource in the schools for the family therapist. The opportunity for the school, family, and therapist to consult and collaborate regarding intervention strategies enhances the likelihood of success. The therapist serves as a model and a bridge to foster collaboration between home and school.

One approach to engage therapists, parents, and schools to work together in the best interests of the child has been termed the "wraparound" process (Kerr & Nelson, 2002). The wraparound process is an intensive level of positive behavioral support. It is based on individualized, needs-driven planning and services. It is not a program or a type of service; it is a commitment to integrate family, school, and community and create services on a "one student at a time" basis.

Many parents who have children with behavior problems may be defensive about admitting to these problems as, in the past, it was fairly common to attribute children's behavior problems to poor parenting. The wraparound process empowers families to advocate for their child by being included as equal partners with professionals in planning and implementing services (DeChillo, Koren, & Schultz, 1994; Friesen & Wahlers, 1993). When parents are full participants in developing a team-based wraparound plan, their resistance tends to disappear. The family-centered focus regards parents as a source of support and strength as opposed to dysfunction and pathology (Duchnowski, Berg, & Kutash, 1995).

The emphasis on strength-based planning and the focus on strengthening desired replacement behaviors align the school, therapist, and parents into a unified front. From this coordinated position, the therapists and parents involved can develop positive, behavioral interventions that will encourage the student to cooperate rather than provoke resistance. Solutions can often be accomplished by substituting a different behavior that is incompatible with the targeted behavior. These changes can evoke a shared sense of increased power and control for all involved, the sign that everybody wins.

The wraparound team consists of the people who know the student best, including the family therapist, school professionals, and family members. Together they develop an individualized intervention plan. School professionals will usually involve the classroom teacher, the school counselor, and an administrator. Services must be culturally competent and the composition of the team must fit the student's culture and community. The plan is needs driven rather than service oriented, as it is driven by the needs of the student rather than the services traditionally available in schools. It also typically encompasses services that extend to life domains beyond the school (e.g., family, living situation, recreational interests, emotional status, medical concerns, legal issues, safety/crisis response). The plan is based on the needs identified by the student, family, therapist, and school staff. The student is encouraged to participate as is appropriate for his or her developmental level (Eber, 1995).

Instructions

School systems adhere to county, state, and federal mandates regarding student support services. The school support team identifies factors interfering with a student's academic progress; aspects of his or her physical, intellectual, social, and emotional health will be considered. Strict guidelines provide a framework for the level of assessment and intervention for each student that is "staffed" or brought to the formal attention of the school support team.

Inquire As to How the Referral Process Works

Referrals are usually submitted to the team by either the teacher, who is most concerned about the student's success at school, or a parent, who is most concerned about the student's success at school and at home. Family therapists can serve as facilitators and encourage parents to utilize the services and resources of the school. Family therapists, with parental consent, should be welcome contributors and team participants. Each SST will have a designated coordinator, usually a head teacher, school psychologist, or school counselor. The coordinator is in charge of notifying interested parties, facilitating meetings, and maintaining records and case notes. Obtain a copy of the referral form.

Identify Team Members

Full-time members of the team usually include the learning specialist, the school psychologist, the school counselor, and a representative from administration. Other significant members are in attendance as warranted for each case, for example: referring teachers, parents, and relevant service providers, such as the school nurse, special education faculty, occupational therapist, speech therapist, law enforcement, social services, family therapist, etc. Contact faculty central to the SST and discuss the case and your interest in working with the family and school. Request a meeting of interested parties.

Promote a Comfortable and Positive Rapport

Everyone should have equal space at the table. All parties should agree to conduct themselves responsibly and professionally. Family therapists and school professionals are trained in communication skills and conflict mediation. They have an opportunity to work together to support the family and forge an alliance to provide services that are in the best interests of the child.

Explore Areas Impacting the Student

Each participant will have an opportunity to present his or her concerns and ask questions. The family therapist can encourage and facilitate parental involvement and help clarify policies and procedures throughout the process. The team coordinator should summarize the issues identified and have participants prioritize concerns. Schools are required to provide services and intervention in the least restrictive environment. A least restrictive environment essentially means that interventions are progressive in nature; they attempt to empower the student with as little disruption to the routine as possible. The methods, process, and procedures provide specific criteria to follow. Students are to remain in the regular classroom and participate in the standard curriculum as much as possible.

Collaborate in Developing a Plan of Action

After a constructively guided discussion, participants will, ideally, arrive at a consensus regarding intervention goals. Interventions in the wraparound process are focused on strength-based planning and capitalize on the student's assets and skills. The focus is on strengthening desired replacement behaviors which is central to behavioral support. Family therapists can contribute their experience and expertise in helping to develop intervention strategies.

The school environment is rich with intervention resources, and school staff can be helpful in many ways. The school principal is typically regarded as the major disciplinarian in the school. Positive discipline can be a potent tactic, especially positive reinforcement such as recognition and praise. The school counselor can also provide reinforcement and coordinate services. Other students may be used as models, tutors, reinforcing agents, and monitors for wraparound plans (Fuller & Olsen, 1998). Structure, resources, and supports for each targeted student must be flexible and creative. Each participant should take a portion of the responsibility for the plan of action and contribute to the solution.

Follow-up and Accountability

Intervention strategies are reviewed and adapted on a regular basis with the optimal goal of students no longer requiring supplemental services. Student progress is monitored by the team coordinator at regular intervals to document continuing progress, alterations or amendments to the intervention strategy, and current level of functioning. With parental permission, family therapists can consult with the school periodically to keep informed as to the student's status.

Involving yourself as a therapist in the schools not only helps your client. It has the additional advantage of increasing your visibility to, and interaction with, school staff. Volunteering to present topics of interest to parents and educators is an opportunity to further develop your referral and resource network. Remember, in working with school staff, adults need support and reinforcement, too. Find out what your client's teachers need, set up communication channels, and be sure to show your appreciation for their assistance.

Brief Vignette

Kim, a third grader, constantly dawdled and daydreamed in class. She often failed to complete her school assignments. The teacher asked the school counselor to visit with Kim to see if she could help identify something to motivate Kim to do better in her studies. When approached by the school counselor, Kim did not seem particularly troubled about the teacher's concerns. To gain more specific information about the nature of the student's problem and how it was being addressed in the classroom, the school counselor observed Kim in class on several occasions. The counselor noted that Kim often left her seat, talked with others around her, or went to the teacher's desk to ask for help. The teacher was very benevolent toward Kim and patiently gave her many reminders when she failed to be on task. When Kim did apply herself, she completed her work without difficulty.

Kim's teacher attempted to involve her parents by asking them to encourage Kim to complete her unfinished work at home. The parents were given a feedback checklist to record which assignments had or had not been completed. Over the next few weeks, Kim's classroom performance went unchanged and incomplete work was returned from home only sporadically. The teacher complained that the parents were failing in their promise to ensure that Kim's homework would be completed. Kim's mother reported difficulties from home and complained that the homework was disruptive to their family time in the evenings. Sometimes Kim had two or more hours of homework to finish, with most of the homework being incomplete work from the day's assignments.

In addition, Kim's mother was concerned that the father was too harsh on Kim. He would not let her eat supper until the homework was completed, and that meant sometimes Kim wouldn't eat until an hour or two after the family did. Kim got tired and hungry, and was often cranky in the evenings. Kim's mother was beginning to blame the school and the teacher for the stress and strain on her marriage and family.

Kim's mother requested the school handle the academic expectations for Kim. She explained that she and her husband were in family therapy to work on their relationship and that this additional stress was unwelcome. The school counselor suggested that the family therapist attend a conference at the school. Hesitant, the parents agreed. The school counselor obtained a release of information and contacted the therapist. A student support team (SST) meeting was scheduled. In attendance were Kim's parents, Kim, the teacher, counselor, and therapist. The wraparound model was introduced and determined to be a useful framework.

Each participant described the problem from his or her perspective and identified what he or she would like to change. Kim's mother wanted a calm environment at home. Kim's father wanted the mother to be more firm in her discipline. Kim's teacher and school counselor wanted Kim to succeed academically and be emotionally healthy. The family therapist wanted parents to collaborate more effectively regarding their parenting responsibilities. Kim wanted to be left alone and didn't understand why everyone was making such a fuss.

The parents and family therapist explained to the members of the SST that one of the areas they were working on was that the mother was abused as a child and found being assertive difficult, if not impossible. Her submissive posture manifested in her relationships with both her husband and her children. The teacher identified that she tended to be lenient with Kim in the classroom. She saw Kim as emotionally fragile and felt Kim could not handle a direct confrontation. The school counselor reported that her observations revealed Kim had many social strengths and that she completed her work when she put her mind to it. The therapist reiterated discussion points from the parents' last session, which addressed the importance of unified parenting, collaboration, and compromise.

As the case unfolded, it was apparent that Kim responded to the covert messages she received from the teacher and her mother. The message was that she was somehow not capable of doing her work in a timely manner. Once the teacher became aware of her own contribution to the problem, she raised her expectations and gave Kim more firm and direct instructions. The family instituted a "TLC time" at home. At 8:30, for the half hour before bedtime, the family engaged in unconditional *tender loving care* time where they played games or read together. This gave Kim's mom a chance to focus on quality time with the family and provided a break from the more structured disciplinarian role she found so taxing. She continued to work on assertive skills such as limit setting and boundaries in therapy. The school counselor developed a contract with Kim and reinforced her for staying on task. Kim earned social privileges by completing her work on time. For example, Kim could eat lunch with a friend and the school counselor, volunteer in the kindergarten class, be the office helper, etc.

As the mother and teacher became clearer and more direct in their requests, and as the tension at home diminished, Kim felt trusted and responded well to the structure. Had the family therapist not been involved, significant aspects of the situation and valuable opportunities would have been missed. The most likely scenario would have been home blaming school, school blaming home, while Kim continued to wander. The wraparound process brings home, school, and community together for the benefit of all.

Suggestions for Follow-Up

Outcome measures of behavioral goals need to be identified and measured often. Home-based positive behavior support programs can be successfully implemented with regular consultation. Parent education groups may be a useful strategy, combining instruction with behavioral principles and procedures with specific problem-solving consultation. Ongoing collaboration among the school counselor, the family therapist, and parents should continue as needed. The team coordinator can flag files to develop a follow-up schedule. A typical schedule might involve the team meeting weekly, to biweekly, to monthly, and eventually replace contact with periodic phone calls. Alternately, the membership of the team may progressively become smaller as objectives are met and some services are no longer required.

Contraindications

This process will be appropriate in many cases, but as is true with any therapeutic strategy, the wraparound process is not the answer to all school-related problems. Depending on the level of behavioral difficulties, additional community resource providers may become central team participants (e.g., medical, judicial, social services). When used appropriately and carefully tailored to the circumstances and the persons involved, this approach can be a powerful and effective intervention tool for use with students and families.

Readings and Resources for the Professional

Barth, R. S. (1991). *Improving schools from within: Teachers, parents, and principals can make the difference.* San Francisco: Jossey-Bass.

Gestwicki, C. (1999). *Home, school & community relations: A guide to working with families* (4th ed.). Albany, NY: Delmar Learning.

Senge, P. M., Cambron-McCabe, N., Lucas, T., Smith, B., Dutton, J., & Kleiner, A. (2000). *Schools that learn: A fifth discipline fieldbook for educators, parents, and everyone who cares about education*. New York: Doubleday.

Bibliotherapy Sources for the Client

Berger, E. H. (1991). *Parents as partners in education: Families and schools working together* (5th ed.) Upper Saddle River, NJ: Merrill/Prentice Hall.

Farber, B. (1999). *Guiding young children's behavior: Helpful ideas for parents & teachers from 28 early childhood experts*. New York: Preschool Publications.

Senge, P. M., Cambron-McCabe, N., Lucas, T., Smith, B., Dutton, J., & Kleiner, A. (2000). *Schools that learn: A fifth discipline fieldbook for educators, parents, and everyone who cares about education*. New York: Doubleday.

References

DeChillo, N., Koren, P. E., & Schultz, K. H. (1994). From paternalism to partnership: Family/professional collaboration in children's mental health. *American Journal of Orthopsychiatry, 64,* 564-576.

Duchnowski, A., Berg, K., & Kutash, K. (1995). Parent participation in and perception of placement decisions. In J. M. Kauffman, J. W. Lloyd, D. P. Hallahan, & T. A. Astuto (Eds.), *Issues in educational placement: Students with emotional and behavioral disorder* (pp. 183-195). Hillsdale, NJ: Lawrence Erlbaum Associates.

Eber, L. (1995, April). *LASDE EBD network training developing school-based wraparound plan*. LaGrange, IL: LaGrange Area Department of Special Education.

Friesen, B. J. & Wahlers, D. (1993). Respect and real help: Family support and children's mental health. *Journal of Emotional and Behavioral Problems, 2*(4), 12-15.

Fuller, M. L. & Olsen, G. (1998). *Home-school relations: Working successfully with parents and families*. Boston: Allyn & Bacon.

Kerr, M. M. & Nelson, C. M. (2002). *Strategies for addressing behavior problems in the classroom* (4th ed.). Upper Saddle River, NJ: Merrill/Prentice Hall.

– 31 –

Loss of a Client to Suicide: Suggestions for Before and After a Client Suicide

Charles F. Vorkoper
Judy Meade

Type of Contribution: Activity

Objective

Many of us have a strong reaction to the word "suicide." It brings up thoughts and feelings based upon our past personal and professional experiences, our beliefs, and our own fears of death. The thought of losing a client to suicide is anxiety producing and may be a nightmare for many clinicians. In a national study, 97 percent of clinicians were afraid of losing a client to suicide, second only to fear of physical assault (Pope & Tabachnick, 1993)

"There are two kinds of clinicians, those who have lost a client to suicide and those who will lose a client to suicide" (Marshall Swartzburg, MD, personal communication, 1981, in Jones, 1987, p. 127). The suicide of a client has been described as an "occupational hazard" for clinicians (Chemtob, Bauer, Hamada, Pelowski, & Muraka, 1989, p. 294). It can happen, and it will happen, given the work you do. As caregivers, you are likely to work with suicidal clients and are vulnerable to losing a client to suicide.

There is the possibility of litigation after a suicide. Our task is not to expand on the legal aspects of this issue but to stress the importance of practicing from a position of confidence and not fear. We are required to practice to the "standard of care." Berman and Cohen-Sandler (1982) described the standard of care as follows:

> Essentially, it is the duty of the hospital [the clinician, in our context] to prevent suicide through the use of reasonable care and skill. "Reasonable" is considered by law to be the "average standard of the profession"—"the degree of learning, skill and experience which ordinarily is possessed by others of the same profession." (p. 116)

You are encouraged to become aware of the dynamics of suicide legal protection and understand ways you can lessen the risks.

Clinical reports describe the negative consequences for clinicians who neglect themselves and their grief after the suicide of a client. Jones (1987, p. 127) says when a client dies by suicide the danger for the clinician may include loss suffered on both personal and professional levels. There may be "depressive" and "narcissistic" difficulties in resolving the loss with drastic consequences. These may include total renouncing of the profession and its responsibilities. He suggests the possibility of heightened suicide risk among professionals who are the survivors of client suicide. This may be similar to the same phenomena among most suicide survivors.

Tanney (1995) believes the clinician impacted by a suicide, sooner or later, will experience another client who is suicidal. This crisis of the first loss provides an opportunity to learn painful lessons shaping and modifying the clinician's attitudes and his or her helping behaviors with future suicidal clients. The clinician's awareness enables changes in his or her clinical practice that will increase his or her clinical effectiveness in the future.

Tanney (1995) finds a small number of clinicians who will discontinue all work with persons at risk. Some clinicians may leave the field all together. If this is not possible, they will avoid assuming responsibilities for suicidal clients. The degree of these avoidant behaviors depends upon how well the survivor experiences have been integrated into the clinician's work.

We have experienced clinician survivors who report periods of depressed affect for months after the suicide. Some clinicians report family disruptions in which family members feel cut off by the clinician's isolated experience even though the experienced isolation has no relationship to family members. Excessive screening for the possibility of suicidal risk in future clients can be a difficult outcome. Sometimes exaggerated interest in the subject of suicide is a way to neglect other professional issues. Although you never can be fully prepared to deal with the suicide of a client, steps can be taken to mitigate the impact of this tragedy. This chapter is written in the hope that you will use the information to protect yourself personally and professionally. These suggestions will strengthen your practice and your clinical work in preparation for the possibility of a client suicide.

The interventions described in this chapter were developed as a result of our personal experience of survivorship, as well as the shared experiences of other clinician survivors. We have been supported and taught by other clinicians who have shared their experience and pain. We have been enriched, personally and professionally, by these connections, conversations, tears, and readings. The first half of the chapter suggests prudent actions that will help lessen the negative impact and strengthen your clinical work. The second half suggests important activities after the death of a client by suicide. These approaches are not intended to be a comprehensive list. They are actions that have been helpful in our personal lives and in our clinical practices.

Rationale for Use

A suicide occurs every seventeen minutes. Official statistics list approximately 29,000 suicides per year, with a working assumption that suicide is underreported. Estimates are that the real numbers are twice that. Deaths which may have been suicides may be ruled as accidents. It is said that at least six lives are greatly impacted by each suicide, thus adding at least 184,000 new suicide grievers each year (McIntosh, 2003). "A suicide griever has lost someone they cared for deeply to suicide. They may be a parent, child, spouse, sibling, other relative, partner, or friend" (Salvatore, 2004).

Clinicians are included in the group of survivors and share many of the same experiences as described by other survivors. Unique factors in clinician response to suicide include fear of blame by the family, censure by colleagues, damage to reputation, and publicity. Many frequently harbor doubts concerning their adequacy and competence after a suicide. The struggle for learning and reorganizing after this kind of death is a common experience.

Richard McGee believes "suicide is the most difficult bereavement crisis for any family to face and endure in an effective manner" (Jones, 1987). Jones similarly believes, based upon his own experience and working with other clinicians, that the suicide of a client is the most difficult bereavement that a caregiver will have to endure.

When a client dies by suicide or lives after a suicide attempt, the impact on the caregiver is significant. Jones (1987), citing Litman (1965), writes that the suicide of a client is a crisis, both personally and professionally, compounding the loss and grief. The most common bereavement response in a survey of 200 caregiver survivors was denial with no subsequent bereavement movement through the process and with no support in mourning (Tanney, 1995). As we have seen in the literature, a need exists to prepare for the possibility of suicide survivorship.

Instructions

Two sets of instructions are provided within this chapter. The first set are to help you prepare before a suicide; the second set of instructions are for the aftermath of losing a client to suicide. Interns, supervisees, or supervisors are encouraged to see Spiegelman and Werth (2005).

Before a Suicide

You are invited to thoughtfully prepare for the possibility of a client suicide. The following list of instructions is offered. These are not intended to be for every clinician or every situation. It is our hope that you will find these ideas helpful and add to them to strengthen your clinical practice.

Self-knowledge support. Examine your beliefs and past experiences with suicide. If you have lost someone to suicide, a family member, friend, colleague, or a client, now is the time to address healing and grief. It is the ethical and responsible thing to do for yourself and your clients. If you have not addressed your loss, this can be a liability in clinical work with clients. Critical signs may be missed and cognitive and emotional abilities may be clouded in making clinical decisions. The results can be costly.

Educational support. Few training facilities or degree programs provide adequate training in assessing and treating the suicidal client. Therefore, clinician self-education is critical and can be accomplished by attending local, state, national, university, and/or professional organizational sponsored conferences or workshops on assessing and treating the suicidal client. (See the "Readings and Resources for the Professional" section at the end of this chapter.) Continual education on this topic needs to be a regular part of your professional life. Providing adequate training for clinicians is a concern that is being built into a number of state suicide prevention plans. The state suicide plans have been stimulated by the National Strategy for Suicide Prevention.

Peer support. You need a personal, informal group of peers with whom you can be open and honest. Due to the confidentiality issues of this profession, you are in a unique position and cannot debrief your work at the end of the day with family or friends. It is critical to have a professional family that is supportive and trustworthy. This peer group must be competent to confront and will not judge in a way to invite shame. This group should never be in a position to directly impact employment. Bosses, supervisors, or subordinates are unlikely persons to provide this support. This group needs to be part of your professional life on an ongoing basis. Long-term relationships are ideal as they provide safety and offer the support one needs. If such a group is not in place, now is the time to begin building such relationships. This trust and support can be built and provides easy access when a clinical situation arises.

Consultation support. Consult, consult, and consult. It is important to consult regularly and often regarding clients, especially those who are suicidal. When treating suicidal clients do not attempt to work in isolation. Seek paid supervision when needed from a competent clinician, preferably a suicidologist, and document your clinical work. When a client is suicidal he or she is unable to think clearly, may be distrusting, and may not see the seriousness of his or her problem. When working with the suicidal client, it is vital to work in collaboration—for your client and for self-protective reasons.

The peer group can also serve a consultative function and can offer expert assistance with clients. This requires the group to be competent to deal with various clinical issues. A group that knows one another well personally is uniquely able to notice clinical blind spots and challenge one another regarding clinical work.

Family support. Many training programs do not prepare clinicians for the possibility of losing a client to suicide. Thus, it is important to prepare yourself and your family in advance of a suicide. If a suicide occurs, the family can become concerned and may not know how to respond in a supportive way.

Educate your family about suicide survivorship. As a clinician you may behave differently and may appear preoccupied, sad, anxious, or even depressed. These responses may be confusing and concerning to your family. It is true that each person grieves in a unique way. The timing, sequence, and behaviors of grief will be idiosyncratic.

It is unethical for clinicians to discuss details of their clinical work with family. However, adult family members should be knowledgeable of the occupational hazard of the profession and of the dynamics of losing a client to suicide. Consider sharing the following information:

- the dynamics of losing a client to suicide;
- reassurance that you have taken professional and legal steps to protect yourself and them as best you can; and
- the resources you use for professional assistance, including trainings, peers, consultation group, consultants, attorney, insurance resources, etc.

Legal support. Some practical arrangements are important whether you anticipate a suicide or not: Do you have an attorney with whom you have an ongoing professional relationship? If not, now is the time to develop a relationship. Does your malpractice insurance carrier have a regular arrangement for a legal response? What can you expect from this carrier?

Policy support. There are also practical tasks that impact clinicians in the event of a suicide and your clinical practice:

- Maintain good clinical records, adequate documentation, and follow HIPPA rules.
- If you work for an agency or business, find out if a protective structure is in place for you to receive help and support if needed. Ask how the agency or business will take care of itself if the deceased's family members express anger by attacking you or the agency.
- If you have questions about existing policy and practice about suicide or if none exist, now (before a suicide) is the time to create policy and practice.
- Provide your clients a direct way to contact you through an answering service, cell phone, or pager.

Client-relationship support. It is impossible to intuitively know if a client is suicidal without asking the question and exploring for suicidal ideation. While it is true that we can ask and never be sure, we can educate ourselves, complete a risk assessment, seek consultation, and document our reasons and rationale for our clinical decisions. Consider carefully the issue of "no-suicide contracts" with clients. They are not to take the place of appropriate suicide risk assessment and treatment planning. Clinicians are not free of the risk or responsibility when the client agrees to a contract verbally or in writing. Little research has been conducted investigating the protective possibilities of these contracts. However, they can be seen by the client as a powerful statement that the clinician cares and will attend to the needs of the client. There are verbal reports claiming that clients have viewed such contracts as protective (Goldsmith, Pellman, Kleinman, & Bunney, 2002). (See the "Readings and Resources for the Professional" section.)

Take suicidal ideation very seriously. It is imperative to be overt when asking clients questions regarding their suicidal ideation. In your risk assessment, ask if a plan for their suicide exists. No data indicate that asking clients if they are suicidal plants the idea in their minds. These questions often give the client permission to talk about his or her thoughts and feelings. Some clients may experience this as reassurance that the clinician takes them (the client) seriously. If the client is not suicidal, then asking the question has done no harm. If suicidal ideation exists, then the clinical work that follows is to address this core issue.

Personal support. You must practice what you preach and get invested in utilizing good self-care skills. This requires accepting that you are a human being and acknowledging that you may experience losses, illness, anxiety, depression, and even suicidal ideation. It is important for you to ask: "Am I suicidal?" If this question shocks you or yields an "I am" answer, it is time for you to enter therapy and get professional help.

Clinician suicidal issues, if they exist, are significant countertransference problems in work with clients. It is likely suicidal clues will be missed. In these cases, you risk making your clients part of your suicidal issues.

After a Suicide

The following ideas are presented in a short, terse, instructional manner. There is a reason for this style. These directions are intended to be read as a part of recovery after a suicide. You will likely not remember much detail of past instructions. This is common for persons in response to loss.

Immediate personal response. You will be in shock initially—your version of shock. This is a normal grief response and is part of being human. Remember, the shock will pass and life will go on. Your body will act like all human bodies and take a "time-out" after you have been hit. You have experienced a personal and professional blow. You may experience sadness, anxiety, fear, anger, and guilt, to name a few. Any and all feelings are okay, and remember, they are just feelings.

Personal support. Contact your trusted peers and allow them to be supportive. Remember, you are in shock, grieving, and journeying through unknown territory. This path should not be walked alone.

Immediate consultation. Remember that confidentiality remains intact after the death of a client. Seek legal consultation before exposing any information. A signed release by the appropriate next of kin is required before any information can be shared about a client.

Here are important items to be considered after a suicide. Each situation and each clinician is different; therefore, this list is intended to be suggestive. Contact your liability insurance company and inform them of the death of your client and consult with your liability insurance attorney.

1. Contact a professional attorney for legal consultation. You may be faced with unfamiliar decisions in the days and weeks to follow. Your immediate response to a decision may change once you have talked with peers or attorneys.
2. Ask for help in dealing with the surviving family. There are no black-and-white answers to this, as each situation will be different. You may be faced with the following questions:
   - Do I attend the funeral?
   - Do I send flowers?
   - Do I send a card?
   - How do I acknowledge my sympathy to the family?
   - Do I meet with the family?
   - Do I work as a clinician with the family?

   Ask peers and legal consultants for help with these questions. Do not forget that you are grieving along with the other survivors.
3. Allow peers to assist you in dealing with your administrative tasks.

4. Document the facts in case notes about the client death and consultations (Speigleman & Werth, 2005).
   If the client was in group therapy, consider having a peer colead the group.
   Seek consultation about what is said about personal grieving to other clients.

Family care. Your family needs to know about your loss. Inform them that you may not be as emotionally available as usual because you are grieving. Consultation with peers to help deal with your response to your family may be necessary.

Time care. Take time off to grieve, to consult, and to begin the healing process. A week is not too much time. Be prepared to be patient with yourself and focus on your grief process. If grief becomes a problem at work, bring in peers for support and consultation. Sometimes innocent issues that clients bring up trigger strong reactions. If you experience anxiety, depression, or have suicidal ideation, please seek professional assistance at once.

Suggestions for Follow-Up

Consider a consultation after the suicide. For many mental health professionals the grief process brings up the need to know more about what happened. Many questions and a desire to know as much as possible about the suicide and an evaluation of clinical response is a common experience.

We invite you to consider participating in a case review or psychological autopsy a few months following the suicide. The person selected to do the case review is extremely important and should be knowledgeable about suicide and therapy. This is the time to review the events of the suicide and your clinical work. Finding clinical errors or omissions can be relieving because they take away the ambivalence that is a part of the grief. Accepting your helplessness and lack of control over other's decisions and behaviors is an important part of working through your loss.

The point of this consultation is to address the client's death, your personal and professional response, the family's response, and other events since the death. It is a time to evaluate and learn; Tanney (1995) said,

> "For the better" most survivor caregivers indicate that they have learned valuable lessons. They no longer minimize complaints of suicidal ideation or suicidal behavior, and are willing to initiate explicit questions and exploration surrounding the potential for self-harm. They are willing to assume greater responsibility and to be more active in their encounters with the persons at risk. At the same time they appreciate that their therapeutic efforts have limitations and these are accepted without becoming discouraged. Many caregivers ultimately acknowledge the difficult and painful experience of losing a client to suicide as an important "rite of passage" in their growth as an effective and care giving helper. (pp. 112-113)

This consultation is hopefully another step toward healing, closure, and forgiveness. It is a time to practice benign self-forgiveness. The goal is to help yourself through this difficult rite of passage to the other side—to acceptance, knowledge, and strength.

As long as you are a clinician, you will never be free from the possibility of losing a client to suicide. The aftermath of a suicide will continue to bring up feelings of guilt or incompetence, and often leave unanswered and unanswerable questions (Berman, 1995). You are quickly reminded of your humanness and your lack of control over others' decisions. Clinician survivors and the literature indicate that sharing this experience with others is helpful and healing. Iris Bolton, whose son died by suicide and the author of "My Son, My Son" (Bolton, 1983, p. 100) talks about the "hidden treasures" in the loss. It is our hope and belief that you, in time, will find healing and treasures in the loss.

Brief Vignette

Lyle's first response was numbness when he learned his client died by a self-inflected gunshot wound. He reached out to people at the agency where he worked and no one seemed sympathetic to his crisis. Despite Lyle's twelve years of experience, he felt alone and devastated. He was well trained and respected in his community. To his surprise, the shock and violent details of the death led to obsessive anxiety. The agency conducted an administrative review, which felt like a criminal trial, with a verdict of "guilty." In despair, he searched the Internet and found contacts created by the American Association of Suicidology. He was referred to a therapist and given a useful bibliography list. He sought treatment and focused on his feelings of sadness, guilt, anxiety, incompetence, and grief. Lyle had previous losses and acknowledged that losing a client to suicide was the most difficult of these losses. To satisfy his demand to know "why," he attended workshops on assessing and treating the suicidal client and searched the literature. His fear of a lawsuit followed him day and night. He attended the local Survivors of Suicide group who, although not rejecting him, would not let him get emotionally close. Lyle remembers feeling alienated, alone, and with periods of despair he describes as an "emotional crash."

One year later he is reaching out to clinician survivors and is integrating this experience into his life and his work. He lives with the knowledge it could happen again. He has developed a support system, joined a supervision group, and increased his clinical skills in assessing and treating the suicidal client. He sees life as tentative and believes no person can be trusted to stay with him, as they can die. Lyle has a new acceptance of his limitations and his lack of control for others' decisions. This tragedy has been a learning experience, one he hopes to share with others who share the same experience.

Contraindications

Your response to client suicide is a major and vital professional and personal task. A client suicide initiates you into an unwanted professional club. You may have tried all the tasks mentioned in this chapter and may continue to experience guilt, anxiety, and fear. If your personal and professional life continue to be compromised, please, be a good caretaker to yourself and seek professional help immediately.

Readings and Resources for the Professional

Internet Sources

American Association of Suicidology. http://www.suicidology.org. (Note the link to a Clinician Survivor Web site.)

American Foundation for Suicide Prevention. http://www.afsp.org.

Centre for Suicide Prevention (maintains a large database of bibliographic materials on the subject of suicide). http://www.suicideinfo.ca/csp/go.aspx?tabid=5.

QPR Institute, Inc. http://www.qprinstitute.com.

Suicide Prevention Action Network USA. http://www.spanusa.org.

U.S. Department of Health and Human Services, Public Health Service. (2001). *National strategy for suicide prevention: Goals and objectives for action.* Rockville, MD: U.S. DHHS; also available at www.mentalhealth.org/suicideprevention, reference document number SMA 3517.

Publications

Bonger, B. (1991). *The suicidal patient: Clinical and legal standards of care.* Washington, DC: American Psychological Association.

Bonger, B., Maris, R., Berman, A., Silverman, M., Harris, E., & Packman, W. L. (Eds). (1998). *Risk management with suicidal patients.* New York: Guilford Press.

Goldsmith, S., Pellman, T., Kleinman, A., & Bunney, W. (Eds). (2002). Programs for Suicide Prevention. *Reducing suicide: A national imperative* (pp. 291-292). Washington, DC: National Academies Press.

Michel, K. (1997). After suicide: Who counsels the therapist? *Crisis, 18*(3), 128-130.

Quinnett, P. (2002). *Counseling the suicidal people: A therapy of hope.* Spokane, WA: The QPR Institute, Inc.

Richman, J. (1986). *Family therapy for suicidal people.* New York: Springer Publishing Company.

Shea, S. C. (1999). *The practical art of suicide assessment: A guide for mental health professionals and substance abuse counselors.* New York: John Wiley & Sons.

Bibliotherapy Sources for the Client

American Association of Suicidology. http://www.suicidology.org.

Ellis, T. & Newman, C. (1996). *Choosing to live: How to defeat suicide through cognitive therapy.* Oakland, CA: New Harbinger Publications.

Jamison, K. R. (1995). *Night falls fast.* New York: Vintage.

QPR Institute, Inc. http://www.qprinstitute.com. (Note: *Suicide: The forever decision* is available for download from this site.)

Quinnett, P. G. (2000). *Suicide: The forever decision.* New York: The Crossroad Publishing Company.

References

Berman, A. L. (1995). To engrave herself on all our memories; to force her body into our lives: The impact of suicide on psychotherapists. In B. L. Mishara (Ed.), *The impact of suicide* (pp. 85-99). New York: Springer.

Berman, A. & Cohen-Sandler, R. (1982). Suicide and the standard of care: Optimal versus acceptable. *Suicide and Life-Threatening Behavior, 12*(2), 114-122.

Bolton, I. (1983). *My son . . . my son: A guide to healing after suicide in the family.* Atlanta, GA: Bolton Press.

Chemtob, C., Bauer, G., Hamada, R., Pelowski, S., & Muraoka, M. (1989). Patient suicide: Occupational hazard for psychologists and psychiatrists. *Professional Psychology: Research and Practice, 20,* 294-300.

Goldsmith, S., Pellman, T., Kleinman, A., & Bunney, W. (Eds). (2002). Programs for suicide prevention. In *Reducing suicide: A national imperative* (pp. 291-292). Washington, DC: National Academies Press.

Jones, F. A. (1987). Therapists as survivors of client suicide. In E. J. Dunne, J. C. McIntosh, & K. Dunne-Maxim (Eds.), *Suicide & its aftermath: Understanding and counselling the survivors* (pp. 126-141). New York: W. W. Norton & Co.

Litman, R. (1965). When patients commit suicide. *American Journal of Psychotherapy, 19,* 570-576.

McIntosh, J. L. (2003). "U.S.A. suicide: 2001 official final data," Suicide Data Page: 2001. Retrieved December 9, 2003, from http://www.floridasuicideprevention.org/PDF/2001datapg.pdf.

Pope, K. & Tabachnick, B. (1993). Therapists' anger, hate, fear, and sexual feelings: National survey of therapist responses, client characteristics, critical events, formal complaints, and training. *Professional Psychology: Research and Practice, 24,* 142-153.

Salvatore, T. (2004). Suicide loss FAQs. Available at http://members.tripod.com/~LifeGard/ssfaqs.html.

Spiegelman, J. S. & Werth, J. L. (2005). "Don't forget about me": The experiences of therapists-in-training after a client has attempted or died by suicide. In K. M. Weiner (Ed.), *Therapeutic and legal issues for therapists who have survived a client suicide: Breaking the silence* (pp. 35-57). Binghamton, NY: The Haworth Press.

Tanney, B. (1995). After a suicide: A helper's handbook. In B. L. Mishara (Ed.), *The impact of suicide* (pp. 100-120). New York: Springer.

Index

Page numbers followed by the letter "f" indicate figures.